Addiction and Pastoral Care

Addiction and Pastoral Care

Sonia E. Waters

William B. Eerdmans Publishing Company
Grand Rapids, Michigan

Wm. B. Eerdmans Publishing Co.
4035 Park East Court SE, Grand Rapids, Michigan 49546
www.eerdmans.com

Published 2019
Printed in the United States of America

25 24 23 22 21 20 19   1 2 3 4 5 6 7

ISBN 978-0-8028-7568-6

Library of Congress Cataloging-in-Publication Data

Names: Waters, Sonia E., 1972- author.
Title: Addiction and pastoral care / Sonia E. Waters.
Description: Grand Rapids : Eerdmans Publishing Co., 2019. | Includes bibliographical references and index.
Identifiers: LCCN 2018043572 | ISBN 9780802875686 (pbk. : alk. paper)
Subjects: LCSH: Substance abuse—Patients—Pastoral counseling of. | Drug addicts—Pastoral counseling of.
Classification: LCC BV4460.3 .W38 2019 | DDC 259/.429—dc23
LC record available at https://lccn.loc.gov/2018043572

Contents

Foreword

Addictions are complex and perplexing. They are made up of a confusing combination of biological, psychological, sociological, relational, and spiritual components, all of which coalesce to shape and form the life experiences of those who find themselves trapped within any given addiction. The complexity of addictions tempts us towards simplicity. "Addiction is *nothing but* a manifestation of sinfulness and selfishness." "Addiction is *nothing but* disease processes within the brain." "Addiction is *nothing but* misplaced desire." Human beings like to try to explain difficult phenomena. If we can explain something we can control it. If we can control it, it is no longer a threat. Simplification and reduction may make for comforting forms of explanation, but in so doing they risk masking the complex reality of the phenomenon and closing down potentially important areas for reflection and intervention. One of the main contributions of this book is to help us recognize the need for an interdisciplinary approach to addictions that holds on to the crucial realization that acknowledging the complexity of addiction is vital for authentic understanding and faithful intervention.

Addictions carry deep moral connotations that are highly significant in terms of understanding, reaction, and response. In her work on the meaning of illness, Susan Sontag pointed us towards the significance of metaphor for understanding illness.[1] Illnesses such as cancer and AIDS, she argued, are not like influenza. Their meaning is not confined to their biomedical origins. Rather, they are very much social diseases that are deeply impacted by cultural meanings. As such they have a problematic tendency to draw to themselves certain metaphors and connotations that further increase the suffering of individuals living with these conditions. For instance, the military language that we use around cancer sufferers can be deeply challenging. Often people living with cancer are encouraged to do *battle* with cancer, to *fight* it, to perceive it as the *invading enemy within* that needs to be *eradicated* so that they can be freed to live. Living with cancer is war. But what if I want to befriend my cancer and live with it peaceably? Likewise, AIDS, which is nothing more (and nothing less) than a virus, attracts to it metaphors and assumptions such as *deviance*, *addiction*, *homosexuality*, and *promiscuity* that have nothing to do with its biological root. Bodily illness is transmuted into social stigmata which lead to the marginalization and alienation of sufferers for whom the enforced cultural metaphors cause distress and misidentification.

Those living with addiction experience all the difficulties that Sontag highlights. But there is also another dimension to their social suffering. Alongside these linguistic and cultural issues is an ontologizing of addiction wherein the person is assumed not just to suffer from an addiction, but actually to *become* his or her addiction. If one has measles, one is not normally referred to as "a measle." But if one has an addiction, one is often given a new name: *addict*. The term *addict* is rich in metaphor and stigma. The ascription of the term baptizes people into a social role wherein their real names are overpowered by their collective social name. But what exactly is an addict? When we talk about addicts, we are not talking about people who are somehow other than ourselves in the way that New Yorkers may be different or other than Scotsmen! Addicts are not a people group, and addiction is not a cultural marker. People with addictions are people in pain. Many of them need and desire the love of Jesus, and their healing requires them to learn how to love themselves more fully in order that they can recognize the love of God and come to love and be loved by their neighbors. One of the important things that emerges from this book is the reminder that addicts have names and that these names matter. Addictions are complicated.

Sonia Waters has gifted us in *Addiction and Pastoral Care* with a fascinating and important book that takes very seriously the multifaceted nature of addictions and the centrality of theology as a way of understanding and responding to this profound human experience. Moving us through a variety of fields from neurology to systematic theology, she takes us on a wonderful interdisciplinary expedition that will undoubtedly change the ways in which many of us understand and respond to people living with addictions. Readers of this volume will not only find some rigorous, fresh, and deep perspectives on addiction, they will also learn the kinds of theological and pastoral responses needed to respond to the complexities of addiction and to help guide people back toward their one true desire: Jesus. Much has been written on addiction within the pastoral literature, but in terms of its deep theological emphasis and breadth of knowledge and wisdom, this book offers something new. Readers with an interest in addiction and addiction studies will not be disappointed by what they encounter here.

John Swinton
Aberdeen University

Acknowledgments

In the pages that follow, I owe the greatest debt to the drug addicts and alcoholics—both active and in recovery—who have shared their stories and taught me so much about faith. I have also inflicted the progression of my ideas upon my students at Princeton Theological Seminary over the past four years, and they have blessed me with their intelligence, creativity, and patience. I am greatly indebted to the Rev. Stephen Faller, chaplain supervisor at Capital Health, who supervised my chaplaincy at a local rehab. Rev. Matthew Rhodes, chaplain supervisor at Princeton-Penn Health, also read and commented on the counseling skills in this work. Chaplain Rhodes and Rev. Mary-Jane Inman have let me try out various versions of these ideas on their chaplain interns at both Princeton Health and at Trenton Psychiatric Hospital. Rev. Jan Ammon, Princeton Seminary's Minister of the Chapel, read through the whole manuscript and added much editorial and pastoral input. These ministers, whose vocations bring them daily to the center of so much suffering, remain an inspiration to me.

Professors Bonnie Miller-McLemore, Deborah Hunsinger, and Dale Allison offered crucial feedback at the beginning of this project and championed me in its pursuit. I cannot thank them enough for offering their time and encouragement to the formation of this book. Robert Dykstra also read an early version of the Gerasene chapter and has been a supportive mentor throughout my time at Princeton Seminary. Clifton Black kindly offered me mountains to read on the Gospel of Mark. My pastoral theologian colleagues from the "New Directions in Pastoral Theology" writing conference also patiently suffered through an earlier version of my thinking on addiction and the Gerasene demoniac. They have inspired my writing and encouraged me in this pursuit.

My partner, Rev. John Mennell, also read and critiqued several chapters and survived me as I completed the writing process. Without his influence, nothing would be linear. Former students Jennifer Herold and Mads Benishek edited and critiqued earlier versions of this manuscript, and Mads used his prodigious organizational talents to be the primary copyeditor for my manuscript. Finally, special thanks to my spiritual mentor Fran JFG,[1] who, when I asked what would happen if she went back to using, said, "I'd lose everything. But most important, I'd lose my soul." I couldn't have said it better myself.

Introduction

When I say the words "heroin addict," what picture do you get in your mind? What people are engaged in this behavior? What do they look like, and where are they? What is wrong with them? What can they do to solve the problem? How does that solution actually unfold? Now, try the word "alcoholic"—or what about "crack addict" or "marijuana addict"? What picture do you get in your mind? What people are engaged in those behaviors? What do they look like, and where do they come from? What is wrong with them? What can they do to solve that problem? How does that solution unfold? Now, add another question: What part does the pastoral caregiver play in that problem, or in the unfolding of its solution?

I ask my students these questions on the first day of our class on addictions. I tell them not to give me their "Christianly" view—the one that they think they are supposed to give me. Instead, I want the first thing that comes to their minds: what they grew up thinking about addicts, what they heard in school, at home, and in the media. I ask for their unfiltered thoughts about why or how people become addicted and why or how they recover. In a class of about fifty students, I can get dozens of different perspectives. Together we write on a large whiteboard themes that are personal, social, and theological. We list contrasting debates between addiction as a habit, a brain disease, or a psychological problem. We see how our thoughts about addiction intersect with stigmas about poverty and homelessness, assumptions about race and gender, and political rhetoric from the war on drugs. We see them inevitably tied to questions of sin, will power, and weakness of character. We admit to stereotypes about delinquency and failure: addicts as the dregs of society. We point to personal consequences, such as loss of family, home, and sometimes even life.

Substance addictions are fascinating because they are positioned—or perhaps, more accurately, *constructed*—at the converging point of so many other discourses. Everyone, from neuroscientists to social workers, from public-health advocates to the police force, has something to say about the causes and cures of addiction. There is an official diagnosis of "Substance Use Disorder" in the *Diagnostic and Statistical Manual of Mental Health Disorders* (DSM-V), suggesting that these addictions are mental health conditions.[1] But, unlike most other mental health conditions, addictions are openly treated as a crime. They are expressions of individual suffering and broken family systems but they are also the province of politicians and presidents, who promise to keep the streets safe for our youth. They fuel the inordinate incarceration of African Americans and Hispanics in the war on drugs. They are attached to images of homelessness, prostitution, and degeneracy. They evoke our deepest assumptions about how human beings express agency and responsibility in the world.

When students discuss the role of the pastoral caregiver in the problem's solution, we need a whole new board to write their responses. We hear about the "ministry of presence," the "power of prayer," "faith healing," "planning an intervention," and "offering exhortation." Some swear by Alcoholics Anonymous (AA) and others by Celebrate Recovery (CR). People share with others a host of homegrown ministries that originate from their local churches. They tell stories about loved ones who were healed and loved ones who never got clean. They talk about fears of not being good enough as caregivers. Sometimes they admit that they are not sure what to do with addicts. After all, they can be confusing people to be around: sometimes they are pitiful and emotional, and sometimes proud and untouchable. They say one thing and then they do another. At some level they seem detached from the chronic behaviors that are taking over their lives. Most of us have seen friends and families, parents and parishioners disappear into this senseless, repetitive excess. We invest in their recovery, we try to help, and then they fail us. At least, that is what it can feel like, if we are honest.

Addictions are a pastoral challenge because we don't really know how an addict heals and we don't know how to relate to an addict who is in that process of healing. If addictions are so multivalent, then easy solutions evade us. How we define a problem affects how we view the solution, and these differing definitions across the board lead to very different solutions: from medicine to conversion, from exorcism to social activism, from doing everything to doing nothing. By the end of a very full whiteboard, it is also clear that both our first definitions and our later solutions produce a certain way of seeing the person before us—as a criminal, a victim, a moral agent, or a medical patient, just to name a few.

The process of healing from addictions is complicated, and it evokes complicated feelings within us as pastoral caregivers. But I usually try to make it even more complicated on our first day of class, just for fun. At some point in that class conversation, I rather unfairly lob the question of theology into the middle of the room. Right now, what is your theology of addiction? How do you see addiction through the lens of your faith? By now, the students are annoyed. Many students believe that addiction is a disease, and so they are not sure what to say about it theologically. Maybe they've just been trained to make a bifurcation between science and faith. Or maybe they assume that a "theology of addiction" necessitates a theology of sin. If this is a medical problem, it seems outside of the purview of theology. Others don't want to lose some notion of sin: they believe that people should be responsible for their actions. After all, they assure me, sin doesn't mean that addicts are bad people, because we all sin. The only problem is that, if we all sin, then it is not a particular theology of addiction.

If pressed to say something Christian about addictions, students on both sides of the issue—addiction as a sin or addiction as a disease—usually find themselves talking about the age-old themes related to free-will sin. Addiction is idolatry, desire gone awry, gluttony, the pursuit of pleasure, a turning away from God. These themes don't quite fit the idea that addiction is a disease, but people who hold to the disease model don't know what else to say about it, spiritually speaking. Christians think about the spiritual life in terms of spatial metaphors: we draw near, turn away, become lost, get separated, or distance ourselves from God through our actions. These are also related to sin, since we are responsible for the direction in which we turn. But a focus on the direction of the individual spiritual life does not take into account the many descriptions of addiction that we wrote on our first board: the broad multivalence of its personal and social causes, its myths and stigmas.

If you were to see the state of my whiteboard at the end of that first class, or the annoyance of my students, you might agree that addictions are confusing. They suffer from a lack of conceptual clarity. We will review the diagnostic criteria for substance use disorder in chapter 1, but even this list of symptoms is based on subjective experiences (personal consequences, time spent in the behavior) that are not easily measured. How many consequences do you need to have before you become an addict? Do you have to use drugs or alcohol every day? Can you be successful in your job and still be an addict? Are you doomed to have a lifelong disease, or is it merely a life-cycle phase? Frankly, addiction is a constructed category: someone noticed these particular behaviors, argued about them with their fellow researchers, and organized them into the *Diagnostic and Statistical Manual-V*. This allows certain people to get an official diagnostic label of substance-use disorder and thus gain insurance or health-care benefits. While medical and mental-health institutions want to standardize such diagnoses for addictions, ultimately only the individual can know whether or not she has a problem with substances. Combine the personal experience of substance abuse with all the other social and political intersections on the board, and two people could be talking about two very different things when they have a conversation about addiction.

Addiction across the Board

Pastoral theologians like to start with lived experience. We try to build a picture of the human situation—particularly situations of suffering— in order to more fruitfully engage the resources of the faith in understanding and addressing that situation. This is not a one-way street; the human situation also has its own theological weight. Lived experience and its broader context teach us about ultimate concerns, about the God-human relationship, and they also correct or critique what is missing in our theologies through their cries for justice.[2] Finally, practices of community and care are a part of our lived experience, which is why the question of how one heals, or how the pastoral caregiver or community is involved in that healing, is a crucial part of the equation. These practices hold implicit theologies and value systems that need to be brought to the surface for further reflection.[3] For instance, practices of addiction care—from DSM-V diagnoses to drug court to Celebrate Recovery—assume very different types of people and describe different problems. Certain understandings of humanity and its problems are enabled by these practices of care, and other expressions are limited. So pastoral theologians construct a particular version of a sick person from the multiple theories available.

As I develop a picture of addictions in this book, I try to honor the lived experience across our classroom whiteboard, scattered as it is with its personal, social, political, and spiritual issues. To sustain some order in this approach, I move from the individual brain to its attachment relationships, and then out into the social world. The individual and his or her inner life is a part of the picture of addiction and has long been a source of pastoral theological reflection as a "living human document."[4] This means that individual experience offers its own source of knowledge, like a written text that enters into conversation with the spiritual and theological texts of our faith. But my whiteboard looks more like what Bonnie Miller-McLemore calls a "living human web."[5] Each individual is located in a web of constructed meaning. Problems may feel like individual issues and may cause individual suffering, but a person's subjectivity—how she experiences or interprets the experience of self and other—is formed by how she is situated within the structures and ideologies of her communities and contexts. My aim is to take an issue that is often highly individualized and trace its webbed connections to the relational and social contexts that make one vulnerable to addiction, create its stigma, and complicate its recovery. This broader picture will then inform my Christian reflection on aspects of addiction and its care.

The living human web also expands pastoral theology into responses that address the socioeconomic and political suffering of the marginalized. We can pay attention, not just to the person, but to the systems of oppression within which they are situated. African American pastoral theologians such as Archie Smith, Edward Wimberly, and Lee Butler have long advocated for a pastoral theology informed by African American history, culture, and the experience of historic and institutional oppression.[6] Ryan LaMothe also broadens the scope of pastoral theology into political theology, including the lived experience of global market capitalism.[7] Racial and socioeconomic oppression play a large role in the story of addiction, especially through the war on drugs and its inordinate policing and incarceration of African Americans, Hispanics, and poor whites.

So while I will be offering individual listening skills in chapters 6 and 7, I am building a picture that considers our broader work as pastoral caregivers, including how we use Christian practices, form caring communities, and engage in political advocacy. The image of the web suggests that we are not atomized individuals closed in upon ourselves. Instead, we are multiply connected to personal, social, and political experiences of both vulnerability and resilience. This can help us understand the individual better but it can also expand our caring work to the social, political, and economic suffering that might complicate addiction. Issues of racism and homophobia, poverty, and the economic insecurity embedded in the shifts of global-market capitalism are all a part of this web. Addiction is not a cause of social decay; rather, it is a symptom of the suffering that grows when we ignore God's call to justice and care for the vulnerable.

As I expand outward from the personal to the social, I describe addiction as an emergent condition arising from how multiple vulnerabilities organize themselves around the repeated behavior of using. It is not just one cause that creates an addiction, but a dynamic tangle of vulnerabilities that catch the individual in the net of addictive behavior and can accelerate the progression of the condition as it grows. I focus on the progress of addiction because I think that it adds a dimension to the pastoral care of addictions that has been undertheorized in Christian writing. There are manuals that help pastors identify the end-stage condition of substance use disorder, there are personal spiritual reflections that connect addiction to the inner life, and there is a recounting of the debate between those who see addiction as disease and those who see it as a moral choice. But we have not really considered that the very emergence and progress of addictions have theological weight: how self-regulatory, ritual behaviors attempt to manage what I call a "legion" of personal, relational, and social sources of suffering. Addictions progressively eat away at the soul, affecting the sufferer's hold on reality, his moral decision-making, his sense of self in relationship to God, and his sense of a right relationship with the world.

As I build this more webbed picture of addictions, the themes of multiplicity, progression, identity, and loss will recur throughout these pages. They culminate in a detailed discussion of the Gospel of Mark's Gerasene demoniac in chapter 5, which I use as a metaphor for the complex interrelationship of personal experience and social suffering in addiction. These dynamics teach us something about our own more complicated role in caring for addicts. From the outside, it may seem like addiction is a single self-harming action, where it is obvious that giving up the addiction means claiming a happier, healthier life. This is not so obvious to an addict. From the inside, many addicts experience a threat to their behaviors as a threat to the way that they have organized their understanding of the self and its relationships. Death is involved in addictions, from the original losses and sufferings that compelled their engagement to the identity that must die in order for addicts to recover from their hold. Thus to lose the addiction is a process of grief. This truth will evoke some themes that travel across these pages: that we do not easily "get over" such a loss; that recovery is a process of changing identity; that woundedness and death are the slow, ambivalent sources of new life.

I know that the classroom whiteboard could be organized differently. If you do not hear your story within these pages, it doesn't mean that your experience of addiction is less real for you. Not every person will claim that relational and social losses were a part of their addictive behaviors. Not everyone thinks that addictions cause permanent changes to the brain.

Addiction is a highly contested concept. In the end, I am not able to tell you what addiction ultimately "really is." Instead, I hope to offer a compelling version of how we might imagine it to be. I believe that this version is a faithful attempt to capture addiction's complexity and also to encourage our compassion. I am trying to embrace pastoral theologian Elaine Graham's criterion of "usable but not innocent" for my choices toward interpretation. Her pragmatic perspective maintains that we recognize "the tentative and provisional nature of our claims to 'truth,' yet we still maintain a commitment to 'usable knowledge' as a working and strategic hypothesis."[8] I hope that this book represents a strategic hypothesis for addiction that will help pastoral caregivers more broadly to serve the individuals and communities that come to us for care.

Addiction Organized

In chapter 1, I provide some foundations that will organize my thoughts on addiction throughout this book. First, addiction is relational; second, it is motivated by the problem of pain, not the desire for pleasure; finally, it is an emergent condition that progressively takes over the will. Addictions do not arise from one cause but from how multiple personal, relational, and social vulnerabilities organize around substance use, as we attempt to regulate negative affect and manage stress. I argue that addictions are one of a class of spiritual bondage that I call a "soul-sickness." They are signs of the soul in distress. Over time, addictions injure the soul, progressively estranging the individual from self, other, and God. I introduce the image of the Gerasene demoniac's legion to symbolize the existential and spiritual suffering of this condition, and I will continue to use the term "legion" to represent the multiplicity of addiction throughout this work. Like the Gerasene's legion, addictions emerge from many forces that have organized into one voice. They combine and overtake the self in ways that are self-destructive and socially stigmatizing, similar to how we might imagine the Gerasene's demon possession.

In chapter 2, I explore how addiction progresses through our brain functioning. Neurobiological perspectives suggest that addictions create a chronic state of stress and negative affect in the user, leading to a kind of spiritual bondage where the individual attempts to escape the stress of using with yet more substance use. I review the dynamics of neurotransmission, tolerance, withdrawal, and craving. I use a simplified image of instinctual and executive "neighborhoods" in the brain to talk about what researchers call hypofrontality. This is the diminished connection between the part of our brain that initially takes in information and codes automatic responses and the part of our brain that processes information deliberately. I review changes to the "reward system" in the brain, which is implicated in both substance abuse and behavioral addictions. The neurobiology of addiction is important for care because I so often hear people confuse addictions with other strong attachments or questionable temptations. I can't count the number of times people have said to me, "But aren't we all addicted to something?" No, we're not. If the growing research in neurobiology is correct, the brain in a state of addiction is not the same as the brain that is not addicted.

Self-regulation leads me to my third premise behind a soul-sickness: addictive behaviors are ultimately attempts to survive pain, not pursue pleasure. In chapters 3 and 4, I focus on the effects of childhood attachment, trauma, and social marginalization on our mental health, in an attempt to develop a more relational model of addiction. Our attachment relationships can fundamentally change our brain and behaviors. Our social relationships can cause chronic stress and emotional distress. When personal and social relationships lack basic empathy, they cannot be accessed for self-regulation or for the construction of a positive self-identity. Theologically, I base these two chapters on the assumption that we are created for relationship with self, others, and God. Other people complete us. These chapters will explore what that profound relationality and its breakage means for addictions care. This focus on self-regulation needs in relational contexts does not remove an addict's responsibility to choose recovery, but it should change our pastoral reflection on addictions. If there is sin in addiction, it is a much more complicated combination of the sins we do and the sins done to us.We should focus on the tragedy of this bargain that we nurse in our vulnerability until it ultimately turns against us.

Having built this picture of addiction in chapters 3 and 4, I return in chapter 5 to the image of soul-sickness, using the story of the Gerasene demoniac as told in the Gospel of Mark. A soul-sickness is an emergent condition that arises from a legion of individual and social vulnerabilities, taking over the voice and will of its host over time. By using this story as a kind of allegory, we can explore the personal and social dynamics of this growing force from a spiritual perspective. We can also consider how Jesus responds to the Gerasene's legion in order to further encourage our own compassionate response to the individual who suffers from addiction. As an overtaking of the will, addiction has symbolic resonance with the biblical understanding of possession as a condition that affects the body and mind, the soul and its social relationships. Postcolonial studies on the Gerasene further suggest the effects of a violent, oppressive context on his condition, and they remind us that he is rejected and left at the edges of society. In accounting for the social and personal suffering behind addiction more fully, we begin to see that addiction is a particular kind of neurobiological possession that arises from our own sins but also the sins of others in a profoundly relational world. It offers an account of the possessive, self-protective nature of addiction, as the legion pleads for its own survival, dreading the torment of healing.

While I focus on substance addictions throughout this book, I do pause in each chapter to relate its themes to broader addiction issues. In chapters 2 and 3, I give a brief treatment of other chronic behavioral conditions that might have similar dynamics or antecedents, with an emphasis on pornography addiction and eating disorders. In chapter 4, I address the broader political issue of the war on drugs and mass incarceration, because this is associated with racism and with society's treatment of the marginalized. In chapter 5, I outline some family responses to the addict. In chapters 6 and 7, I review some basics in multicultural counseling and mental-health awareness. None of these excurses from the main topic are sufficient to address the complexity of the issue, but I hope that they will encourage readers' further exploration and will enrich their understanding of addiction care.

Shifting to skills in chapters 6 and 7, I explore a staged model of care to better address the challenges of this progressive condition. I use Change Theory and Motivational Interviewing to help caregivers understand how long-term behavioral changes are made and how to encourage and support a person toward those changes. Medical professionals have used these skills to help motivate better self-care in chronic health conditions, such as diabetes or HIV infection. They are also becoming popular for conceptualizing mental-health diagnoses, such as schizophrenia or bipolar disorder, where a person's compliance with medication and lifestyle changes help support long-term recovery.

Motivational Interviewing offers the pastoral care provider clear advice for working with ambivalence, raising consciousness regarding problematic behaviors, and supporting an addict in relapse prevention. It encourages the pastoral caregiver to strategically disengage from argument and power-struggle, and to pay more attention to the values or goals that might lead a person to change. Change Theory understands the decision to change chronic behaviors as a staged process. There are different tasks that an individual must accomplish with respect to each stage as one seeks to tip the decisional balance toward lasting change. This framework will help pastoral caregivers plan conversations and spiritual resources according to the addict's readiness for change. These strategies cannot promise recovery. But they can fulfill our calling to care for souls in distress, companioning with them as they seek the fullness of the good that God wants for their lives.

Finally, as we explore substance addictions, I hope that you will find other connections to your pastoral care. Addictions teach us much about the pathos of being human. They teach us about the fragility of our humanity and our need for others. They teach us about the power of symbolic ritual to tell stories of self-hate, abuse, and social disconnection. They prove our resilience in the face of impossible situations. They show us the lengths that we will go to try to survive our lives. They teach us how very much we need others to love us, and how personal and social environments that lack empathy do more than just hurt our feelings, but seek to destroy our souls. Working with chronic behaviors humbles us. We cannot solve them but we can walk with someone as she journeys through the crucible of this suffering.

Terms and Conditions

When I consider the living human web of addiction scattered across my whiteboard, I also have to consider who I am as the puller of these strings. I am not merely weaving these pieces together from a place of objectivity, but entangled in the midst of my own webbed history and its cultural and spiritual influences. I bring my own cultural and political biases, my history and context, my theological preoccupations, and my hopes for healing to the human situation that I describe here. I am formed by my place as a middle-class white woman in America, and by my childhood in an immigrant family living in different states across the nation. The former informs my privilege, the latter my interminable curiosity about others. I am influenced by being a teenage convert to evangelicalism, by my calling as a priest in the Episcopal Church, and by my current residence and teaching position at a Presbyterian seminary. You will hear traces of all those formational spiritual contexts in this book. I am influenced by the pastoral theologians whom I have cited in the acknowledgments, and also by my conversation with addicts and alcoholics in recovery.

My thoughts about addiction are further formed by my particular involvement in 12-step practices, a culture with its own narratives and traditions that has shaped my subjectivity. This means that I might notice certain themes or be primed toward certain stories through my own formation in both Christian and 12-step spiritualities. But this is not a book about the Twelve Steps. I am not a spokesperson for AA World Services and do not represent its program. My interpretation of 12-step sayings or activities is influenced by the peculiar hybrid of my Christian academic-practitioner brain. Sometimes I will refer to quotes or sayings in the 12-step tradition that I think express spiritual wisdom. But not everyone finds 12-step recovery useful for their healing. Each person needs to consider what can help him address the broader dynamics of addiction, such as avoiding triggers, changing learned behavior concerning the habit, addressing personal trauma, increasing connections to ethnic or group identities and cultures, and finding new ways to manage affect regulation and stress.

Let me forge ahead into terms for the following chapters. In the course of this book, I will refer to the individual who is struggling with a substance-use disorder as an *addict.* I will also try to move between pronoun sets for the individual addict: "she" and "he" in the singular, we and "they" in the plural. I understand that the word "addict" can be viewed as a stigmatizing label. In recovery circles, people sometimes prefer to say something like "I have the disease of alcoholism" or "I have/had an addiction" or "I am recovered" (or "in recovery"). I've met many people who toggle in their speech between using the label as a part of their identity ("I'm an addict") and speaking of their addiction as a kind of externalized or personified third-person force ("My addiction is trying to fool me today"). People find many creative names to call themselves and ways to describe their condition.

For the sake of clarity and brevity in this book, "addict" seems to be the best choice for a term that is so often repeated throughout these pages. I will also refer to addiction under the more general umbrella of "chronic behavioral condition," since I believe that substance addiction is spiritually connected to other types of ritual self-harming behaviors used for self-regulation. I personally find the technical diagnosis of substance-use disorder (SUD) unappealing, but when I use the word "addiction" I am generally assuming this clinical understanding, which ranges from mild to severe. I want to avoid the diagnosis of substance-use disorder because some people remain "subclinical," not scoring enough symptoms for an official diagnosis because they are highly functioning. Some also have enough privilege and economic security to avoid the practical or relational consequences on the DSM-V symptom list. Ultimately, the individual is the one who has to assess whether her level of substance use is problematic to her goals for her life.

When I use the term "recovery," it connotes formal and informal strategies that addicts engage toward changing an admitted problematic level of use. When speaking of recovery, I am focusing on abstinence but also leaving room for intentional harm-reduction strategies if these are what the individual discerns as her goal. This means limiting the amount or mitigating consequences because one knows one has a problem. Medication-assisted treatment, such as taking methadone, suboxone, or naltrexone, is very helpful for some people, though best practices also advise some kind of counseling along with the medication. It is also possible for some people to "age out" of heavy use or quit without formal treatment.[9] Each person must decide what best meets his needs. If someone fails in repeated attempts at moderating or quitting, it might be a sign that he needs more structured therapeutic help to recover.

Throughout this book I will offer some of my experience listening to addicts in 12-step meetings, nonaffiliated recovery small groups, and individual discussions with people in recovery.[10] I have changed personal names and details and in some cases have amalgamated stories to ensure anonymity. They include conversations in my official capacity as a priest, professor, and chaplain. But they are more often from AA/NA friends and acquaintances whose stories have touched me and subsequently have influenced my thinking about addiction. I did not systematically gather these, and they do not qualify as research that might prove what addiction "really is." Instead, they represent the formation of my own interpretive horizon. These stories came forcefully to mind as I was beginning to be troubled by oversimplified and often stigmatizing comments about addicts that I heard in Christian environments. Reflecting on these stories helped me to form the questions that I asked about addiction and they deeply influenced my concerns about the state of our Christian witness in addictions care. They have formed my thinking about the particular effects of a soul-sickness, and I wanted to bring those voices that have influenced my thought more fully into this work.

At a more affective level that is difficult to describe, I am influenced by the pathos I have seen in addiction and its recovery. Some addicts are in the middle of onerous drug-court probation, or they have lost custody of their children and are in a local jail-like treatment program or halfway house in my area. They are trying to find basic resources just to survive. Others have all kinds of privilege but are spinning in cycles of relapse, breeding chaos upon chaos. Some are coerced into rehab, full of bravado and resistance. Others are numb and desperate with no belief that they can change. There are some who recover with grace and tenacity. Others appear full of insight until they suddenly disappear into relapse or death. Almost everyone seems to have a story of a loved one who overdosed or committed suicide. And everyone has a pained look when other members of the group call themselves hopeless. As one woman with a week of sobriety said, addicts feel for other addicts because they see themselves in their struggles. Over and over in these encounters, I have been struck by the idea that Christians bond as saints. We don't share the true ugliness of our lives, our personal and moral failures, with other Christians. We seek to be good, to be appropriate, to be worthy of love. But addicts bond through their sins. Whether in rehab, AA/NA meetings, or out on the streets, they tell each other their stories of suffering. I have been changed by their experiences of struggle and grief.

Chapter One

Addiction as Soul-Sickness

> Addiction is a primary, chronic disease of brain reward, motivation, memory and related circuitry.
>
> —Board of Directors,
> American Society of Addiction Medicine

> Addiction is about our hungers and thirsts, about our ultimate concern, about the clinging and longing of our hearts, and about giving ourselves over to these things. When it is in full cry, addiction is finally about idolatry.
>
> —Cornelius Plantinga,
> *Not the Way It's Supposed to Be: A Breviary of Sin*

A man takes his seat in a circle of chairs and begins to tell his story. He describes passing out and waking up in dangerous places, the lies he told himself, and the shame he felt for what he did to his family. He describes growing up with a punishing God who was counting his sins—a God whom he had already failed by the time he was twelve. At that age, he was already sure that he was destined for hell, a real place with "burning coals and a fire-poker." He claims that he used drugs to get rid of this thing he called "angst," a growing sense of being uncomfortable in his own skin, his mind going a mile a minute, the need to shut off his consciousness. But at the end of decades of drug abuse, he lived in mental anguish. He quotes a familiar saying: "I can't use but I can't stop using." It took him three more years to manage one year sober. It took him longer to imagine a higher power as a loving universal force that would help him face the sins of his past without the overwhelming shame that turned him back to using.

Another man in the circle describes forty years of manipulating friends and family, therapists, and supervisors—all to continue drinking. He admits that he grew up Catholic and believed in God, but found this inconsequential to his increasing need to drink. The spiritual nature of his problem was evident in his brittle denial and his complete lack of empathy for others. Interventions did not work and pleas from his wife and daughters only taught him to be more secretive. He used his considerable intelligence and creativity to hide his continuous alcohol consumption, drinking from the moment he left for work to the moment he passed out at night. Beer during the morning commute, airplane bottles of vodka in pockets, a portable minibottle of cheap wine in his briefcase, hard liquor in the door of the car, wine while making dinner, and extra beer hidden in the golf-club bag in the garage. He describes the moment when he was finally sent to rehab. He woke up on the bedroom floor one morning and could not get up. His wife tried to help him, but he was a dead weight. He just did not care. His daughter called the ambulance, but could not rouse his interest. He just did not care. He did not care whether he went to the hospital or stayed home, whether he lived or died. He had felt that way for a long time now. Nothing held any meaning for him.

Addictions are a dilemma of relational estrangement and spiritual bondage. They infect body, mind, and soul. There is a popular misconception that people pursue addictions for pleasure: they "chase the high" of drugs or alcohol. But addictions look more like these men's experiences of psychic pain and spiritual hopelessness. They are conditions of profound suffering. When people tell their stories of addiction, they usually describe lives that, in the language of the Twelve Steps, had become completely unmanageable. After some time in recovery, they can look back and see that their thinking had become distorted. They describe a growing sense of helplessness concerning their choice to use substances. They point to their actions, their living standards, or their treatment of others that, in hindsight, appear insane to them. They were no longer themselves. They no longer cared if they lived or died. They were caught in a ritual loop that left them completely self-absorbed and yet in a strange way ancillary to their own minds and bodies. They were suffering from a progressive physical and spiritual sickness.

As pastoral caregivers, we often encounter addictions at the end stage of the condition because this is often when people come to us for help. But if you listen to stories of people struggling with addiction, what you will hear is the progression of suffering. Not everyone who uses substances becomes addicted, and it does not occur to early users that this solution to the problem of the self could spin out of their control. Some people use drugs or alcohol recreationally for most of their lives with little consequence. Others look back on heavy use in high school or college as a kind of rite of passage that gained no obsessive hold on them as they aged. Perhaps they had no genetic component that was activated by substance use, or they had a secure enough sense of self, family, education, or environment to gain new coping skills as they grew into adult roles. Substance use gradually disables our functioning, so there are times across its development when people can regret the consequences of their heavy use and make a decision to stop.

For others, somewhere in the midst of their behaviors a mysterious need grew. The Faustian bargain within this easy solution began to unfold. They found that they gave more and more of their time, organized their days, or planned their relationships around their use of the substance. They interpreted the withdrawal and craving related to the drug as more anxiety, rage, or pain, which they then medicated by more use. Other causes came into play: painful losses, adult traumas, economic troubles, social failures, or the piling up of experiences of discrimination. They developed a tunnel vision, finding only this one solution for every problem. They began using in isolation rather than celebrating with friends, or as some describe it, they were alone even when partying with others. Substance use increased in response to the growing neurobiological, physical, and practical problems that the substances themselves created. Its sometimes devastating effects on relationships, employment, or the daily practical needs of living required more soothing with the old solution. Decision-making abilities were further damaged by the neurobiological and emotional consequences of continued use. Over time, these multiple dynamics organized into a single desire, into one all-encompassing compulsion.

Addiction, Relationality, and Soul-Sickness

When people in recovery talk about their addiction, what I see is this intense, building sense of suffering. It twists through a person's life and grows into its own dynamic force. In this chapter, I will review some of the common discourses associated with addiction: the moral and the medical model, the diagnostic criteria, and the many proposed causes of addiction. Ultimately, we will use this experience of progressive suffering to reframe addiction as a *soul-sickness.* A soul-sickness arises from many interacting vulnerabilities and progresses into one all-encompassing condition of pain. It is not derived from one individual cause, but the result of a multitude of sufferings that merge together under a common self-destructive solution. Addictive behavior self-organizes into an active evil that sticks to, corrupts, and entwines with a person's state of being. Addiction is not a sin. Rather, it is a spiritual bondage. It is not a free-will action. It is a condition of the soul in distress.

There are some particular premises behind my belief that addiction is a soul-sickness. The first is that we are created in brain, body, and spirit to be profoundly relational.[1] From the beginning, God created us for interdependence, placing us in the circumference of other bodies: first, the body of our attachment figures, and later the body of the social world. As children and as adults, we continue to need others to become whole. This core relationality ties into our need for self-regulation, which is the second premise of this work. I believe that self-regulation is the primary motivation for engaging in addictive behaviors. These behaviors help us to regulate overwhelming or uncomfortable negative affects—in other words, to manage our emotional states, including feelings that seem to rev us up, depress us, or just leave a vaguely uncomfortable anxiousness, like the "angst" that my friend describes above. In the same vein, addictive behaviors help us to cope with stress. They help us to transform our sense of self when relating to others, whether we wish to feel exciting, sociable, or connected. So they help us to manage discomfort or pain within personal and social relationships. While these might sound like individual problems, we seek ritual attempts at self-regulation because we were unable to access our relational worlds in order to achieve that regulation. We did not internalize the skills that we needed to self-regulate amid complex contexts. Or worse, our relational or social environment was the direct source of our suffering.

Think of ice cream or chocolate for a semi-innocent example of self-regulation. Some of us use them to reward ourselves, to feel better after a hard day, to enjoy something very pleasing to the taste, to get a sugar boost, or to symbolically "be good to ourselves"—even though these sweets are nutritionally bad for us. They change how we feel, and so they are little outer band-aids for self-regulation. Other relational connections could have helped us manage whatever sense of stress, boredom, or loneliness that we were feeling; for example, calling a friend, having a cat on our lap, or a worship service. Yet the sweets call to us and the vulnerability of seeking social support is too great to bear. Better sit in front of the television with chocolate (speaking for myself) than trust another human, let alone my fickle cat. Chronic behaviors like addictions are these tendencies writ large, but the dynamics are obviously more pernicious. They begin as attempts to self-regulate. Over time they create something greater than the sum total of the habitual action. Addiction is a force with its own goals and demands, a will that entangles into our own and now must be survived.

This book is primarily about addictions to substances, but I believe that addictions are one of a class of chronic behavioral conditions—ritualistic and self-harming—that have similar effects on the soul. These include eating disorders and other behavioral addictions, such as gambling, internet, or sex addictions. These chronic behaviors have different mental health or medical classifications, but they manifest similar spiritual characteristics that we can gather up under the rubric of soul-sickness. They are all behaviors that begin as ritual attempts to survive something unbearable that is happening in our inner or outer world. They appear to help us, but they are really self-harming. They infect us, compromise the will, then take over the will, and finally turn against us. While I make only brief references to other behavioral addictions, I hope that much of what I am offering here will help the reader frame her or his compassion for these and other chronic conditions. They are not about pleasure, but about pain. In all of these cases, the goal of the caring relationship goes beyond simply "getting over" this behavior. We must consider how past wounds have a habit of pressing into the present. We must respect the suffering of mind, body, and soul that exists beneath these behaviors.

How We See Addictions: A Brief History

I want to begin by explaining some of the history behind how we understand addictions, and why it is important to create a new image of the soul in addiction. What difference does "soul-sickness" make? Simply put, definition drives care. How we frame a condition changes how we view the problem and imagine its resolution. As a very near-sighted person, I know this well. I have a drawer full of glasses in all different shapes and sizes, and each pair changes my vision. I'm keenly aware that my frames and lenses make a difference in the details that I can see. The frames create a border, limiting the breadth of my sight. The lenses bring that particular area into focus. This small area becomes my focal point: it is the clearest reality that I see. So it controls what information becomes important to me. It organizes my field of vision and thus limits the questions I ask of the world. The problem with a pair of glasses is that, after a while, we forget that the frames are there, organizing what we see. In the case of addictions, this means that we enter into theological reflection as if certain assumptions are agreed upon regarding the personality of the addict: what addiction actually is, what causes it, and what solutions best address it. These assumptions frame our vision and limit our ability to see addictions differently.

Addiction is classically viewed through two main frameworks: it is either moral choice or medical disease. The moral side of the argument has framed addiction as an issue of free-will choice. The lens has focused on themes related to sin against God or the sin of criminal behavior against society. It asks questions about the inner life: sins of pleasure or pride, the weakness of will or the force of desire. In contrast, the disease model challenges the idea that addictions are an issue of free-will choice. It has framed addiction as a neurobiological disease. Its lens has focused on themes related to individual health and medical cure. It asks questions about the "hijacking of the brain" by powerful drugs, genetic vulnerability, and the use of pharmaceuticals and empirically tested treatments in recovery. Getting to know a little about these frameworks is important, because they function behind the scenes in much of our theological reflection on addiction. They have implications for how we approach addiction care for the individual and also for how addicts are stigmatized in society.

On the moral side, addictive behavior—or more particularly intoxication—has been an exemplary sin through the centuries. Jesus suffered its stigma as a man who spent time with the wrong kinds of people: he was considered "a glutton and a drunkard, a friend of tax-collectors and sinners" (Matt. 11:19; Luke 7:34). Drunkenness, carousing, and being enslaved to drink make regular appearances on the lists of sin in the New Testament, perhaps drawn from popular Jewish and pagan sources that were concerned that individuals monitor their self-control.[2] New Christians were encouraged to separate themselves from the ways of the world and from practices that appeared pagan, including the moral laxity of social clubs, banqueting, and the celebration of pagan rituals (e.g., 1 Pet. 4:3; 1 Cor. 5:10–11; Rom. 13:12–14).

The great theologians of our faith continued to frame intoxication as an issue of individual free-will action. Through that frame of reference, they focused on attendant questions of desire, pleasure, and appetite. Augustine believed that Christians must order the will and its desires toward God as their ultimate concern. He did not approve of those who were "enslaved to any habit of wine-bibbing," and he was well aware that excessive drinking could progress, moving the soul away from its true direction toward God as one drew closer to the lesser pleasures of the flesh.[3] For Aquinas, drunkenness fell under the general moral sin of gluttony (extreme appetite). Its special problem for the very rational Aquinas was how it hindered our ability to reason. The sin of drunkenness was one of free-will intention. If you knew that the amount of alcohol you imbibed would lead to intoxication, you were responsible for that sin and any other sins that you might commit while intoxicated. If you did not know the strength of the wine, were ignorant of the amount, or did not realize that it would get you drunk, you were considered outside the culpability of intention.[4]

For the Reformers, drunkenness remained a work of the flesh and an expression of how the nature of man is corrupted by the "old Adam" of sin.[5] Luther loved his beer, but he would have preferred some pragmatic limits for the local lords.[6] He claimed that drunkenness was a common sin of Germans, "for we probably can't stop it, and yet it's such a disgraceful nuisance that it injures body, soul, and goods."[7] The Geneva Catechism outlined a similar model of temperance, based on the sin of gluttony. The individual should show temperance in appetite, not eating or drinking more than the body requires. Drunkenness, in particular, was "an infamous vice, which renders a man brutish, injures his health, shortens his life, reduces him to poverty, and by depriving him of the use of reason, may plunge him into the most dreadful crimes."[8] Here we see the themes that will recur throughout the centuries, connecting intoxication to moral corruption and social delinquency.

The moral model thus grew from teachings on intoxication and located the problem within the inner life. It also moved on a spiritual continuum between love for God and love for the pleasures of the flesh. Christians like the philosophical idea of a *telos* to human nature, that we are created to move toward a goal that expresses our essential selves. Like a hammer is meant for a nail or a flower moves toward the sun, human beings are created to move toward what completes them. Augustine believed that we were created to love God. As he famously said, our hearts are restless till they rest in God.[9] Calvin claimed that the chief end of human life was to know God.[10] The Westminster Shorter Catechism affirms, "Man's chief end is to glorify God and to enjoy him forever."[11] Movement in the wrong direction is sometimes called concupiscence or disordered desire. So we are either moving toward the true pleasures of God in temperance or toward the lesser pleasures of the flesh in addiction. Our actions, seemingly unhindered by contingency or context, draw our desires in a line toward a singular goal—one way or the other.

Labeling inner sin has a tendency to leak out into social stigma, so the moral model also branded certain inebriates as corruptors of society and dangers to others. In the nineteenth century, the Prohibition movement against "demon drink" expressed this growing stigma. Drunkenness was associated with the lower class. It represented the breakdown of the family: the problem of irresponsible or abusive husbands and impoverished women and children.[12] Rev. Lyman Beecher, one of the founders of the American Temperance Society, claimed that alcohol "obliterates the fear of the Lord, and a sense of accountability, paralyses the power of conscience, and hardens the heart, and turns out upon society a sordid, selfish, ferocious animal."[13] He warned that the laboring classes, "perverted by intemperance," would ultimately put American democracy at risk.[14] Prohibition was also considered a way to enforce the emerging Jim Crow social order and to provide the "moral uplift" of African Americans. [15] For instance, in the Texas prohibition debate, to disagree with prohibition "left African Americans vulnerable to a pernicious form of moral exile" by white evangelicals, which threatened African Americans' right to take part in the political process.[16]

Opium was added to the moral and racial stigma in the mid-nineteenth century, particularly as a result of campaigns against Chinese immigration. White people regularly took opiates in the form of tonics or prescriptions from pharmacies, and that practice often resulted in abuse or addiction.[17] But the Chinese were stigmatized for smoking opium and for corrupting white women and youth in their opium dens.[18] These claims—along with accusations of criminal behavior and job stealing—culminated in a set of laws that effectively banned Chinese immigration to America from 1882 to 1943. The moral model was a way to ascribe an immoral identity to a group of people, which would then justify controlling or removing them as a corrupting influence on society.

The growing drug wars of the twentieth century continued to use moral and racial rhetoric to enact social control. As early as 1911, Dr. Hamilton Wright, America's first opium commissioner, made the connection between cocaine, crime, and African American drug use.[19] By 1914, the Harrison Act restricted the importing and marketing of cocaine and opium. It essentially made these drugs illegal, as doctors were convicted for prescribing maintenance opioids to addicts.[20] In the 1930s Harry Anslinger's crusade against heroin and marijuana also focused on African Americans.[21] In the 1970s, the Nixon administration declared a new war on drugs, most famously connecting drugs to social marginalization and racial control. Nixon's domestic policy advisor, John Ehrlichman, was said to have claimed that by "getting the public to associate the hippies with marijuana and blacks with heroin, and then criminalizing both heavily, we could disrupt those communities."[22]

By the 1980s the drug wars had shifted to crack cocaine, but the connection between drugs and race remained. Racial stigmatization was most clearly evident in the Anti-Drug Abuse Act of 1986 and 1988, which led to a five-year sentence for simple possession of five grams of crack cocaine, which was considered to be a problem in poor African American neighborhoods. A comparable sentence required 500 grams of powder cocaine, which was considered a drug of the white elite. This crusade against drugs was used to justify greater harassment, searches, arrests, and incarceration of African Americans.[23] In the two decades after 1980, drug arrests in America increased by 170 percent.[24] Today, African Americans, Hispanics, and poor whites remain the ones most likely to be serving time in jail or prison as a result of this so-called war.[25]

The medical model has had a briefer history in America, growing out of attempts to develop a cure for alcoholism. It began with the writing of Dr. Benjamin Rush (1746–1813), whose first study of the problem of alcohol involved drunkenness in the Continental Army. He was the first to consider chronic drunkenness as a progressive medical condition and to consider abstinence as the ultimate goal for cure.[26] In 1864, the New York State Inebriate Asylum in Binghamton became the first hospital for addictions in the country.[27] By 1870, a group of professionals had gathered to create the American Association for the Cure of Inebriates (AACI), hoping to create a new medical specialty that offered compassionate care to alcoholics.[28] Doctors and researchers also began to assert that opium addicts presented a clear medical trajectory and symptomology. Treatment included a variety of methods for medically monitored detoxification, with some advocating exhortation and education to avoid future relapse.[29] Yet even in these discussions, doctors distinguished between higher class victims of iatrogenic addiction and the criminal or morally degenerate addict. In the 1930s, the Alcoholics Anonymous movement called alcoholism a disease of craving, like an allergy that sets off a chain reaction in the body after one drink.[30] The addict was not weak-willed but powerless over this cunning disease. However, the 12-step cure for this allergy remained spiritual, including belief in a higher power that blurred the lines between alcohol's effects on body and soul.

Throughout America's history, there has been a conflation between the moral and medical models, from Lyman Beecher toggling between the terms disease and sin, to a law passed in 1929 to "confine and treat" heroin addicts in federal hospitals, to the current drug court treatment system that seeks to both punish and cure.[31] Today, advocates are pushing for a purely scientific return to the medical account, seeing addiction as a neurobiological disease rather than a moral sin or crime. Reams of studies test for genetic predisposition, scan the brain, and generally abuse rodents in an effort to discern why certain individuals would take drugs to excess. Some groups, such as the Substance Abuse and Mental Health Services Administration (SAMHSA), emphasize that addiction is a neurobiological disease that is best addressed by a combination of psychological and medical treatments.[32] Other researchers seek new pharmaceuticals to rebalance the brain without the help of a therapeutic context or a higher power. Framing addiction as a disease and not a crime is a major point of advocacy against the war on drugs.

Limits of the Moral and Medical Models

When we compare the moral and medical models of addiction, we can see that there are clear reasons to be cautious about the moral model. Most obviously, research shows that people do not choose to become addicts. We are learning more and more about how the functioning of the brain and nervous system propels addictive behaviors. This understanding of the neurobiology of addiction suggests that addiction is a condition with its own dynamics rather than a daily succession of free-will choices to get intoxicated. Second, for pastoral caregivers, the moral model does not help us understand the particular spiritual suffering that surrounds this chronic condition. It focuses on the moment of choice and not on the spiritual bondage of the one addicted. It flattens out the complexity of a condition that grows from both the sins we do and the sins done to us.

But, perhaps most importantly, the moral model of addiction must be dismantled because society has used the many meanings covered under this model to stigmatize and marginalize distinct groups of people. In the United States, it has attributed an immoral and criminal identity to the Chinese, to African Americans, and most recently to Hispanics, who are accused of poisoning America's youth with drugs.[33] It is used to justify anti-immigration laws, invasive policing tactics, and inordinate incarceration. The moral model is too easy an excuse for the powerful to enact their own sin against the most marginalized of our society.

The medical model is a helpful starting point because it enables us to challenge the stigma of addictions and to advocate for medical treatment instead of criminalization and punishment. But when it is held with its own religious fervor, this model can overfocus on the brain to the detriment of the body and soul. It can seem to suggest that our brains simply malfunction from the power of the drug, as if our brains and behaviors are not profoundly connected to our emotional and social lives. It risks reifying addiction as a kind of virus or organ dysfunction, instead of a dynamic progression of behaviors, different at different stages of substance use, which addicts experience in relation to their personal resources and broader social context. There is a slow uprising against the insistence that addiction is a medical disease, which claims that, while brain changes may occur, they are based on the way the brain learns and can be reversed.[34] It is at most "disease-like"—but not an actual disease.

Furthermore, while pharmaceutical interventions do help manage safe withdrawal from substances, they can't teach us how to live a healthy and happy life without our addictions. There is a huge financial incentive for pharmaceutical companies to claim that their drugs can cure addictions, whether by blocking cravings or patching the genetic holes in our brains. But focusing on brain scans and drug trials does not begin to address how addiction is attached to the realities of our interpersonal and social worlds.[35] So, while pastoral caregivers need to be informed about the neurobiological condition of addiction, that is only part of the story. If we are created for relationship—to love God and to love others as ourselves—pastoral caregivers have much work to do to help encourage emotional, relational, and social healing for the person seeking recovery.

Since pastoral theologian Howard Clinebell wrote his classic book on the pastoral care of addicts nearly two decades ago, Christians have continued to debate whether addiction is a moral failing or a disease, or whether certain actions proceeding from substance use could be considered sin or symptom.[36] Our frames prevent us from seeing much beyond these borders, and our lenses keep us focused on the same questions. We end up debating who is at fault (the will or the brain) and thus who or what single cause can heal the problem (a conversion or a medical treatment). But what if theological reflection has something to say to the whole of the condition—its genesis, its grasping attempt at self-regulation, its neurobiological reorganization, and finally its possessive hold? A soul-sickness is the spiritual oppression that takes shape within these multiple-emergence points of addiction. My hope is that we can develop a different vision in order to better address the spiritual causes and effects of this progressive condition.

The Emergence of Addiction

I find the Gerasene demoniac in the Gospel of Mark to be a particularly apt image for understanding addictions, since one of addiction's defining characteristics is multiplicity. Just as the Gerasene is infected with a legion of demons, addictions arise from a legion of vulnerabilities related to the addict's personal history and broader context. No singular cause makes someone become an addict. Instead, an addiction develops over time as multiple factors organize around the addictive behavior and lock it into place. Reviewing this multiplicity will prepare us for the chapters ahead, when we discuss the brain in chapter 2 and the specific relational and social causes of addiction in chapters 3 and 4. This story will also build the foundation for our understanding of a soul-sickness. The idea of many-into-one, this emergence into a self-organizing condition, expands how we understand the spiritual challenge of addictions as pastoral caregivers. The addict is not trying to manage a single, individual choice to use drugs or alcohol in excess. Instead, he is battling something bigger, which has come into being from multiple sources of suffering.

So, what causes addiction? Let me begin with an extended example: the opioid epidemic. Not surprisingly, a multitude of explanations exist for this problem. Some people focus on iatrogenic addiction: opioid abuse that begins with legitimate medical use and grows into an addiction. It is estimated that between 8 to 12 percent of patients prescribed opioids for chronic pain develop an opioid use disorder.[37] From an individual perspective, we could claim that patients using opioids were genetically predisposed to addiction. Or, if we considered context, we could focus on the overprescribing of prescription narcotics by doctors. For instance, in 2010, enough prescription painkillers were prescribed to medicate every American adult around the clock for a month.[38] If we took a further step back in causes, we could find broader economic reasons for the overprescribing of opioid medications, including the behavior of the pharmaceutical companies who engage in aggressive marketing campaigns to encourage opioid prescribing and use.

But perhaps the problem is the strength of opioid street drugs and their availability. Heroin is readily available and much cheaper than pills. Decreases in the price of heroin have been associated with increased hospital admissions for heroin-related overdoses.[39] News stories also tell us about the dangers of heroin and new fentanyl-based substances that are one hundred to ten thousand times more potent than heroin.[40] So the problem is the power of the drug both to hook us and to kill us. Multiple-substance use is actually another part of the overdose problem, as many overdoses are linked to a combination of opiates with alcohol, antidepressants, or hypnotic drugs.[41]

Another cause of the opiate crisis may be social modeling and peer influence. The sharing and trading of pills for recreational use appears to be an increasingly acceptable behavior in high-school and college groups. In fact, opioids are competing with marijuana as the drug of initiation for youth. In 2015, they rivaled marijuana as the most prevalently abused drug, and the number of individuals reporting current misuse of prescription drugs is more than those reporting use of cocaine, heroin, methamphetamine, MDMA (mollies), and phencyclidine (PCP) combined.[42] If we step further back, we might find broader socioeconomic reasons for this growing use among the young. For instance, in one account, heightened prescription opioid and heroin use signals the end of the proud manufacturing towns of the Midwest, including the social ennui and lack of opportunity that is leading these youths to an increasingly available supply of Mexican black-tar heroin.[43]

These voices of alarm are not the end of the story. Others will say that the real issue remains the public perception of delinquent behavior. Opioids are being covered in the news media now only because white, middle-class kids are getting addicted.[44] We are arguing for changes in laws or additional funding for treatment only because it is now viewed as a white problem. America has a long history of connecting drugs to minority populations in order to criminalize them. Now that there are too many overdose deaths to ignore its effects on white and middle-class users, a kinder and gentler treatment has come into focus. News stories tell us about white opioid and heroin addicts who are college kids and schoolteachers, people with hobbies and friends—in other words, good people who suddenly became victimized by the power of the drugs.[45]

Finally, opioids have unique effects on the brain. They help to remove not only physical pain but also emotional pain, which might be why they are so compelling. The anterior cingulate is a relational part of the brain that is responsible for our attachment bonding. It lights up when we feel the pain of social rejection or social separation.[46] It is also the region with the highest concentration of opiate neurotransmitters, since opiates rise when we bond with our attachment figures. Along with our bonding and security needs, the anterior cingulate is the place where we feel the affective aspects of pain. In other words, the emotional response to pain resides in a different part of the brain than the registering of physical pain. This combination of attachment need and affective pain may explain why we really do feel better if someone holds us when we are physically hurting.

Studies show that when this area is flooded with opiates, animals stop making distress calls to their mothers, which is just about the saddest thing I have ever heard.[47] Imagine a drug that can take away your feelings of social pain or your need for security and soothing while under stress: you are alone, but you no longer care enough to cry for help. The ability of opioids to remove emotional and physical pain, along with the harrowing childhoods of many heroin users, suggest that this is a very appealing drug to medicate pain that comes from childhood maltreatment or trauma.

Which answer is the correct one? In fact, "all of the above" is the more accurate explanation. A combination of risks, different for each person, emerges into an addiction. As the opioid debate suggests, there are many risk factors that make individuals vulnerable to addictions across the life cycle.[48] First, the power (or potency) of substances is part of the problem, which is why the federal government rates drugs for their addictive potential and makes some illegal. Mental-health issues are also strongly correlated with addictions, such as ADHD, depression and bipolar mood disorders, borderline and antisocial personality disorders, and schizophrenia. Genetics are estimated to make up anywhere from 40 to 70 percent of addiction propensity.[49]

However, these individual factors are also influenced by the addict's broader environment. Families greatly influence addictions, especially substance-using caretakers. They may model substance use for the next generation or cause chaotic, neglectful, or abusive environments for their children. In fact, childhood maltreatment and trauma are closely linked to the early onset of substance use and future addictions. Some advocates also want to widen the net from the family to argue for broader social modeling. Our culture glorifies substance use, making it available and appealing. Anti-tobacco laws work from this assumption: they attempt to limit smoking in public places, and they use rising prices and social shame to curb the appeal of smoking. Finally, social stress makes individuals vulnerable to substance use. Substances help us manage negative affect, so we may use them as a coping skill in situations of trauma, economic insecurity, or social oppression.

None of these causes makes someone wake up an addict. Instead, they paint a more complicated picture of a person's progress from substance use to addiction. It is a much more haphazard process than we usually imagine, as the disorder grows from our attempts at managing a variety of risks during the course of our lives. We enter into substance use as we experiment with how to navigate our personal and social worlds. As we use, we find that the substance does something for us. For some, drugs and alcohol medicate psychological suffering from histories of abuse, neglect, or trauma. Or we used them to manage the symptoms of a mental-health condition. Others may have suffered social anxiety or shyness, or just wanted to fit in with a crowd in high school or college. Most found that substances helped them manage negative affect, such as depression, loneliness, or rage. In all of these cases, individuals did more than seek pleasure. They sought a change in their sense of self so that they could better live in their own skin and relate to others.

People may experience the progress from recreational use to abuse and into addiction very quickly—in a matter of a few months or a few years. Or they may progress slowly across decades. There are certainly those who have high genetic vulnerability, mental illness, or lives of extreme trauma who flash quickly into addiction's hold. But even here, if we look more closely, we will find that more than one factor has led to their initiation into substances and the escalation into abuse. There are others who manage problematic use across a lifetime, sometimes gaining control for short periods before dipping back into further abuse of substances. They may never reach an official diagnosis of substance-use disorder, but their behaviors affect their physical and spiritual health and hurt those they love. For others, after decades of problematic use, multiple losses and consequences surround them and they seem to lose all control, falling into a single-minded focus on their addictive behaviors.

So addictions emerge over time as multiple aspects of one's life reorganize around the use of drugs and alcohol. Rather than a string of daily choices to use a substance, it is better understood as the emergence of a self-organizing system.[50] Self-organizing systems do not build in a linear manner from singular cause to its effect. Instead, multiple factors interact with each other, balancing out into a system that is beyond any single cause. Different areas of the brain adjust to the drug, and to each other, as the brain's many functions seek to find a new balance. Habits and behavioral cues, the rise and fall of emotions, and the daily aesthetics of living also get folded into the use of the drug. Relationships fall to pieces, stress is actually heightened instead of managed, and negative affect is increased rather than soothed. A person needs more drugs to feel normal. The new system balances around substance use and locks in place. Once created, the addict does not have to make a daily choice related to any one vulnerability, such as ceding to natural impulsivity, feeling the daily influence of a social group, or even responding to the trauma that led to first use. Addiction has self-organized into its own system and strives to keep this new balance. In the language of possession, the addict now fights a separate force: an organized, self-perpetuating condition that seeks to choose for her.

Symptoms of the Sickness

What are some signs of this emerging system? Addiction is called a disease, but we cannot take an X-ray or have our blood tested to diagnose our condition. Instead, it is expressed through a multiplicity of symptoms or behaviors that affect our ability to manage our lives. The *Diagnostic and Statistical Manual* (DSM-V) criteria offer a range of severity for what they term "substance use disorder," which flows on a continuum from mild to moderate to severe, depending on the number of symptoms present in the person's life. The

DSM-V is the official manual to diagnose many mental health conditions. Most of its diagnostics are concerned with the length of time for a behavior, how many symptoms a person has, and how much the behavior is getting in the way of daily functioning. As an example, the diagnosis for "alcohol use disorder" includes the following characteristics, which are similar for any substance disorder diagnosis.[51] People can be diagnosed with a mild disorder if they have two to three symptoms, moderate with four to five, or severe if they have six or more symptoms on the list.

DSM-V Symptom List for Substance Use Disorder

1. Alcohol is often taken in larger amounts or over a longer period than was intended.
2. There is a persistent desire—or unsuccessful efforts—to cut down or control alcohol use.
3. A great deal of time is spent in activities necessary to obtain alcohol, use alcohol, or recover from its effects.
4. There is craving, or a strong desire or urge to use alcohol.
5. Recurrent alcohol use resulting in a failure to fulfill major role obligations at work, school, or home.
6. Alcohol use continues despite having persistent or recurrent social or interpersonal problems that are caused or exacerbated by the effects of alcohol.
7. The person gives up important social, occupational, or recreational activities or reduces these activities because of alcohol use.
8. Recurrent alcohol use in situations in which it is physically hazardous.
9. The individual continues alcohol use despite knowledge of having a persistent or recurrent physical or psychological problem that is likely to have been caused or exacerbated by alcohol.
10. Tolerance, as defined by either of the following:
    a) a need for markedly increased amounts of alcohol to achieve intoxication or desired effect;
    b) a markedly diminished effect with continued use of the same amount of alcohol.
11. Withdrawal, as manifested by either of the following:
    a) the characteristic withdrawal syndrome for alcohol;[52]
    b) alcohol (or a closely related substance, such as a benzodiazepine) is taken to relieve or avoid withdrawal symptoms.

Note again the theme of multiplicity. A person struggling with substance abuse can experience many symptoms. There are neurobiological effects, including craving, tolerance, and withdrawal. There are relational and social effects, including social and interpersonal problems, poor emotional regulation, and withdrawal from other interests. We also see something of the spiritual condition of the disorder. We lose a sense of our responsibility to self and others as we fall deeper into addictions. We lose a connection to values and relationships. We are also spiritually oppressed by something evil, since an identifying characteristic of addiction is that it is self-destructive as well as other-destructive. It continues despite consistent adverse consequences and risk of physical or psychological harm.

It is good for pastoral caregivers to know the common symptoms of addiction, because people often minimize their substance use even when they come to pastoral care worried about their behaviors. They might need help making the connection between their practical problems and their substance use. We have a stereotype of the addict as homeless or antisocial, but many people who qualify for a mild or moderate substance-use disorder are able to function well enough to fool themselves and others about the extent and consequences of their use. Keeping this list in mind can further help pastoral caregivers notice when multiple problems are arising for a parishioner that may suggest a problem with drugs or alcohol. As I will discuss in chapters 6 and 7, we can gently open the conversation about how substance use might be affecting a person's life. We can help an addict verbalize how the use of substances might have led to consequences in her life, maybe for the first time.

Finally, as we look at this long list of symptoms, we see that addictions truly affect the health of the soul. The DSM-V list has moral implications: addicts may use substances without concern for their responsibilities, sacrifice relationships and values, and may use even to the point of self-destruction. While the state of addiction is not a sin in itself, these moral sins—the ways that we hurt others and ourselves—are certainly a part of how this condition unfolds. At the same time, we have to be careful not to confuse the *causes* in the last section with the *symptoms* in this section. When we see these symptoms in someone we serve, we might decide that she is morally weak, selfish, angry, or irresponsible. By doing so, we confuse her actions with her character. We internalize her symptoms and assume that her personality caused her addiction. She may currently seem like all of those things right now, but that does not tell us who she was or who she could be if freed from the soul-sickness that lives through her.

I remember a man talking about his addiction after many years of sobriety, sharing all of the selfish ways that he had lived his life. Suddenly and passionately he said, "But that is not who I am anymore." He knew that he had cared for others and had wanted to care even then, but drugs and alcohol had him in chains. He might disappear from work for a day or leave for an errand and never return that night to his wife and children. The addiction had strangled his care for others. He was, he repeated, in chains. When he got sober, the part of him that wanted to care was set free. It could flower. He could be in love with his family and feel their love in return. As we will discuss in the story of the Gerasene in the Gospel of Mark, it is important for us to know which voice is doing the talking, because so often it is the voice of the addiction that is taking the lead in people's lives. If we understand that moral problems are often symptoms of the disease, we are better able to meet the addict with compassion and walk the longer road toward a full physical, emotional, and spiritual recovery.

Desire, Pleasure, and Soul-Sickness

If multiple threads self-organize into addiction, this complicates how we see addiction's spiritual effects. It means that we need to broaden our frame to the context and causes through which addiction emerges. We see addiction less as a drama focused on the inner world of faith and more about how we attempt to survive pervasive experiences of suffering through our relational and social worlds. A soul-sickness is the infection within the soul that emerges as the addiction takes hold. The experience of emergence "from many into one" suggests that something new comes into being—something within but also beyond a person's will. It is a state of spiritual bondage.

What does this framework help us see differently as pastoral caregivers? When attempting to reflect theologically on addiction, Christians have largely remained informed by the moral framework and have focused their lens on the movement of desire toward or away from God. One of the epigraphs at the beginning of this chapter, a quote from Cornelius Plantinga's *Not the Way It's Supposed to Be,* is a classic summary of Christian thought on intoxication.[53] Plantinga is sympathetic to addiction as a tragic and complex condition, but when considering the spiritual effects of this condition, he ultimately returns to the drama of the will and its appetites. It is the choice to make substances rather than God our ultimate concern. It is a result of the disordered longing of our heart and the lassitude of a will given over to pleasure. Terry Cooper, in *Sin, Pride and Self-Acceptance,* also describes the movement of desire through the sin of pride, claiming that addicts move away from trust in God to "habitual, destructive enjoyments of inferior goods as replacements for God."[54] While he mentions Reinhold Niebuhr's distinction between pride and self-escape as two kinds of motivations behind addiction, he does not consider that there might be sufferings outside of the self that the individual is trying to manage through that escape. The focus remains interior, and in the end it is pride and self-reliance that fuel addictions, as individuals rebel against God to follow their own pleasures.

Augustine's idea of misdirected desire also is used to describe addictions as a kind of longing for our true union in God that has gone awry. Desire that is properly ordered through our actions moves toward its divine resting place, while disordered desire moves the passions toward poor substitutes, such as alcohol. We find this story of desire in contemporary authors such as Gerald May's classic *Addiction and Grace.*[55] While an addiction affects the brain and psyche of the individual, it is also a sign of disordered desire. We fall away from God as our ultimate concern and fall into idolatry. We become attached to our addictions, and they become a false god to us. These themes are also behind the more nuanced account of James Nelson's *Thirst: God and the Alcoholic Experience.*[56] Nelson honors the paradoxical experience of addiction as both a medical and moral problem, but the spiritual framework remains largely inside of the individual. Addiction tries to fill "a yearning we can't quite name and yet are quite aware of," and God is the source and destiny of this yearning desire.[57]

The ordering of desire is a very appealing image of the soul and its spiritual dilemma, as it is pulled to and fro between God and the pleasures of the flesh. It certainly seems as though addicts replace worship of God with the worship of a substance. It seems that they desire pleasure in their craving for intoxication. Their appetite seems insatiable because they can't seem to moderate it, and their attachment seems obvious because they won't easily quit. In the pride of will, they can definitely be difficult to help. However, we are defining the problem through its *symptoms* again. We are not talking about what causes addiction, but about its effects: craving and withdrawal, dependence and tolerance, tunnel-visioned motivation, and changes to personality and spiritual health. All of these seem to mimic pleasure-seeking or misdirected desire. Perhaps it feels natural to put the addict on this telos between God and the flesh because it is human nature to desire things that are destructive to us. We can then make the addict fit into our theologies of the spiritual and moral life. After all, don't we all struggle with bringing our lives into conformity with God's will? Don't we all fall into temptation?

Yes, we all do. And that is exactly why this is a bad framework within which to perceive chronic behavioral conditions like addiction. The framework is both too universal and too particularly focused on one explanation for the addict's suffering. To the former point, this is a universal account of the movement of the soul toward or away from God. The account can be beautiful and sweeping, as in Augustine, or precise and particular, as in Aquinas. But as a general proposal about the individual movement of the will, it is not suited to making particular pastoral sense of the forces that combine in a chronic behavioral condition like addiction. I certainly affirm that human desire should move toward its ultimate and proper end of loving God, but using this framework to understand addiction erases what is distinctive about addiction as a spiritual malady. Addicts do not score high on the DSM-V standards for substance-use disorder because they felt a universal restlessness of the heart and thought that alcohol or heroin might be better than God at solving that lack. They were caught in an effort to survive their inner and outer worlds, and that effort turned decidedly against them.

This gets us to the latter point, the particular focus on desire. Disordered desire misinterprets addiction as a pursuit of pleasure. This is based on the idea of intoxication as a pleasurable experience, which is actually a problem applicable to the recreational use of alcohol, not to the experience of addiction. At first blush, the pleasures of intoxication seem to fit nicely into the idea of the pleasures of the flesh. Lack of ability to moderate or stop also seems to fit into the problem of gluttony or appetite. We can certainly see all of these features within the experience of an addict. The problem is, again, that we are confusing symptoms with cause. The moral model is about what motivates the addict. Pride, pleasure, appetite, and desire can be ancillary to the experience of addiction but not its primary motivator. The primary motivator is pain. It is personal and relational suffering. It is the cycle of withdrawal and craving, which functions outside of conscious willing. It is spiritual distress. Addiction is not an enjoyable experience. It is not an attempt to run to pleasure. Rather, it is an attempt to manage pain.

Let me repeat that definition drives care. As I have mentioned above, deciding that addicts are especially sinful (after all, they had a choice) leads to especially judgmental or punitive individual and social responses. Deciding that the addict faces a temptation to indulge excess appetite "just as you and I do" (after all, we are all tempted) risks assuming that the addict can think about and execute behavior change just as you and I are able to do. Deciding that an addict failed the test of desire and gave in thoroughly to pleasure risks our discounting of the pain of his experience. We thus thin out the whole drama of his relationship with God into one line toward or away from his heart's desire. Finally, this telos sets up a spatial problem to our suffering. Is the addict really walking on a line away from God and toward the flesh? Does he need to return to God, or has God never left him as he struggled to survive his life?

The Framework of a Soul-Sickness

How can we think about the spiritual effects of addictions outside of this broad concept of human desire? If a soul-sickness follows the emerging and progressive medical condition of addiction, then we can see in it certain identifying markers. It is the result of behaviors that were harnessed in an attempt to survive a problem in self-regulation. It arises from a dynamic combination of personal, relational, and social vulnerabilities. It affects moral, emotional, and neurobiological functioning. As it clicks into a homeostasis, it becomes self-protective and self-perpetuating, eroding the quality of life and the will of its host over time. Addictions are tragic because they turn on us. The many gains that the individual received from using, such as managing emotions, dealing with stress, or easing social belonging, are exactly what she loses once the addiction takes hold. In the irony of the sickness, she ends up using more substances to manage the suffering that the substance itself inflicts.

A soul-sickness is the spiritual oppression that unfolds in the wake of this progression. We become estranged from ourselves and others. We are not really present in our own skin. We are unable to take in information from the world and respond to it accurately. We are trapped in the dysfunction of our brains and bodies. The soul-sickness further isolates us from others, and guilt and self-loathing inhibit a positive relationship with God. Sometimes God seems unable or unwilling to save us. Over time, our relationships begin to fail, our empathy dulls, and our moral compass sways off balance. The substance becomes our primary relationship and our greatest need. It is less a weakness of the will than the feeling that we must survive something evil that has taken over our functioning. It is that double-mind of Paul in Romans 7, where it is no longer I who does it, but sin that dwells within me (Romans 7:20). Many people in recovery describe the moment when they knew that they were enslaved to the cravings of their use. Yet this knowledge was not enough to change their now chronic behaviors. The addiction had emerged into a self-organizing system and had a life of its own.

In this way, the dynamics of addiction do not flow out of humanity's fallen pride. They flow out of our fallen fragility. Rather than a line between cause and effect, it is better imagined as getting caught in a net. Imagine a meshwork of attachment vulnerabilities and social sufferings, poor stress-regulation and poor social skills, impulsive choices and genetic propensities that together knot the addict into this emerging condition. Finally, pleasure is not the main motivating factor, but pain. Pain propels us to substances as a solution. Pain wraps around our use as the addiction takes hold. The spiritual problem of addiction is not in its free-will sin as much as its slow privation of the good. It is an opportunistic infection. The addict has been fed upon by evil and needs Jesus to save him from a bondage that is progressively unwinding his mind, body, and soul.

Within this spiritual framework, we also need a scriptural lens to help us focus what we know about addictions. Mark's Gerasene demoniac—possessed by a legion of demons and abandoned in the tombs—captures this sense of multiplicity and emergence, suffering and self-regulation (Mark 5:1–20). Much like addiction, the Gerasene's legion is an active and victimizing force. It is a spiritual condition but also possesses the body and mind. It seems to be happening partially against the man's will and yet also through his will. It is both individual and social because, in the Gospel of Mark, demon possessions gesture toward the deep political suffering of an oppressive empire. Possession is also unclean, separating the individual from any relationship with the religious world. Finally, a possession is a torment to heal, as the personal and the social are knit back together without the behaviors that have become a part of the person's identity. The legion thus becomes a metaphor for what is binding, dangerous, and oppressive about addiction.

The Gerasene demoniac also knows something about evil and its effects. He has already lost everything, yet his demons persist. Though some sense of sin is involved in this abject character howling among the tombs, it is not the primary problem. He is controlled by a force greater than himself. So the Gerasene does not need to repent and return from his sin. He needs to be met and healed in his soul-sickness. Jesus comes to him as he is, in the midst of the legion's attempt to protect itself from change. Perhaps this last point is the most important for our pastoral care. As Jesus bargains with that legion of demons, we see the process of care in a different light. It is not one choice to change, but a progress toward healing. It is not a sudden and miraculous cure or a quick resurrection. It is staying with the ambivalent process where life grows tentatively from death. It turns out that addiction is not about our movement away from God, but about God's staying with us even as we suffer. It is God's faithfulness to us even when we are estranged from the good, when we are oppressed and in spiritual distress.

As we discuss the neurobiological changes, childhood losses, and social oppressions that are a part of this condition, keep in mind the image of a growing legion. A soul-sickness helps us to imagine what shape evil takes when it latches onto our vulnerability. Moral sin is involved in this model, because chronic ritual behaviors compromise our moral decisions over time. But the larger picture is the emergence into a possessive force that slowly takes over the self. This possessive nature of the soul-sickness is evident when users begin to dream about stopping in some distant future or begin to rationalize their ability to control or manage the substance. It is the growing insanity of promises sincerely made and by midday callously ignored. It is the experience of waking up in the middle of the night, full of shame and recrimination, but then turning back to the substance the next day even as they talk about leaving it. Due to the denial and physical dependence associated with addiction, it can be weeks, months, or even years before a well-considered choice is made to stop the use. In this sense, it is not surprising that the word "addiction" comes from the Latin *addictus* (meaning "to be enslaved"). The expression "don't give the devil a foothold" is good advice.

Chapter Two

This Is Your Brain on Drugs

> Who has woe? Who has sorrow?
> Who has strife? Who has complaining?
> Who has wounds without cause?
> Who has redness of eyes?
> Those who linger late over wine,
> those who keep trying mixed wines.
> Do not look at wine when it is red,
> when it sparkles in the cup
> and goes down smoothly.
> At the last it bites like a serpent,
> and stings like an adder.
> Your eyes will see strange things,
> and your mind utter perverse things.
> You will be like one who lies down in the midst of the sea,
> like one who lies on the top of a mast.
> "They struck me," you will say, "but I was not hurt;
> they beat me, but I did not feel it.
> When shall I awake?
> I will seek another drink."
>
> —Proverbs 23:29–35

It might seem strange to begin a chapter on the brain with the Bible, but Scripture agrees that intoxication takes a man out of his right mind.[1] Wine might be a gift from God that gladdens the heart, but too much of it makes the brain foolish, and the ensuing physical and mental consequences hold a surprising consistency across the generations. Proverbs 23 gives us the most detailed symptom list for drunkenness in the Bible, and its description of craving, habit, and consequence agrees well with our own conception of alcoholism today. The alcoholic suffers woe, sorrow, strife, and complaining.

He has the red eyes of a permanent hangover, the seeking for more and more of the substance, and the craving when he awakes. Alcohol leaves the drinker unable to think through actions or realistically understand their effects. Life seems random and victimizing. His sense of reality is altered: he sees and hears strange things. He is unable to account for the passing of time. He suffers physical injuries and emotional confusion. He does not learn from his mistakes because he is not fully conscious of how he is hurt or damaged as a result of his drinking. Consequences do not deter him and he only wishes to repeat the cycle again.

From ancient days to the DSM-V today, people have noted the effects of substances on an individual's ability to function in the world. They note the obsession and excess, an inability to perceive reality, and the seeming inefficacy of consequences to deter the repetitive behavior. They witness the degeneration of decision-making and moral capacity. The individual addict seems to have lost his right mind. How does that happen? In this chapter I want to talk about how a decision becomes a condition: it's a story about your brain on drugs. If you were born before the 1980s, that phrase should evoke an old TV message about an egg cracked into a frying pan. This, it claimed, is your brain on drugs—simply cooked to a crisp. But if you were born after the 1990s, you may have a better image. Your brain on drugs is less like an egg in a frying pan and more like a computer that has caught a very bad virus. Drugs do not fry the brain; they rewire it to function differently. Scientists are studying many areas of the brain for the effects of heavy drug use; I will briefly explore these areas of functioning:

1. Brain signaling, or neurotransmission (different by drug, but all affecting dopamine levels);
2. The reward center of the brain (nucleus acumbens, mesolimbic dopamine pathway, and the ventral tegmental area);
3. The stress system (amygdala, insula, HPA-axis that creates stress chemicals like cortisol, the nervous system);
4. The executive brain (prefrontal cortex).

In case this list triggers unpleasant memories of your high-school biology class, let me give you reason for courage. We do not need to diagnose or fix the brain as pastoral caregivers. But some information on the brain will help us get a better feel for the dilemma of the addicts we serve. We can read Scripture on drunkenness and get a basic picture. But Scripture will not tell us why many generations of people have noted these same effects.

Caring about the whys behind a behavior is a way of being faithful to a holy curiosity about the other. By "holy curiosity," I mean the honor that we feel when we are allowed into the life of another child of God. We are called to be curious about who that person is and how she is experiencing her life. The brain is a big part of the why of addiction, so we can show our love to others when we seek to better understand their brains. These basics can help us plan care in light of common neurobiological symptoms of addiction, such as anxiety, depression, denial, a quickened stress response, and an emotional reactivity that may be related to the swings of the brain's chemical balance. Learning about the brain can also give us a more compelling picture for our theological reflection as we consider the progress of the disease. Most important for pastoral care, remember this: the brain that first chooses to take the drug is not the same brain that, years later, has to make the decision to stop taking it.

For the addict's progress to possession, the changes of the brain represent what neuroscientist George Koob calls the "dark side" of addiction. The move from recreational use to addiction proceeds from an *impulsive* to a *compulsive* stage of using. The impulsive stage is what we usually imagine when we think of intoxication. The positive effects of casual drug use sensitize what is called the "reward center" of the brain. The reward center says, "Do more of this!" The drinker or drug user feels motivated to repeat these effects over and over.[2] In this stage, we want to repeat an action for its expected effect, or positive reinforcement. It is the kind of chasing after pleasure or escape from pain that society—and often theology—think about when they consider intoxication. Some people stay in this stage for a long time and then begin to transition from recreational use into abusing substances. They might experience some negative effects on the health of their mind, body, and spirit, but they often think that they can control their use or stop whenever they want to.

However, the more we use, the more brain systems become implicated in the habit and the harder it is to escape the behavior. Addiction grows from an ever-tightening loop of three recurring phases: 1) binge and intoxication; 2) withdrawal and negative affect; and 3) preoccupation and anticipation to use again (craving).[3] This binge-withdrawal-craving loop produces a state of stress reactivity as the body and brain seek to manage the chemical ebb and flow and try to achieve a sense of balance. Over time, cycles of craving and withdrawal, drug seeking, and intoxication create a chronic stress environment.[4] We are now compelled to use in order to restore the brain's balance and reduce the stress of craving. We have entered the compulsive stage, which means that we now use substances to escape the stress on our bodies and minds that rises when we are in withdrawal. As addiction progresses, it is characterized by the emergence of negative affect—depression, anxiety, irritability—when access to the drug is prevented.[5] Thus, managing stress and negative affect, not seeking pleasure, becomes the primary motivating factor in addiction.[6] Like the Gerasene's possession, the addiction has taken over the person's functioning and now must be survived.

Drugs Inside and Outside the Self

If you are a casual drinker, you may have more points of familiarity with the impulsive stage of substance addiction than you realize. It's in the little things. For instance, imagine you are having a bad week at work. You know that on Friday you will gather at a local bar with old friends to watch the game and drink a few beers. By Wednesday of this bad week, you are feeling deflated and irritable with everyone at work, and you start to fantasize about Friday. You can picture just how the evening will unfold: the shiny glass bar, the attractive fellow sports fans at the counter, and the beautiful amber of the pint. Your aging and worried self, constrained by responsibility and resentment, will slip away. You'll be like a college student again, making loud jokes and yelling at the players on the screen. You can almost feel the slight euphoria a couple of drinks bring. You associate the alcohol with a whole range of feelings having to do with social belonging and personal history.

By Friday morning, you can't wait to escape your life. There's no problem at work that a couple of beers won't solve. You imagine the ritual of gathering at the table, hearing the loud flat-screen TVs, and laughing with friends. You feel a slight fluttering in your chest as you leave the office: it's your dopamine already rising at the thought of the evening. You enter into the bar and your tense muscles relax. You are behaviorally conditioned to this environment, and you already start to feel witty and attractive as you order the first drink. By the second beer, all your fears of failure have slipped away. By the third, you are in your own world, but it is a happy world where you love everyone, feel bonded to your friends, and feel like this is the best game of the season.

Substances don't just give us pleasure; they change our sense of self and our perception of reality. They offer a solution to our stress and help us manage difficult emotions. They help us bond with others and escape the fears and insecurities of our everyday lives. We associate them with a broad range of behavioral cues that connect beer to sports and bars—and to bonding with old friends. We become different persons, or perhaps a different version of ourselves (a different self-state) when we drink or use drugs recreationally. This is the fun me, the witty me, the sophisticated me who drinks cocktails from pretty glasses, or the exciting me who lives on the edge of the illicit. Of course, all of these goals of recreational use don't change reality or really solve our emotional or social problems. They change the brain so that we experience reality differently.

Now imagine a woman in the compulsive stage—Lisa, who is addicted to stimulants such as cocaine.[7] She may be similar to a casual user in that she associates the drug with a range of aesthetic experiences and changes to her sense of self. She also uses substances to manage her feelings and to forget her problems. But this compelling desire to use is more intense for her than for our sports fan above, because Lisa is in the second, compulsive stage of addiction. These goals of transformation are evoked by the inner and outer consequences of the drug use itself. Lisa wants to escape the problems that are piling up due to years of drug use. She wants to manage the emotions that all feel like alarms going off in her brain, leaving her exhausted and full of self-pity. For the casual user, all the environmental cues of a sports bar on a Friday night might evoke a conditioned response to drink like a college kid again. But for Lisa, many cues inside of her body and outside in her environment— from the neighborhood, to using friends, to a feeling of worthlessness—compel major cravings to initiate drug-seeking behavior.

Lisa also feels it necessary to use because simple pleasures no longer register in her mind as salient or rewarding. She has desensitized the "reward center" in her brain, which is responsible for brightening our world and motivating us to survival goals like food, sex, and social connection. Her brain isn't producing enough dopamine, and she cannot feel much of anything besides a general depression. She has no interest in the daily movements of her world and little empathy for the feelings and thoughts of others. She says that she loves her family, but the cravings make her wish that they would leave her alone so that she could use the way she wants to use. She feels compelled to use in order to manage the withdrawal and craving that she experiences when she does not use. She needs to fix the combination of irritability and dysphoria that makes the outer world dull and meaningless, while also leaving her inner self restless and discontent. Her brain pushes her to return it to balance with the drugs that originally made it imbalanced.

Even though she promised her family that she would not use again, that promise requires a level of future planning and self-regulation to which she no longer has access. As a craving hits, her evolutionarily older brain that seeks to satisfy survival needs takes over. Her rational or executive functions seem to fall asleep. The future fades away, and she is stuck in this present moment, feeling physically and emotionally uncomfortable without the drug and its ritual. She starts rationalizing. After all, she has been doing pretty well for a month or so. She thinks she can control it this time. And besides, no one has to know. The instinctual brain has supplied the unbearable craving and the executive brain has furnished the excuses.[8] She decides to use cocaine—just this one more time.

Lisa feels better already as she drives to the usual dealer's house, and she starts to feel that life is exciting and bright again. This is the rise in dopamine in the reward center of the brain that is motivating her to seek the drug. She used to party with others, but now she returns to her empty apartment to use alone. She takes the drug and feels euphoria and relief. She feels powerful, capable, complete again; or, at the extreme, it simply relieves the withdrawal symptoms, and she feels more of what she now refers to as "normal." The next morning she awakens to a horrible depression, an aching body, and self-loathing. But this does not prevent the habitual, seemingly automatic compulsion to begin the ritual cycle of behaviors and use again.

The Rewiring of the Brain

Lisa is trying to manage the rewiring of her brain from chronic substance use. The brain is wired with connected neurons that stretch in webs or gather in bundles in different parts of the brain. Each neuron has a sending end and a receiving end (axon and dendrite, if you remember that high-school biology class). There is a little space between them called the synaptic cleft. The synaptic cleft is like a busy canal ferrying chemical signals called neurotransmitters from the sending end of one neuron to the receiving end of the next. Neurotransmitters are chemicals such as dopamine, serotonin, or glutamate, and they are stored in the warehouses called vesicles on the sending end of the neuron. When neurotransmitters are released, they swim across the canal and connect to the ports on the receiving end. There are specialized ports for each neurotransmitter category, so dopamine cannot attach to serotonin ports, or vice versa. Once the neurotransmitter plugs into the port and sends its signal, it unplugs again and floats around the canal until it is pumped back out, returning to the storage warehouses on the sending end to await the next trip over. Pumping it out of the synaptic cleft stops the signal from stimulating the ports on the receiving end, and the communication is terminated. This process repeats from neuron to neuron, axon to dendrite, like a mass transit system hopping from canal to canal across the brain.

Drugs work directly on this wiring system. They don't really add a substance to the brain. More insidiously, they change the natural process of neurotransmission signaling from one neuron to another. Some drugs mimic the neurotransmitter, some stimulate the output from the sending end, and some block the signal from being pumped out of the canal at the conclusion of the process. Different drugs are identified with a different major neurotransmitter, most affect other signals along with it, and they all seem to create a rise in dopamine.[9] So, for instance, cocaine's major neurotransmitter is dopamine. When Lisa snorts cocaine, the drug blocks the end stage of this process: the pumping of dopamine back out of the neuron's canal. The synaptic cleft gets flooded with the dopamine it already has in the system. The little dopamine signals attach, disengage, then swim around the canal, stimulating the ports at the receiving end over and over again until they are broken down metabolically by other bodily functions, such as liver and kidney functions.[10]

The brain was designed to be in intimate relationship with its environment, and it fights the effects of drug abuse right at the shores of our synaptic cleft. Since it can't get rid of the drug-induced overflow of neurotransmission, the receiving end adjusts by creating fewer ports to receive the signal. Or the sending end synthesizes fewer chemicals to store in the warehouse, so that fewer signals can enter into the canal in the first place. This is an attempt to desensitize the brain from the influx of signals. It cuts down the stimulation, but it also means that now Lisa needs more of the substance to get the same high. She has developed tolerance. It also means that when she is not using, her brain is communicating with fewer signals. So Lisa needs at least some of the drug to feel normal. In fact, she begins craving the drug because she doesn't feel "right," or good at all, when she doesn't take it. This is dependence. Her brain has incorporated the drug as part of its daily functioning and experiences stress when it is out of balance. So the problem with this amazing balancing act is that once it rewires to the environment of heavy drug use, the brain then seeks the addicted balance rather than a healthy one.

Dependence and withdrawal go hand in hand. Withdrawal is partly the effect of the toxins on the rest of the body, such as the liver and kidney. In terms of the brain's balance, it is also the swing to the other side of whatever stimulant or depressant your drug use has provided. For instance, imagine that you are a heavy user of alcohol. Alcohol is a depressant, so your body will make less of this natural depressant, gamma-amino butyric acid (GABA). Your body will also try to balance the depressant with more glutamate, which is an excitatory neurotransmitter. This is the brain's attempt to manage the effects of alcohol. I describe this process as driving a car with the parking brake on (not hard for me to imagine since I forget to release the parking brake about every other morning). I press at normal levels on the accelerator, expecting the car to go, but it is inhibited by the depressant of the parking brake. So I press harder on the accelerator, putting more excitation on the car to get up to normal speed. I have to add the glutamate of the accelerator to balance out the GABA of the parking brake. But my new balance is dependent on both the acceleration and parking brake together. When I suddenly become aware of the problem and release the parking brake, the accelerator frees up and the car jerks forward. I've overcompensated, swinging in the opposite direction. That jerk forward is the withdrawal, as when an alcoholic wakes up in the morning feeling jittery, anxious, or irritable. Not enough GABA, too much glutamate. Now imagine putting that parking brake on and releasing it, up and down, jerking backwards and forwards, over and over every morning for years. It would get to you after a while, as well as damage your car. People who are addicted to substances live in the chaotic loop of withdrawal, intoxication, and craving. This is not a mere chasing after pleasure; it is a chasing after a new normal. Addicts are trying to restore their brain's homeostasis with more of the chemicals that have created the problem in the first place.

In terms of our pastoral care, the most important thing to remember in all of this talk about neurons is that the brain that first chooses to take the drug is not the same brain that, years later, has to make the decision to stop. This is crucial to our compassion. It is also important to our application of "change theory" and "motivational interviewing" (discussed in later chapters) to realize that the addict's brain is not necessarily functioning in the same way as ours are. When considering change, they are not simply rationally assessing a decision to stop or limit a problematic behavior. They are deciding whether or not they are able to enter into the torment of rebalancing a brain that has already organized itself around the substance use.

Wiring is not the only story of this reorganization. There is a little more to report about why our motivation becomes so focused on the substance once the brain gets rewired. There are many theories on how drugs affect the brain, but I will focus next on our instinctual and executive functions, and our reward center, because these are related to the cycles of impulsivity, deadened sense of reality, and chronic stress that are characteristic of addiction. These experiences are particular to how I understand addiction as a spiritual oppression. To me, what seems particularly spiritually evil about addictions is that they progressively cause more of the exact problems that they first appear to cure. We begin to use for the benefits I have described above: affect and stress regulation, the transformation of self-states, and the management of self-other relationships. Over time, drug use dysregulates these functions, making us more emotional and impulsive, tunnel-visioned on the drug, and stressed out even when nothing stressful is happening. Drug use also appears to weaken the prefrontal cortex, the region of the brain involved in executive functions, such as decision-making, inhibitory control, and self-regulation that could help us better manage this compulsion to use.[11] This is the tragedy of addiction: the insidious flip from something that helps us manage our lives to something that must be managed. This is where the possession takes hold.

"Your Mind Is an Unsafe Neighborhood; Don't Go There Alone"[12]

I lived for a while in Pasadena, California. In Southern California, you get to know a suburb or town by learning which freeways you have to take to get there. Freeways are known by their number alone. The 210 freeway intersects the middle of Pasadena and the 110 rises north from Los Angeles to dead-end into it. The 134 is transformed into a random offshoot of the 210 along its side, and the rambling Huntington Drive pokes along underneath it. Pasadena is a relatively tiny patch of land, but there are distinct neighborhoods, such as Old Town in the center, South Pas bordering San Gabriel's sprawl, or the north slope of the foothills, with its sleepy rows of houses. Every day these neighborhoods organize around the flow of traffic. If there has been an accident further up on the 210, you would see some backed-up cars escaping to the surface streets. If it's a Friday evening, you would skirt off Colorado Boulevard before you hit the crowded stretch of touristy restaurants and shops in Old Town. If it's a holiday weekend, the wide Huntington Drive would suddenly become congested as it headed toward the Huntington Library and Garden. If it's rush hour, you would not try to merge onto the last rickety mile of the 110 unless you had a death wish. Most of traffic life and its movement are dynamically related, based on how systems adjust and compensate for an unequal flow of energy or a stressor on one part of the system.

Your brain has its own neighborhoods that are threaded through with the information traffic of your neurons, and it adjusts dynamically to inner and outer stressors. The old neighborhood is responsible for more instinctual processes.[13] It is the gatekeeper to much of the information we take in from our environment through our senses.[14] It scans for what we should avoid or approach, initiates fight-flight-freeze behavior, and seeks survival needs like food, sex, sleep, and safety. It evokes basic emotions and attachment needs, it codes sensory memories with emotions, and it helps to develop habitual responses to the world. It also triggers the stress response of our central nervous system. On the other side of the freeway, the new neighborhood is our executive brain. It is responsible for making thought-out decisions, analyzing information, linear thinking, delayed gratification, managing emotions, using words, and interpreting life events.

It is not that these neighborhoods or their functions are mutually exclusive. It actually takes a variety of brain areas together to create something as complex as a memory, a feeling, or a behavior pattern. For instance, the prefrontal cortex has a direct connection to our limbic and nervous systems and helps to regulate the more immediate impressions and reactions from the instinctual side of the brain.[15] The instinctual side also takes in immediate sensory impressions, but these become coded into autobiographical memory through the work of the executive brain. So our brain is a balanced system. We need to be warned of danger in the moment and to pursue impulses that give spice to life, but we also need to learn how to self-soothe, to delay gratification, and to plan for our future. There should be traffic between the instinctual and executive neighborhoods, so that we can have emotionally rich and sensual lives, but also the kinds of lives that are goal-directed and meaningful.

While we need both neighborhoods to talk to each other, sometimes one side will take over because its skills are more useful in that moment. For instance, if you are on a hike and see a long, slithering object on the ground, it is time for the instinctual brain to do its split-second work. You jump away with a rush of adrenaline, crying out some form of gibberish, before your mind can even form the word "snake." (This just happened to me yesterday, so I know whereof I speak.) It is not the time to assess whether or not the snake might be dangerous. It's the time to jump away from danger. You already possess a snake-schema in the brain, developed from reading the book of Genesis, seeing snakes on TV, or experiencing snakes in real life. Since the brain has already coded long thin slithering things on the ground as a danger, there is no need to move this sensory impression to the executive brain and decide how to feel about it. You react before you think. But let's say you see this object from a good five or ten yards away or you perceive that it is strangely lifeless. Then the brain might quickly assess, even as you shudder, that the snake is a stick. (Or, in my case, a snake that has passed on to its great reptilian reward.) You could hear your prefrontal cortex say to yourself, "Whoa! What is that? Is it a snake?" as you peer from a safe distance and analyze the situation. Your limbic system may have gotten your heart rate up, but the instinctual brain has passed this information to the executive to make a decision about it. Your executive brain was able to delay your reaction and calm your emotion before you started screaming at the top of your lungs.

Substance abuse is associated with exaggerated bottom-up and compromised top-down neural network functioning.[16] In other words, the instinctual brain has taken over, and its functions and assessments are taking precedence over the balancing work of the executive brain. The executive brain is having a hard time keeping the instinctual brain regulated and under control. Neuroimaging studies, particularly on cocaine addicts, suggest that they suffer from what is called hypofrontality, or reduced metabolism in the prefrontal cortex. Hypofrontality suggests that the executive functions go off-line in drug addiction, leading to poor impulse control, lack of resolve, and faulty decision-making.[17] This poor communication between instinctual and executive brain may be an issue of temperament for those who appear to be born with higher impulsivity or risk-taking traits.[18] I will also argue that childhood attachment makes a big difference on how our brain communicates and self-soothes. It is also possible that these problems with communication are caused or exacerbated by the drug itself.

Studies further suggest that drinking alcohol reduces the connectivity between the amygdala (alarm system) and orbitofrontal cortex (prefrontal cortex region), which means that, when someone is intoxicated, the regulatory part of the brain is interacting less with the alarm system of the brain during the processing of socioemotional stimuli.[19] If you remember the usual flow of a night of heavy drinking during college, you will be familiar with the impulsivity and emotional dysregulation that alcohol can cause. The college party stories of some of my cheekier seminary students have brought this memory vividly to mind for me. At some point in the evening, someone gets mad about an insult that did not actually happen; two people suddenly find each other incredibly attractive for no apparent reason; and someone else streaks naked across the college campus because it seemed like a really good idea at the time. There is, as with Proverbs 23, a lack of ability to take in information and read it correctly, and there is also a lack of the risk/reward assessment needed to respond to impulses appropriately. The old neighborhood that takes in information is not talking to the new neighborhood that would make a more thoughtful assessment of it. This problem can become chronic with chronic use, compounding stress upon stress—or, more accurately, unreality upon unreality.

The Progress into Possession

Substance use appeals to our instinctual brain because we usually first associate the effects of intoxication as a reward: something that enhances positive emotions, increases our sociality, or soothes our stress. The problem is that when our neurotransmission adjusts, the old neighborhood adjusts along with it. The nucleus acumbens is the major reward center in our brain, and it runs on dopamine. It receives input from dopamine pathways that arise from an area called the ventral tegmental area (VTA) at the base of our brain.[20] In Koob's compulsive theory of addiction, this is the area of the brain that locks the cycle of addiction in place, as the user progressively develops a tunnel-vision concerning the process of craving, seeking, and withdrawing from substances, compelled by negative affect.

The reward center does what its name suggests. It provides good feelings for pursuing and gaining certain survival needs like food, sex, or safety. It works with some other structures in the old neighborhood of the brain to create conditioned responses to outside stimuli. Addictive drugs increase dopamine neurotransmission, causing a rise of that beloved chemical in the reward center of the brain. This dopamine spike does not only make us feel good, it helps award salience to certain behaviors and pursuits over others.[21] In other words, it makes us notice, need, and be motivated toward particular goals that we have found rewarding in the past. Dopamine rises in anticipation of a good meal when we are hungry. It is a part of that slight euphoria we feel when the world seems bright, benevolent, and interesting. It motivates us to pursue our sexual urges. It encourages us toward behaviors that keep us safe, which, depending on our environment, may be dominance, achievement, or attachment to others.

Connecting an increase in dopamine to an action thus helps us to learn. It helps us to connect an experience with the environmental cues surrounding it, leading to a conditioned response when we experience those cues again.[22] Dopamine tells us that this behavior is a solution to a need: Do it again! Environment, action, and reward repeat over and over, until, with repeated experiences, dopamine actually rises at the thought of the action, not just the receipt of the reward. We all get these impulses to engage in conditioned behaviors. On the first truly sunny day of spring I am compelled toward the ice-cream shop in town. I do not have some kind of conscious rationale for why I must have ice cream on that particular day. But on that day, my heart is slightly restless until it rests in a single scoop of praline on a sugar cone. The gentle warmth on my shoulders, the smell of the dry sun, the sudden untangling of my tense chest, and the expansive good mood I feel as I step outside—all are outer and inner cues that are associated with ice-cream-cone consumption. Like Pavlov's dog, I hear that sunny bell ring, and I start to salivate at the counter, dopamine up and ready for a reward.

When we become addicted, this natural learning process in the reward center goes into dysfunction, telescoping our motivation toward one solution to every problem. The world around us and the emotions within us become triggers that cue us toward the craving and pursuit of substances. The triggered behavior becomes more than a slight temptation to eat ice cream. It becomes a survival sense that we must solve what is out of balance in our bodies and minds. We tend to think a craving is like any kind of thought to engage in an indulgent behavior, like wishing we could avoid work for a day of TV binge-watching, or fantasizing about initiating a romance with someone we'd be better off avoiding. We can feel these pulls toward a pleasurable or impulsive behavior, but then we would hope to exert enough responsibility or reality-testing to avoid acting on that temptation. This is how we understand temptation, and so we expect that we can easily execute the same will power over the craving to use.

But addiction cravings are not the same as conscious thoughts and are not consistently overcome by the conscious, thinking part of the brain.[23] They can be as clear as "I must have it now!" or as subtle as a vague sense of discomfort or irritation, like a growing rug burn on the psyche. Cravings are also compounded by the fact that a learned behavior becomes a habit. This is related to another area of the brain, the dorsal striatum, which helps with forming habits and routine behaviors, and may also be involved in how we process emotional and social stimuli.[24] The whole point of habits is that we do them without thinking. They conserve the rest of our brain's energies for new actions or novel stimuli responses.

Much like my craving for praline ice cream, people with a developing dependence on substances are still under the illusion of control. They think that they should be able to control a craving easily—like any thought. They assume that it is an action, instead of a habit carved into the neural freeway of the brain. Humans are meaning-making beings, so when addicts feel compelled to complete the action, the executive brain rationalizes or minimizes the behavior. Sometimes, if they are in complete denial, they may not even see the behavior as a problem at all. But many addicts in the midst of a hangover promise themselves and their loved ones that they are really done this time and ready to stop. They believe it, because at that point they are not in a state of craving. When they are triggered toward the behavior or the cravings hit, they find excuses to do the behavior once more and then assure themselves that it will be better the next time. This creates the illusion of control and agency that protects their egos and also helps them to continue their behaviors. But as their condition progresses and the broken promises pile up around them, they become caught in a cycle of shame, craving, and use.[25]

Shame gets us to the other effect of dopamine desensitization, the growing predominance of negative affect. Our reward center not only inspires our cravings, it also inspires our joy. We have a certain amount of dopamine flowing in our brains most of the time. Along with other neurotransmitters like serotonin and opiates, dopamine keeps our mood up and motivates us to complete important tasks. It helps us to notice the beauty in the world, to enjoy a good meal, to want to contribute to goals in our life, or to spend time with loved ones. Social and sensory goals are about surviving and thriving in our varied and changing environments. But as our brains become dependent on the environment of substances, the neurotransmission in our reward center also adjusts to the dopamine flood and we make less natural dopamine. For Lisa, lower levels of natural dopamine communication mean that the motivational rewards toward basic pleasures (food, sex, attachment, social connection) become drastically less salient, and the satisfaction of the simple enjoyments of living are dulled. This is called anhedonia or dysphoria: an inability to feel pleasure and a generalized sense of depression. Lisa uses to no longer feel bad, but also because she can no longer feel good.

Chronic Stress in Addiction

In addition to less natural dopamine, addicts can have a greater sense of being under stress. Substance abuse throws our stress system off balance. Addictive substances are toxic to the system, and it takes time and strain on the body to metabolize and remove their effects—what we commonly call a hangover. The cycle of addiction further puts the brain and body into chronic stress.

Remember Koob's assertion that addiction is not an impulse toward pleasure but a compulsion away from pain: the binge-withdrawal-craving loop produces a state of stress reactivity as the body and brain seek to return to a sense of balance. But there's more: this cycle can also change how the stress system works, so that the addict responds with stress to situations in life that are not necessarily stressful. For some addicts, this means that they become more easily dysregulated or reactive emotionally as they seek to balance the brain.

Let me give you a basic outline of the "fight-or-flight" portion of the stress system in our instinctual brain, because it can also become dysregulated from other chronic stressors that we will be discussing, such as childhood maltreatment or the pervasive effects of racial discrimination. Imagine that the amygdala is our alarm switch and the hypothalamus-pituitary-adrenal axis (HPA) is the circuit board that gets the body electrified for fight or flight. The amygdala tells the hypothalamus to send a messenger chemical called corticotropin-releasing factor (CRF). This chemical messenger then signals for the pituitary and adrenal glands to release stress chemicals like cortisol that prepare us to face a threat. Now we are hyperalert, we are full of cortisol and adrenaline, and we are ready to face the threat—or at least to run really fast away from it.

CRF also appears in other parts of the brain related to stress responses, suggesting that this little messenger chemical plays an important role in the regulation of behavioral responses to stress.[26] Both the HPA axis and the CRF messenger are activated over and over by the chronic administration of drugs, and ultimately this system is dysregulated.[27] This constant engagement of the stress system can lead to long-lasting changes in the CRF levels in the brain. We not only become oversensitive to the effects of withdrawal, but we develop a trigger-happy stress system, which is set off by both our inner and outer environment. So it is not surprising that CRF is thought to be related to the stress-induced reinstatement of drug-seeking behaviors. In other words, the poor modulation of our stress response means that stressful environments quickly lead to relapse.[28]

Let's put this picture together for Lisa. While she loves her family theoretically, she feels less motivation toward the rewards of connection to her family. Her natural dopamine is lowered and life feels deadened and meaningless. At the same time, her brain has become focused on the stress of her intense conditioned response to drug use and its attendant physical symptoms of withdrawal and craving. Finally, her stress-system is dysregulated and her reactivity is high: that is, she is unable to take in information from the outer world and read it with any objective distance from her own emotional storm. She cannot reliably engage executive functioning to help reality-test her current situation or to make future-focused goals. When Lisa feels that the last argument with her boss or her neighbor is so stressful that her emotions are unbearable, she feels that she must use again. She does not feel that any form of self-soothing other than the substance will switch off this circuit board in her brain, which is screaming to be put back into balance. She does not feel that prioritizing a child's birthday party, going to work, or paying her bills is half as salient as the real feeling of craving and the discomfort it produces. At this point, Lisa only needs to think about her dealer to begin to feel a spike in dopamine. Her reward system is drawn to rebalance her brain with more drugs, and she feels fully alive only when she uses. So the addict develops tunnel vision toward the drug of her choice.

Excursus: Porn Addiction

The administration of chemicals directly into the body and brain pose a pernicious challenge to our neurobiological regulation. But what of behavioral addictions such as gambling, internet, and sex addictions, or other chronic conditions, such as eating disorders? Since all drugs appear to affect dopamine, one theory is that the reward system in the brain also dysfunctions for particularly strong dopamine-spiking behaviors.[29] Behaviors that involve fundamental survival processes like eating, sex, or social competition might then become similar disorders in the brain. Changes in the reward center, along with poor connections between the instinctual brain and the executive function, may cause individuals to become tunnel-visioned to the behavior. Genetic propensity may also prime an individual's instinctual brain for chronic ritual behaviors. For instance, researchers found that people with a gene that limited D_2 receptors (the dopamine ports we've been talking about) were overrepresented in cases of substance, gambling, and shopping addictions, obesity, compulsive sexual behavior, compulsive internet use, obsessive texting, and workaholism.[30] There are many theories being tested, such as examining changes in the brains of porn addicts, or experimenting with medication to address potential chemical imbalances in gambling addictions or eating disorders.[31]

Gary Wilson, in his book *Your Brain on Porn*, reminds us that sex is a survival instinct, and its pursuit raises the dopamine in the reward center of the brain.[32] He distinguishes the normal pursuit of pleasure from the tunnel-visioned motivation found in pornography addiction. Sexual pleasure such as orgasm is experienced through our opiate neurotransmission, but attention, motivation, and seeking sex comes from our old friend dopamine in the reward system of the brain. Searching internet porn is an intense activity of seeking, and the action of pursuing increasing levels of stimulation causes a surge of dopamine as the internet porn surfer clicks through the websites. It is a behavior that awards our attention because there is always a new sexual novelty to seek on the next page or the next click.

Internet porn acts as a "supernormal stimulus" because it includes abnormal levels of sexual intensity, surgically enhanced bodies, novelty, surprise, and anxiety in terms of taboo-breaking. These stimuli get tied into our brain's instinctual search for novelty and anticipation of reward. Studies in supernormal stimuli also suggest that an object that is unnaturally and extremely stimulating will become cued to sexual arousal beyond a natural stimulus in the environment. Sexual cues get attached to the extreme images or actions of the pornography. It progresses into more and more pornography and more hardcore visual images as the brain develops tolerance to the stimuli. Porn also combines sex and aggression, usually physically and verbally aggressive or dominating behavior toward women. As a survival instinct, aggression is also a potent inducer of dopamine, and the combination of sex and aggression may compound the progression of the addiction.[33]

People also engage in sex addictions to manage negative affect and stress. As sex therapist Robert Weiss explains, "Sex addicts don't use compulsive sexual fantasies and behaviors to feel better; they use them to distract themselves from what they are feeling in that moment."[34] Sex addicts use fantasy and sexual behavior to numb out and escape from stress and discomfort. This includes pain arising from depression, anxiety, abandonment fears, or early life trauma. The cycle becomes triggered by "pain agents," or cues in the inner and outer world of the addict—emotional discomfort, unresolved conflict, stress, or a need to connect.[35] This begins the craving and motivation to engage in the behavior. The progress is thus similar to drugs and alcohol: we use the behavior over and over as a self-regulatory tool, we cue more triggers into the use, and we develop tolerance. We then need more and more radical images or experiences to raise our chemical high. Shame and self-loathing actually keep individuals stuck in cycles of pornography use or sexual acting out, since they seek to manage this negative affect with more of the behavior. So sex addictions include progression and a sense of possession. We are looking for Koob's compulsive stage: tolerance and dependence, negative affect and stress during withdrawal, and cravings that compel the individual to use again in an effort to return to homeostasis.[36]

It is important for pastoral caregivers to minister to potential sex addicts with caution and discernment. Just because someone has had affairs, visits prostitutes or strip clubs, uses porn, or masturbates does not mean that he is a sex addict. For Christians, these actions may conflict with their values and cause great shame. They may believe that they are sex addicts, even though they are not spending excessive amounts of time, it is not escalating or out of control, and it is not significantly getting in the way of daily living.[37] Their sexual acting out may be attached to other sources of pain that need to be explored, but they are not yet suffering from an addiction. On the other hand, actual sex addicts may minimize their behavior or hide the full extent of the problem from us, because it feels shameful to them or they fear that we will judge them. If a behavior is embarrassing or hard to talk about, it is fair to assume that pastoral caregivers will hear only the bare minimum of the whole story. We might want to assure the person of our support and ask some open-ended questions about the behavior's effects on the person's life so that we can develop a fuller picture.

The last two chapters of this book will offer skills for this kind of nonjudgmental engagement. While we can broach the subject of our concern and point out the dynamics that we see, it is unwise for us to make any definitive pronouncement that someone has or doesn't have an addiction. This is a realization that must ultimately come from the individual and should include an assessment by a professional trained in these conditions, especially for behavioral addictions or eating disorders. If a person is troubled by sexual behavior or suffering from a sexual addiction, a therapist with experience in counseling sex addicts can help him explore his sexual history in order to determine the best course for healing.

The Brain in Pastoral Care

At some point during this chapter, you may have been asking yourself, "What does all this talk about the brain have to do with pastoral care?" Everything! Definition drives care. Again, it is crucial for caregivers who want to show compassion to understand that the brain that makes the first decision to use is not the same brain as the one that needs to make a final decision to stop. If the caregiver has never had such a condition, changing the behavior might seem like an easy decision. But if we have never been addicted, we are assessing that decision with a different kind of brain. If an addict like Lisa comes to us when she feels sick in her own skin, she may talk in disconnected or irrational ways. She may seem full of self-pity, stressed out from simple daily living, or angry at someone for what seems to us a small thing. She may seem unable to focus, complaining about events that don't seem serious enough to warrant her last binge on cocaine. Or she may just offer us a cheerful wall of denial and claim that her behavior is really under control.

As we listen, our first reaction might be to see her as immature or resistant about her behavior. We might decide that she does not want to stop. We may be offended by what her selfishness is doing to her family. We might want to quickly offer advice, exhort her to change, or try to fix her problems for her. Or we might feel hopeless, and so decide that she is hopeless too. I know that, as pastoral caregivers, we wish to appear that we are always compassionate and wise, but admitting these first suboptimal reactions is an honest part of the business of care. We can be tempted to read the surface of what someone says or does through our own values or brain functioning.

It will make a significant difference to our care-planning if we realize that Lisa has lost a connection between accurately reading stimuli in her environment and initiating an appropriate response. What she says in the moment might make no sense to us, but it makes perfect sense to her brain right now. Exhortation, preaching, and argument rarely work against a soul-sickness, because one of its primary characteristics is this sense of cyclical unreality. It is a condition that refers to itself and not the realities in the outside world. If we know that her stress system is dysregulated in this way, we can take the momentary storm in stride and start thinking about developing coping skills and emotional regulation over time. Avoiding argument and rolling with resistance—two strategies of Motivational Interviewing—will make more sense if we keep in mind that Lisa's executive brain is busy forming really good reasons why she should give in to her cravings. Instead of delving into her feelings about what seems like circular self-pity or trying to argue her out of irrationality, we can begin asking about actions Lisa can take in the face of this craving moment.

Knowing about the brain also helps us develop a long-term focus for recovery. When Lisa returns from this lapse, do we decide that she is weak-willed, manipulating for attention, or doesn't really want to change? Or do we understand that the neighborhoods in her brain aren't really talking to each other as clearly as they should, and her unconscious behavioral cues—from a sunny day to a sense of loneliness to a using friend—trigger a drug craving so compelling that she hasn't even identified these triggers as a problem? What a difference it makes to our pastoral care if we realize that she has to unlearn much more than the use of drugs. She must learn a whole new set of tools for daily living, including new coping skills to manage stress and to regulate her emotional well-being. Spiritually, the connection between changing behaviors and changing the self is not so new to us. It is discipleship. We become a new creation in Christ, but after that we must be formed over time through the practices of our faith. So, rather than focusing on what appears innate or dysfunctional about her, we can help Lisa reconnect to her relationship with God as a shelter in this storm. We can begin to coach her toward applying Christian principles to her life, as she learns new ways of engaging her executive brain over the compulsion to use.

Chapter Three

Addiction, Attachment, and Trauma

> Addictive and compulsive behaviors are not a moral failing but a neurobiological result of trauma and attachment loss, and are perpetuated through social oppression and marginalization.
>
> —Gabor Maté,
> *In the Realm of Hungry Ghosts: Close Encounters with Addiction*

> Our liquor is but a symptom.
>
> —Anonymous,
> *The Big Book of Alcoholics Anonymous*

In the beginning, humans were created to be held by an environment. A whole world was brought out of nothing, so that God could place the human in its midst. We were created for union with our environment, with each other, and with the God who walked the paths of the garden with us. The "us" is the important part. We were created in relationship to each other. The first pronouncement God makes about us is that it is not good for the human to be alone. We commonly focus on the assumed gender of that Genesis account, but perhaps we should return to a more fundamental message. The human is not a complete creation until there are two of them. We cannot become or continue to be human outside of relationship with another. This shouldn't be surprising. We are created in the image of a triune God, whose own Godhead is grounded in the relationship between the members of the Trinity. Each member of the Trinity is, in the words of the Council of Chalcedon, distinct yet consubstantial (sharing the same substance or essence). We are distinct in our genetic dispositions yet consubstantial in how those potentials unfold, only coming to developmental fullness through other human beings. So it is only after two of us are created that the Triune God can put up their collective feet and take a rest.

The Fall represents the end to our hope for union. Humans will now be in enmity with the earth, with its creatures, with the pain of their own bodies, and with each other. They hide from God and from each other with a pathetic self-protection. The story of the Fall is not simply the story of a breach of contract on the part of humanity, but an account of longing and loss. Paradise is lost and a union with the environment breaks apart, fissuring our souls along with it. So the Fall is not just juridical but relational. We carry an ancient memory of why we were created, that our essential humanity is vulnerable and deeply dependent on others. We carry a memory of our need for each other and God, along with the old habit of turning away from both to protect ourselves in a way that ultimately only harms us. This is the tragedy at the heart of our human frailty. But the other side of this tragedy is our possibility. When we are faithful to another child of God, our mutual need for each other is also our greatest strength.

Since that first creation, every infant also comes to completion through relationship with others. We are our baby's first experience of Paradise, and we are the environment that God has provided for our child. Infants begin life in union with their caretakers, and they use their caretakers' caring ministrations to regulate the novel flood of their inner and outer experiences. The security found in comfort- and contact-seeking, what developmental theorists call attachment, is a basic human need that begins in infancy and extends into adulthood.[1] The infant's future sense of self, his confidence in exploring the world, and his patterns of relating are formed by this first, all-encompassing environment. As an infant grows, he internalizes the patterns learned in these first experiences and continues to seek places of belonging and relationship in the broader environment to ground him. We need others in order to relate in healthy ways, to love ourselves, to create meaningful lives, and to draw on our social connections to gain resiliency in times of stress. We might lose the intense union of the infant paradise, but we continue to need attachment figures and to seek a positive social environment to thrive into adulthood. Throughout our lives, we only come into the fullness of our minds and bodies within the compass of another.

So what happens if we never get a paradise? I am back in a circle of chairs. We are about twenty people—a fairly rough and teasing lot. We settle down as a speaker shares his story about recovery. The mood in the room becomes reflective as the speaker talks about his struggles with depression, his own parents' mental health problems and how, in the euphemism of abuse, they "used a belt."[2] He talks about a long road through counselors and 12-step principles, both of them laying the groundwork for a new, chosen life.

People begin sharing their stories in response to his, one after another, about alcoholic parents and grandparents, about three other parents who used a belt, one about how trauma therapy became a part of his recovery, two more about how depression and anxiety still overtake their functioning. They talk about issues like anger, selfishness, acting out or acting insensitively that they now realize were grounded in the breakage of these earliest relationships.

Not all identified with histories of abuse or neglect. One speaker claimed a good home but bad genetics. Another spoke of his own fractious temperament. One woman felt that drugs seemed to cause her depression rather than the other way around. There are many paths that find their way into an addiction. But the mention of childhood trauma, family chaos, and neglect are so common in AA/NA groups, that people who do not experience those things often feel the need to clarify that they "actually came from a good family" when they speak. Others will claim that they came from a "good home," but then will tell stories of parental alcoholism and divorce, chaotic families, or bullying at schools—stories that are seemingly disconnected from any criterion of actual good. But in this group the connection is clear: their abuse histories, their mental health challenges, and their practical problems were wrapped into their substance use as it boomeranged across the course of their lives.

The self-medication hypothesis claims that individuals don't actually seek pleasure, but instead emotional and mental relief, through their addictive behaviors.[3] For those who cannot regulate internally or manage relationships externally, addictive behaviors can appear to relieve these problems. A major proponent of the self-medication hypothesis, Edward Khantzian, claims that people become dependent on substances because "they are overwhelmed by or cut off from their feelings, their sense of self and self-esteem is precarious, their capacity for secure attachments and comfortable relationships [is] elusive, and self-care is underdeveloped."[4] Addiction becomes an opportunist, attacking those most vulnerable to its effects.

It might be tempting to see Khantzian's description as a list of interior problems or character flaws. As pastoral caregivers, we need to ask, how does an adult become feeling-averse, suffer low self-esteem, develop poor coping skills, or not know how to receive soothing and nourishment from her environment? She develops these problems, in the first place, by the quality of her attachment figures, and in the second place, by her experience of self in the social world. In fact, most of the issues that people bring to us for pastoral care move beyond the individual to her or his experience of relational and societal injustice. Attachment is one way to understand how these sins affect us at the level of our individual functioning and our adult relational patterns. Through others we become a self and through others we develop the resiliency and sense of belonging necessary for that self to flourish. When relationships in our personal and social world are threatening, fearful, neglectful, or not attuned, it profoundly affects our mental and physical health.

Attachment and Self-Regulation

I first want to spend a little time telling you about attuned and secure attachments, because it is not just what was done to people, but *what wasn't done* that makes the difference. When I say that our ground of being is in others, I'm not exaggerating. It may sound somewhat heretical, since our ground of being is usually considered God. God still wins in terms of philosophy. God is the essential first, the unmoved mover from whom all creation proceeds and is sustained. But being a practical kind of person, I am betting on the adult who cares for us after we have come into this world. This is how God designed us. Whatever essence resides in our bodies and souls at birth, it is not enough to develop our physical or psychic machinery without care from the human other.

Infants are born with immature brains and nervous systems. They have little capacity to manage or reflect on the sudden influx of stimuli that comes with birth, whether feelings of discomfort from inside the body or impingement from outside. They have nascent personality tendencies, but not a self-identity. The majority of their cortex and neuronal connections—and the patterning of relationship that will become their sense of self—will grow through the work of their first caregivers. So while genetics provides the building blocks of who we will become, these possibilities find their potential in our relationships. Perhaps it is this deep interdependence that really expresses what it means to be made in the image of a Triune God.

The recipe for a new baby's brain is deceptively simple. It develops from the surprisingly basic actions that adults tend to do whenever they see a baby. Infants need those exaggerated smiles prompting them to smile, that lilting and pitched baby-voice making them coo in return. They need the playful singsong of face, eyes, and gesture that baby and adult pattern into a kind of mutual conversation.[5] As a parent adjusts in this kind of synchronized play to a baby's response, the child begins to learn what increased positive affect —what he will later call joy, laughter, love, or safety—feels like. His playful relating actually raises opiates and dopamine in the parent and the baby, providing a growth-promoting environment for the child's new brain.

As a mother is attuned to the child's needs for stimulation, she enhances positive affect but tries not to overwhelm the child. She seeks that sweet space of baby homeostasis. Babies are made to be held and played with, but an attuned parent also allows a baby to break eye contact and look away when the connection is too intense. This helps babies to develop a tolerance for ever-higher levels of affect on their excitable little bodies. She also responds to a baby's distress or physical discomfort, transforming negative affect into soothing, feeding, or diaper changing. By responding with these loving techniques, the attachment figure also helps a child down-regulate too much stimulation, supporting her developing nervous system, which is our stress regulation system. A thousand repeated patterns of affect transformation begin to build neuronal pathways between our executive emotional regulation and the instinctual emotional response centers in the brain.[6]

Finally, parents continue to add language to their relationship, speaking to their child like a real person: "Are you hungry?" "That hurt, didn't it?" "Don't worry, I'm here"— even before he can understand. Over time, what feels like random senses and inner experiences get organized into language so that the child can develop emotional and social intelligence. Affect is not emotion: it is just those negative and positive shifts in our physical and mental states that later get patterned and classified through emotional language by our schema-obsessed brain. As we enter into these daily adjustments with our babies, overlaid with verbal communications, we are helping them to develop patterns of relating and to gain a sense of agency about the interplay between outer stimuli and inner response. We also try to remain a secure base for a child's exploration into the world: near enough for him to touch us if overwhelmed, verbally elaborating on his thoughts or feelings about his play.[7] Those rituals of kissing boo-boos, sacramentally applying Band-Aids, or holding a child who seems to be auditioning for chief diva are all the blessings of attachment. Over time, children begin to learn that the negative and positive stimulation in their bodies and minds is manageable and can be changed over time.

All loving caretakers have their good days and bad days as far as attunement goes. But a good parent's general point of view is that his child is a thinking and feeling self in her own right, and the parent is interested and curious about this self. Developmental theorists call this "mentalization," a process where we imagine the mind—the intentions, goals, thoughts, and feeling—of the other as something separate from ourselves.[8] We think about the thinking of others. Attuned attachment figures act on the assumption that they are in a two-sided relationship. They seek to get to know their infant. From the child's birth, they act as though the child has her own needs and wishes and is trying to enter into communication with the adults in her world. They take seriously a young child's need to be comforted concerning overexcited emotions or sheltered from their fears. They try not to belittle or reject a child's needs, nor do they force their own thoughts and feelings onto the child as if the child is merely a mirror of their own mental and emotional life. We all fail at this sometimes, depending on how much of a two-year-old's tantrum we can take. But attuned parents also seek to repair the relationship after a rupture in connection or empathy with their children. This empathic consistency leads to a sense of security over the long haul. The attachment figure can be depended on to respond with appropriate concern and soothing when a child is overwhelmed, fearful, or under stress.

If you have caught the language in these last few paragraphs, you might notice some similar points from the earlier chapter on the brain. The first years of life are about regulatory functions: management of affect, regulation of stress, strengthening the nervous system, and increasing connections between instinctual and executive brain. It is the foundation for learning how to manage the self and to begin patterns of relationship with others. Dopamine and opiates are also triggered in these first interactions, providing a baseline of these growth-promoting and positive chemicals in the brain.[9] As children grow, they start to internalize these skills of self-regulation and self-expression, and they make forays into managing the big world outside of paradise. They further internalize self-other patterns of relating that lay the foundation of their self-identity. They continue from this baseline, taking in new information and adjusting their patterns of relating as they grow. These first years of a child's life are about resilience-building. The more secure our beginnings, the more we internalize positive coping behaviors, and the more buffers we have against the need for an outer regulatory behavior to manage the self and its relationship to others.

In these small daily ways, our attachments help to prepare our bodies and brains to live in a complex inner and outer world. So it is not surprising that a secure attachment is strongly associated with an increase in exploration and play, intelligence and language acquisition, ego resilience and control, tolerance of frustration, self-recognition, and social capacities.[10] As adults, secure children are able to be less reactive, less impulsive, and more reflective about their responses to the environment. In other words, they have a well-functioning central nervous system, are not overwhelmed by their emotions, and have learned how to engage the executive functions of the brain. They have also learned that they can access others in their environment to aid in self-regulation. In summary, then, a securely attached child gains the following skills:

1. managing affect and stress regulation;
2. the growth of social understanding;
3. development of personality; and
4. acquisition of emotional intelligence.[11]

I must confess that I never got the female biological clock that ticks for children. Perhaps it was lost in the mail. But I love to see a happy, confidently relating baby. My own opiates rise a little, but also my faith in humankind rises, and my faith in God's intention that we care each other into completion. It reminds me of that lovely portion of Psalm 139 that expresses a secure attachment to God: "You discern my going out and my lying down; you are familiar with all my ways. You know me so deeply and you are always with me." To be seen and known lovingly by the other, to know that she is near in time of need, leads to a secure sense of self in the world. I love a happy baby, but what disturbs me about the above list is just how quotidian yet profound is a child's pathway to a beloved sense of self. It puts the question in our minds: What happens if none of this loving attunement unfolds?

Resistant, Avoidant, and Disorganized Attachment Relationships

If the above list shows what secure attachments provide, it also shows what insecure attachments threaten to take away. These very areas of deficit leave openings in self-regulation that must be filled by some strategy found outside of the self. Insecure attachments do not predict substance abuse, but they can be a significant risk factor in its development and cause challenges to recovery. Addicts tell a very common story about their childhoods. They say that they felt anxious, uncomfortable in their own skin, were afraid of others, or were socially awkward. Drugs and alcohol felt like a solution that immediately took away this feeling of being somehow "not-right." Just the other day I heard this again: "I was ugly, worthless, disgusting. But when I drank I was like a model, I was funny, and I could talk to anyone. In fact, I wouldn't stop talking. Where had alcohol been all my life?"

Since the child's first environment is that of her parents, the addict may be unaware of the thousands of repeated patterns she experienced over the first few years of life that might have contributed to this general feeling of not-rightness.

There is a debate in attachment theory about whether these feelings arise from child-parent relationships or whether natural temperament plays the bigger part.[12] Children can be naturally fussy, shy, or anxious. But we do not grow straight up from the seed of our genetics. The shape that a genetic propensity takes will be influenced by a child's environment. Attachment researchers argue that even children who are difficult to soothe will gain a positive attachment if the parents continue to work on mentalizing and dependable caretaking. Insecure attachment is also not necessarily a parent's "fault," though there are certainly abusive and neglectful parents. It could be that the parent and child did not have a temperamental match, or the parents were overwhelmed by many other troubles that distracted their attention or increased anxiety in the child. Major losses and bumpy life transitions can affect a child's sense of security, and parents can feel helpless to comfort their children during these times. There are also parents who feel powerless while their children struggle with mental illness or impulsive temperaments that seem to lead them into dangerous life decisions. It does not have to be a fault of the parent, but it is a fact of our human fragility that children are vulnerable to attachment needs and that we as adults are not always equipped to meet them.

Insecure attachments can differ in strength and intensity, but attachment theory commonly separates them into resistant, avoidant, and disorganized patterns. Children with *resistant* attachments find that their needs for safety or attunement are inconsistently met by their caregivers. The attachment figures are sometimes responsive, but at other times they are either neglectful or impinging.[13] They seem to project their own inner states onto children. They are often preoccupied and less able to mentalize their child's inner world, so the attunement between child and adult is often disjointed.[14] Resistantly attached children ramp up the attachment system but can't easily bring it back down. They are unable to be soothed or unable to trust the safety of the environment or the responsiveness of the caretaker. They tend toward impulsivity and high-arousal states, and they have a hard time soothing their stress system once it is set off.[15] They have difficulty feeling sensed and known by the mother, and thus they ultimately have difficulty in knowing the self.[16] As adults, they remain preoccupied with others' ability to love or care for them. They are often overwhelmed by their feelings and tend to act out emotions rather than thinking about them. Alcohol and drugs help to anesthetize this emotional dysregulation and to escape the relationally threatening environment surrounding them.

Children with *avoidant* attachments have caregivers who ignore, reject, or minimize their feelings when they seek soothing and security.[17] Avoidantly attached children don't expect to be soothed by emotionally unavailable parents, and hence they ramp down their attachment system. They organize their behavior to avoid their attachment needs, not learning to communicate or interpret emotional signals. The poor-affect attunement, emotional distance, and rejection that dominate avoidant relationships create a kind of low-affect environment.[18] As adults, avoidantly attached people tend to feel uncomfortable with intimacy and dependency. It is sometimes difficult for them to explore or understand their own emotional makeup or imagine the emotional needs of others. An adult with this internalized attachment model tends to minimize emotional expression, has a limited capacity to experience intense negative or positive affect, and is susceptible to overregulation and overcontrol of emotion.[19] Avoidantly attached people abuse drugs and alcohol partly because it helps disinhibit them emotionally. It also helps them escape their intense inner critic and a deep sense of their own unlovability.[20]

A child who consistently experiences traumatizing, frightening, or frightened behavior from attachment figures may develop a *disorganized* attachment.[21] Caretakers can also perpetuate frightening or chaotic homes where children feel unsafe and unable to manage the emotions triggered by the unstable environment. Sometimes parents who have suffered their own childhood traumas can be emotionally unstable in themselves; they may be a frightening or inconsistent caretaker as they try to manage their own distress.[22] This can create a situation where children are left helpless in their high arousal, unable to influence the caretaker to address their physical or emotional needs. Thus infants are not sensed or known in their distress.[23] Children with disorganized attachments can't figure out how to use the caretaker for soothing or security, since the attachment figure is actually the one causing the problem. The child may not be able to find any kind of patterned response to unpredictable or fearful environments. Disorganized attachments have strong correlations to self-harming behaviors like addiction.

In the legion of vulnerabilities that develop across our lives, we have risks but also resiliences. As children grow, they have opportunities to find positive experiences of attunement and avenues toward self-regulation that can help repair their experience of infant attachment. Some children find mentors through relatives, church communities, or sports teams. Others find a sense of agency through the expression of academic gifts or artistic talent. These positive people and experiences can contribute to resilience in the face of difficult home environments. But early attachment problems do cause vulnerabilities in emotional well-being, social competence, cognitive functioning, and resilience.[24] These vulnerabilities risk combining with stressful relational and social environments, which leads to the need for some strategy for self-regulation. As one attachment therapist put it, from birth we are driven to seek close human contact, and, "to the degree that we are deprived of this and do not possess the ability to accomplish this task, we are emotionally deficient and vulnerable to addiction."[25]

Knowing how our attachment patterns affect our self-regulation is important because pastoral care for addictions should happen before the addiction. Our church communities and our pastoral care leaders can do a lot of resilience-building by helping people become "attached" to God and the church community. This means that the leadership and the community are dependable, consistent, and attuned in their care for others. When children and adults feel that they are seen and heard, they experience a sense of mirroring and belonging. When they take part in worship and leadership, followed by our praise and appreciation for their work, they feel a sense of agency and connection. Rather than focusing on people as problems, resilience studies also suggest that optimism and hope, the development of emotional intelligence, the use of flexible and pragmatic coping skills, and empathy for others all sustain resilience.[26] If churches would strategically address these needs in the ministries they offer and the culture they cultivate, then they could become places of attunement for many.

Childhood Trauma and Disorganized Attachment

Much childhood trauma is attachment-related. It is perpetuated, enabled, or excused by the very caretakers to whom the child must turn for soothing and safety. Childhood maltreatment and trauma can undo most of the gifts we have talked about for securely attached children, including strengthened regulatory functions, emotional intelligence, internalized relational patterns, and a sense of core self. Child maltreatment is a major pathway to early teenage or preteen onset of substance use. Early drinking and cigarette smoking are also connected to adverse childhood conditions. In a longitudinal study of about five thousand children, exposure to child maltreatment was associated with early teen smoking and alcohol use.[27] A twin study (3,761 girls) examined sexual abuse and early-onset substance use. Childhood sexual abuse history was a distinct risk factor for use of cigarettes and cannabis, and is a very strong predictor of drinking at an early age.[28] Another interview study, with 300 intravenous drug users about their childhood histories of physical abuse, found that 40.3 percent reported severe abuse, 34 percent reported mild to moderate abuse, and 25.7 percent reported no physical abuse history. A history of severe physical abuse was significantly correlated with an earlier initiation into alcohol and with the first onset of injection-drug use for this population. All reports of abuse in this study, from mild to severe, were connected to more extensive lifetime polydrug use.[29]

Shane Darke, of Australia's National Drug and Alcohol Research Centre, affirms that distressing affect is the primary motivator for compulsive drug use.[30] He asks: "Are the socio-economic stressors, parental psychopathology and drug use seen in the backgrounds of many heroin users associated with high levels of childhood abuse? The answer is an unequivocal 'yes.'"[31] Intravenous drug users report high levels of childhood sexual abuse, physical abuse, neglect, and psychopathology. Children who have substance-abusing parents are also more likely to have adverse childhood experiences, including physical, sexual, and emotional abuse and neglect, and to begin using substances early.[32] This helps us to understand why "addictions run in the family." Genetics may be involved, but their expression is also compounded by a combination of insecure or disorganized attachments, abuse and neglect, chaotic homes, and exposure to and modeling of substance use. As we will discuss in the following chapter, childhood trauma coupled with oppressive social environments can create a cycle of emotional and practical suffering. The symptoms of trauma cause their own difficulties at work, in school, and within relationships, which then cause more emotional and practical problems, which then trigger more stress and painful affect states.[33] At first, drug and alcohol use can seem like a solution to these painful emotions, but it actually makes them worse and often exposes individuals to the risk of further traumatic events in adulthood.[34]

Post-traumatic Stress Disorder

If deficits in early attachment can cause problems in self-regulation, symptoms of post-traumatic stress can add a chronic state of affect dysregulation to these difficulties. Post-traumatic stress disorder includes three symptom clusters: dissociation or numbing, hyperarousal or hypervigilance, and intrusive memories (or flashbacks) related to the trauma.[35] These are related to how our stress system becomes unbalanced when we experience multiple violations without repair or empathy. We become hypervigilant in preparation for danger, and our stress system turns itself on over and over again, leaving our bodies and brains overaroused and inundated with stress chemicals. When we are completely overwhelmed or trapped in a violent situation, we may also dissociate. This is the "freeze" response of the "fight-flight-freeze" instinct. It is how our nervous system manages our helplessness, especially if we experience no agency during the attack or no place of protection or attunement to our distress after the attack.

Traumatic events also change how we take in information from the world and how we remember trauma. When our stress system is turned on, instinct takes over. Stress chemicals actually shut down the hippocampus, the part of the brain that is responsible for helping us process new memories. The dangerous or violating experience is not stored as a normal memory—autobiographical and in the past—but in clips and pieces like a movie or in bodily sensations, smells, or feelings.[36] Since our experience is not integrated and put in the past as a memory, this experience feels like something that is still happening in the present. Our brain also begins to read unrelated neutral stimuli in the environment—a similar smell, feeling, sound, or voice—as danger. We become hyperaroused, even from neutral stimuli. Intrusive memories are also triggered by associations with these stimuli. Some self-regulation strategy is needed to escape, numb, or feel powerful in the face of these threatening feelings or memories, so traumatized people are at risk of using ritualistic, self-harming, and sometimes other-harming behavior in an attempt to gain affect regulation.[37]

It is misleading to suggest that PTSD arises from one traumatic incident, because childhood abuse is better understood as a pervasively abusive and unempathic environment. The particular tragedy of childhood abuse is that the one who is abusing the child is the one to whom the child would instinctively turn for attachment security and soothing. The stress system is turned on, and you need to transform negative affect, but the one to whom your instincts cling is the one who is causing the stress. So traumatized children may have more intense and longer-lasting emotional reactions to their environment and may have difficulty engaging the body or brain to help minimize or manage these reactions.[38] They may also turn to substances to calm feelings of anxiety or hypervigilance arising from the effects of chronic stress on the alarm system of the brain.[39] Not surprisingly, efforts to deal with these states of arousal have been connected to drug use.[40] Trauma and addiction form a toxic feedback loop. The mental-health symptoms caused by traumatic stress stimulate the compulsion to use. The withdrawal and craving cycle then generates further distress on the mind and body.[41]

Stuck in such a corner, substance users with past childhood abuse histories are also more likely to injure themselves, attempt suicide, or have co-occurring disorders.[42] For instance, in one study on self-harming behaviors and drug abuse, Marina Bornovalova and colleagues study how abuse causes impulsive reactivity.[43] They found that both physical and sexual abuse were related to self-harming behaviors and substance abuse. The link may be that, for some, symptoms of trauma make it difficult to regulate emotions when stressed. The survivor of abuse is not generally impulsive, as if he were born with this character trait. Instead, he engages in impulsive and potentially self-destructive behaviors particularly in the context of negative affect. This suggests again that chronic behavioral conditions like addiction are not attempts to chase after pleasure, but are attempts to survive pain.

It is difficult to parsimoniously measure out the ways that cruelty unravels through our lives, but the one consistent finding is that hardships in childhood lead to harder paths of living. Childhood maltreatment and trauma do not cause addictions directly, but are predictive of the early onset use and abuse that later leads to addictions. It is a distinct vulnerability that interacts with other factors, such as substance availability, peer modeling, and the compounding of other personal or socioeconomic hardships. Not all children follow this path, but some kind of solution must be engaged to manage painful states of being. There may be other compulsive actions that deny the needs of the self, such as workaholism, caretaking, or high-stress lifestyles that involve a sense of running from feeling in the present moment.[44]

When substances are engaged as a coping skill, we need to understand that they are important because they both repair something missing (safety, self-regulation) and help manage the effects of something that is anxiety-producing, arising from histories of suffering. I often hear about how addicts responded to chaotic, abusive, or neglectful homes by gravitating toward substances, trying whatever was available at home or hanging around with older friends or siblings who had access to them. Preference for a drug or alcohol type, the influence of peers, extroversion or introversion, or personal comfort with risk-taking have also affected their particular path. Some claimed that they used as an addict would—that is, in excess and to kill their pain—from the first time someone handed them a substance. Others were able to manage heavy drug or alcohol use for years, until a loss in adulthood, such as a divorce or the death of a loved one, submerged them from heavy use into addiction. Every story of progression is enmeshed within the stories of others and built upon the particular risk factors that surrounded them.

But one thing is painfully clear. These children were attempting to carve out survival from little recourse. Drugs or alcohol seemed like a solution that fixed what felt broken in their inner and outer worlds. Thus, when we think about children and addiction, we have to adjust our vision. We have to see, not an excess of pleasure or prideful sin, but an attempt to survive how the sins of others unraveled their functioning. We have to be willing to change the question from "Why the addiction?" to "Why the pain?"[45] We also have to reconsider what it looks like to change behaviors that have become intertwined with trauma survival or have replaced the benefits that secure attachment relationships bring to our functioning.

EXCURSUS: Eating Disorders

The self-medication hypothesis claims that neurobiological malfunction is not enough to understand addiction's compelling hold. If it were, one would only need to balance the brain and the problem would be solved. Instead, for many people, once one addiction is overcome, another self-regulatory behavior will take its place.[46] It might be another substance, for example, trading drinking for marijuana use; or it might be a behavioral addiction, such as sex, internet surfing, or a gambling addiction. It might be a behavioral compulsion, like anorexia nervosa, bulimia nervosa, or obsessive-compulsive behaviors. People will combine a variety of self-destructive behaviors until the basic problem—the sense of inner emptiness, relational anxiety, and low self-worth at the core of the self—is addressed.[47]

For instance, while eating disorders (EDs) are not classified as an addiction, they are ritual behaviors that are harnessed to manage the self and its relationship with the world. Like substance addictions, they are often co-occurring with other mental-health issues, such as anxiety, depression, or PTSD.[48] Eating disorders are not the same as substance-use disorder, because food does not cause an addiction, and one cannot abstain from eating to solve this problem. But they share some behavioral similarities, including excessive amounts of time and thought devoted to the behavior and the continuation of the behavior in spite of consequences to emotional, physical, and relational health. As in substance addiction, individuals with an eating disorder "may not recognize the seriousness of their illness and/or may be ambivalent about changing their eating or other behaviors."[49] These behaviors take on a life of their own as they progress.

There is also a correlation between eating disorders and adverse childhood experiences, suggesting that some eating disorders are utilized as coping skills. According to the National Eating Disorders Association, an estimated 30 percent of people with eating disorders have also suffered childhood sexual abuse. Being a victim or a childhood witness of domestic violence is also a risk factor for developing an ED.[50] Gregory Jantz, in *Hope, Help, and Healing for Eating Disorders,* further suggests that attachment difficulties may be involved in the condition. In environments where a child is overly criticized, impinged upon, or controlled, food becomes a way to regain some ritual or predictable control over the self.[51] Eating disorders may also develop as a response to cultural pressures concerning women and thinness, or may begin as a way to navigate the pressures of life-cycle transitions, such as entering high school or college. Remember the image of the Gerasene's legion: genetics and personality factors combine with childhood attachment and with environmental stressors in the development of chronic behavioral conditions.[52]

Eating disorders are a very serious mental-health condition: they are a condition of the soul in distress. According to eating-disorder therapist Carolyn Costin, they are wrapped into the management of the individual's emotional life and sense of self. [53] Anorexia behaviors can serve to eliminate the feeling, needing aspect of the self. There is a focus on being unique, special, successful, and in control. Those with anorexia nervosa pursue a perfectionism and mastery of the self, which can be quickly cracked with shame and self-hate when attempts at food restriction fail. Those with bulimia nervosa can feel oppressed by the need to purge, and can feel that this process is compulsive and out of their control. The act of purging itself can become emotionally cathartic and therefore potentially addictive. EDs also develop their own homeostasis where a will beyond the person seems to take over. Like an alcoholic who wakes up and drinks, the "illness can get to the point where nothing particular is causing you to restrict or binge or purge; you just do it habitually. In fact, not doing it makes you uncomfortable."[54]

In the book *Spiritual Approaches in the Treatment of Women with Eating Disorders,* Scott Richards and colleagues claim that eating-disordered patients often struggle with a negative image of God, feelings of spiritual unworthiness, guilt, and shame.[55] They suffer from isolation and have difficulty with trust; in other words, they have difficulties with attachment. Part of our work is to help those in recovery evaluate their image of God and talk about what trust in a loving God might feel like to them. We could also explore themes of acceptance and surrender, because shame, along with intense fear and self-doubt, are central to the need to control eating and food intake. Of course, in this process of exploration it is important for pastoral caregivers to first get to know the negative images of God and self that the individual holds, without moving quickly to offering solutions and advice. Spiritual growth slowly unfolds in recovery as individuals begin to address their condition through eating-disorder treatment.

Putting the Pieces Together

Chronic behavioral conditions related to childhood suffering are particularly challenging because they grow from attempts to manage a wound. They have a mysterious rootlessness, because they are created from past sufferings that began when we were too young to fully reflect on or understand them. Those opaque histories then become patterned into how we manage the self and relate to others in the present. As such, these wounds have a presence but also a peculiar absence. We can know something verbally about our past and possess some general memories. We can use descriptive language such as "I was abused" or "I lived in a chaotic, sometimes violent home" or "No one seemed to care about me"—and *that* is why I started using drugs or alcohol. But this is a past that is also only partially remembered and so cannot be fully articulated. It returns piecemeal in disconnected memories. It lives on in adult behavioral patterns and odd compulsions. It is lodged in the nonverbal part of our brain: the chemical rise of the stress system, the sudden self-loathing, the generalized anxiety and somatic symptoms—all of which have little grounding in conscious knowledge. Maltreated children use drugs and alcohol because of what is known—but also what is not known—about their earliest years.

The other difficulty with trauma-informed recovery care is that chronic behavioral conditions self-organize into their own problem. As they lock into a self-protective cycle, they remain partially fueled by what created them, but they have also taken on a life of their own. They now possess their own self-perpetuating characteristics. So there is a tangle of pains—some from the past and some from the present—that are dynamically related to each other. Recovery is a slow process of loosening the net that has entangled the addict. Sometimes pastoral care in recovery begins with simple things, such as how to survive a stressful situation without drinking or using. We ask what their plans are for that day and how they will take care of themselves as the day's stressors unfold. At other times we notice how the past pushes into the present more clearly. The individual has flashbacks, talks punitively to the self, and feels vague anxieties or sudden emotional reactivities that trace the scars of much older wounds. Then perhaps we ask different questions about why or how that behavior or emotion is coming up in the present. What does this experience or emotion mean to them, or how have they survived it in the past? How can their faith support them? But before any conversation ends, there needs to be a return to the practical. In light of this abusive history, or of this difficult situation in the present, how will individuals plan their time or manage their stresses in order to survive into tomorrow without a drink or a drug?

I am talking to a woman (I'll call her Kim) who has been in recovery for one year. Her home life was chaotic and traumatizing, with an inconsistently available mother and several abusive male relatives. As is the case with many addicts, it was not just the big moments of trauma—it was the whole childhood context. It was a pervasive environment of fear and ignored need that failed to mentalize her as a valued self. It is thus not surprising that her attachment style is highly resistant. Kim repeats the attachment pattern of her youth by seeking help and connection over and over, but it is never enough to calm her high arousal. Her self-identity is of one who is victimized, who needs help and love, but who can never get quite enough to soothe her. By describing Kim in this way, I am not suggesting that she is a "needy female." I am saying that she tells me about her past by how she patterns her present relationships. Kim was early made the "identified patient" in her family: for example, she was on antidepressants since she was thirteen. When she became an adult, more doctors tried to throw more medication at her: Trazadone, Klonopin, Abilify, Xanax. Kim also developed what she called an occasional eating disorder, going through phases of bingeing on food. Furthermore, she drank a bottle of vodka a day for ten years, which was on top of her prescribed medications, and no doctor or psychiatrist ever seemed to notice. It is quite astonishing that she did not kill herself with that combination of prescription drugs and alcohol. This is a profound example of why the disease model without the rest of the body and soul is not enough. Kim was never able to fully feel or integrate her pain, and she lost most of her life to a haze of intoxication.

While I have taken the time to receive her past trauma as the gift of her trust in me that it is, I can't delve extensively into the details of her traumatic memory and guide her through that opaque and threatening place because I am not a trained trauma therapist. If she decides that this kind of exploration is important, she needs a therapist who can be a consistent and professional presence through a long process of integration. But as a pastoral caregiver, I can offer care that is informed by the dynamics of her traumatic past. I can be unsurprised, solid, dependable, and consistent in my care. I can explore who God is to her. It is understandable, in Kim's case, that this meant a lot of recrimination about God's abandonment. But at this early stage, it is more important to help her survive her legion in the present. A common cause of relapse is, unsurprisingly, negative affect or stress. This is experienced neurobiologically in withdrawal and existentially in managing feelings evoked by daily living that were once numbed by substances. But for Kim, it also involved the symptoms of post-traumatic stress. So one simple goal for our time together was to support her efforts at affect regulation.

This was important for Kim because, after a year of sobriety, the first gift that she received in recovery was her anger. It burned bright and random against her work colleagues and general acquaintances. The rage was not actually attached to anything in the present, though she did not know that. It was the flooding of a dysregulated brain and body, set free from the bonds of addiction. It was all of her insecurities, fear of others, poor attachment, chaotic inner world, and self-hatred translated into one overwhelming affective storm. It's not this way for everyone. Some people are very compartmentalized or cut off from their emotions, since any sense of anger feels dangerous to them. Others seem very able to name and talk about their emotional states, and they quickly regain this skill once drugs and alcohol clear out of their system. But Kim's rage had always boiled beneath the surface, numbed through alcohol since she was a teenager. Her emotional life had stood still. Now it broke open.

In pastoral care classes, we are often taught to follow feelings above all else. We get to the root of problems by exploring feelings, and we seek insight and catharsis through the expression of feelings. In addiction recovery, we learn that feelings are not facts. Kim had a feeling-drenched story about her life, and it was one of danger, rage, and abandonment. Every new event was plotted within this basic narrative. Sometimes she expressed a lot of fuzzy, inchoate emotions—depression, anxiety, or irritability. Sometimes she expressed specific diatribes about how co-workers, politicians, and slow drivers on the freeway were all a string of expletives that I cannot repeat in polite company. That doesn't mean that I discount her emotional states. I need to check for the signs of social sins that might be stressors in her life:

discrimination, racism, power issues at work, abuse, and the economic and practical challenges that make living painful. But in the midst of the emotional challenges of early sobriety, it is also tempting for pastoral caregivers to get caught in the undertow. We want to tell someone to stop worrying. We want to explain away the problem for them, or attempt to fix the burning issue being expressed. So what I'm trying to do is avoid what Motivational Interviewing calls the "righting-reflex": the desire to fix, solve, teach, exhort, or control the other.

Kim's emotions are real, but in a different way than we usually think of that term. They are a very real communication of something in the past through which she experiences her present and future. This needs to be held with absolute respect. But while her internal frame of reference needs to be honored, I don't have to follow wherever she leads. Kim is able to step back and reflect on her life, and I can help her strengthen that process. Together we can try to develop an observing eye for her affective storm through basic reflective listening skills. First, I would guess at a feeling: "You feel helpless," or "You are worried about losing your job. Does that sound right?" We are trying to develop some practice in self-observation. Second, we might want to look at the cause or context. I could ask an open-ended question, such as, "Are you afraid of something?" or "Why do you think this affected you today?" I could reflect back a discrepancy in her observations, as, "You seemed positive about your job yesterday, so what do you think changed today?"

Sometimes emotional regulation begins to fall apart when someone is thinking about a future event—visiting one's childhood home or seeing old friends who still use substances. Sometimes it is the past, like dealing with a time of year or a situation that triggers traumatic memory. Or it could be an interaction in the present that evokes the themes of shame or abandonment that are threaded through a person's life. Of course, sometimes people are just lonely and afraid, immersed in an emotional world that they don't know how to address without substances. In the end, the broader goal is to be curious, observant, and grounded together: to name discrete emotions and begin to put them into perspective, so that we disarm what seems global and immersive about dysregulated affect states.

Finally, the goal of affect regulation goes beyond identifying emotions to choosing actions. In sobriety, recovering individuals have choices. Emotions do not have to control their responses. Problems have more solutions than the drink or the drug. Once I have spent time getting to know the situation from Kim's perspective, we can be curious about framing a response. The question is about action: What are you going to do with this feeling? You have choices about your co-workers or the fellow drivers on the road. How does this current response hurt or help you? Or we might identify a family event, a holiday, or a time of the year that is actually the problem. You have to go to a family birthday party next week, so seeing your family again is scary. What fears do you associate with that? What would help you prepare? How can your faith practices support you? Together we begin the work of distancing from the overwhelming affective static long enough to look at the self and identify what is happening and what to do about it.

The final question that ends our session together is meant to be grounding as well as practical: "What are you doing for the rest of the day?" or "How are you taking care of yourself tonight?" People who have spent a good part of their lives checking out of the present need some sense of structure to manage living in that present. As a 12-step person, Kim has heard about some skills to manage life without substances: call your sponsor, go to an AA meeting, call a sober friend, be around positive people, exercise, go for a walk, meditate, do yoga, watch a comedy on TV, enjoy a hobby, cook a meal, eat something with sugar.[56] People come into recovery with only one tool—a substance—and it often feels unnatural to try to use new tools on our old woes. Therefore, small plans for the day are wise, including reaching out to supportive friends and communities that can hold the individual accountable to those plans. The final summary (see Motivational Interviewing skills in chap. 6) needs to affirm Kim's many strengths and then repeat the new story: from how she was feeling, to what she identified about it, to what she is going to do to stay sober today.

By focusing on regulation in the present, I am not trying to avoid talking about the past wound that brought Kim to this point. The wound is all around her. I am trying to remain a secure base, attuned and loving, while we begin the small steps of feeling and thinking together. Learning how to manage emotional arousal and to develop strategies for self-soothing is essential to relapse prevention, especially for adults who experienced neglect, rejection, or abuse as children.[57] Claudia Black, a longtime writer and speaker on addiction and the family, spoke at a conference about what care looks like for young addicts with multiple experiences of trauma. First on her list of treatment goals were skills in grounding and emotional regulation.[58] The life skills for these young people included learning first to pause, to listen, to communicate healthily, and to enter into problem-solving. Learning self-regulation responses are crucial in addiction, because addiction represents someone's attempt to survive stressful and emotionally dysregulating situations.

These skills of pausing, observing emotions, and choosing a response are also new ways of being present to emotional pain as one begins to build a life of recovery. Some addicts report feeling wonderful after their bodies and minds get cleared of the substances. Others feel wonderful for a moment as the chemicals clear, and then the old thoughts and feelings return with no way to numb them. This is important, because we can confuse good feelings with a good recovery. It is hard for anyone—addict or otherwise—to accept that horrible feelings are sometimes inevitable in life. Addicts in early recovery can experience times of heightened depression, anxiety, or rage. They can face many stressful practical problems and personal losses that tempt them to use again. But not every feeling requires a response. There will be feelings up and feelings down, and there will be feelings that Kim can't identify but just seem sticky and uncomfortable. There will be days that she wants to get sober and days that she wants to drink. The strange feeling of restlessness crawling under her skin—the sense of being irritable and discontented with nothing in particular—will also come and go. We can use our role as pastoral caregivers to normalize these emotions and also to structure the discussion about emotions in a manner that associates them with recovery skills. We can also assure people in recovery that if the emotional stressors do not shift—if sobriety has uncovered a mental-health challenge, such as a mood or personality disorder—then this is good information that can lead to a better strategy for long-term care.[59]

Christian Practices of Self-Regulation

Kim's efforts to get to know and respond to her feelings were inspiring, and it leads me to wonder what role spiritual direction could have in helping people who are struggling with self-regulation. In Claudia Black's presentation on trauma-informed recovery, she listed some self-regulation practices that could support trauma therapy for young addicts, including mindfulness practices and bodily activities such as meditation, yoga, tai-chi, labyrinth walks, chanting, drumming, song, the expressive arts, and breath work. Currently, mindfulness meditation is the most popular practice in addiction care for managing difficult emotions and learning how to remain in the present. When addiction specialists talk about self-regulation practices, I am always struck by how many of our Christian practices could be harnessed for recovery if we could help our people make these connections. It is unwise to insist on such practices, but as a volunteer chaplain and a priest, I have certainly talked to people who wanted to know how to bring their faith lives and practices into their recovery.

Our faith has many grounding and centering practices that might appeal to Christian people in recovery who are struggling with emotional regulation and spiritual connection. For individual spirituality, there are rosaries and prayer beads, contemplative prayer practices, and prayer books with morning and evening devotionals. Or one can pray with Scripture, walk the labyrinth, or meditate with icons. There are practices of memorizing prayers or Scripture passages that one can repeat as a mantra. AA sponsors often suggest that people memorize the Serenity Prayer. There are communal practices, such as healing worship services, laying on of hands, Bible studies, or praise services that can help a person new to recovery reconnect with others and God. There are those who bring the creative arts, music, and singing into their prayer lives. Each denomination has a wealth of tools that are about embodied spiritual growth—practices that engage the body, mind, and senses toward healing and spiritual renewal.

Of course, a practice is only centering or stress-relieving if the individual finds it so. When I was in college, I remember being lectured at length about the benefits of contemplative meditation by a priest in my Episcopal tradition. I was not very good at sitting alone and contemplating, but I liked this priest and wanted him to feel useful, so I never told him that this practice held no appeal for me. If he had asked, I would have told him that I liked the Jesus Prayer, and I liked walking while praying it. If he had asked a few more questions, he also would have found out that I was (and remain) lazy. I could have used some help developing a plan to walk and pray more consistently. If he had asked a few more questions, he would have learned that the morning was not the time for contemplation or prayer, or really anything other than coffee. I can only pray after being fully caffeinated. So, while it is unwise to prescribe spiritual practices, we can take the time to get to know a person's spiritual needs. We can ask what is spiritually resonant to him or what has helped him in the past, so that together we can co-create a response that best fits his spiritual growth or his recovery needs. And it is always good to check in, just to make sure that he is still listening.

A Slower Resurrection

The connections between childhood maltreatment and addictions should give us pause before we imagine that addicts have a simple problem, solved by a simple choice to stop using. Addictions that grow from deep relational wounds are indeed a problem, but they also have been a source of survival. People develop a relationship with their addiction, and it becomes part of their identity. In our minds, it is killing them; in their minds, they are often not sure how to live without it. Part of our commitment to the other as a child of God is to respect the fact that an individual's path to sobriety may be as idiomatic as her path to addiction. Changing who we are, integrating our past, responding differently to the present, restoring relationship with God and others—these defy our anxious desire to move quickly to resolution in our pastoral care. Addiction care can be frustrating, because loved ones and care providers really want addicts to change, sometimes with more clarity or passion than do the addicts themselves. By change, we usually mean stopping compulsive and excessive substance use. The choice seems simple to us. We want those who suffer to get over a destructive action and embrace the good God wants for their lives. But for many addicts, recovery is not about removing a single action. It is about managing a way of being that has infiltrated body, mind, and soul.

I know that addiction is a problem, but I have been seeking to adjust the caregiver's vision about this condition so that we can approach it with more respect. I want to suggest that there is something starkly beautiful about our attempts to survive our lives. Chronic behavioral conditions are symbols that contain and communicate histories of relational suffering. An individual's experience of his addiction tells us something about what he has lost, what he longs for, and what he is grieving in his life. For some, addictive behaviors are about the longing for escape, the desire to annihilate consciousness. Others express longing for transformation: to be seen as attractive, funny, connected, and ultimately loved if they can be someone other than themselves. Some behaviors express parts of the self that seek thrill and rebellion. Others are full of chaos and hardship, reliving childhood situations of anger, abuse, and loss.

If we listen more closely, the story deepens. The escapist feels trapped. The life of the party tries to manage shame and self-loathing. The thrill-seeker dissolves into dull and repetitive using, and the vulnerable child is locked behind the hard street persona. Self-harming habits tell complicated stories of suffering and survival. By the time the solution turns against them, there seems to be no way to continue a coherent sense of self without the behavior: to be the person we know ourselves to be in our bodies and histories, while at the same time changing everything that defined the self. As one abuse-survivor said without irony, "I loved the street life. I hated myself, so

I was killing myself with substances." In this man's self-understanding, the love and the killing go hand in hand.

Addictive behaviors contain and communicate suffering because suffering insists on being expressed. A traumatized person's psyche continues to try to tell her stories of early self-other relationships in which she learned to treat herself in neglecting or hateful ways. She internalized the idea that she was worthless, that it was better to escape this body and this need for holding and love. Until we can communicate this pain, our bodies and minds use symptomatic ways of letting our suffering be known. There is something incarnational about how the body refuses to act as if the sins against it never happened. Our words become enfleshed, expressed through the behaviors that hold what was denied language for us. The murdered Abel's blood cries from the ground, and the raped Tamar tears her garments and becomes a desolate woman in her brother's house. Spiritually, addictions are one of these symbolic communications. They are containers for people to hold and express something that was lost to them. They become an intimate part of a person's identity. To lose these behaviors would be another kind of death: a loss of how people construct the self and stay alive in the midst of their suffering.

Shelly Rambo, in *Spirit and Trauma: A Theology of Remaining*, encourages us to remember that trauma is not about easy solutions, and our main goal is not to remove or erase the realities of others' suffering lives.[60] Many times in our theologies of redemption, we move in a linear progression from cross to resurrection. We move from tragedy to victory, from death to new life. Rambo reminds us that trauma does not move in this neat progression. It breaks our understanding of temporality. In the symptoms of trauma that I have described above, the past invades the present, but it does not return as an autobiographical memory, well-formed and set in the past. It lives in clips and pieces of memory inside of us. It is expressed in reactive symptoms and physical sensations. It is perpetuated in our relational patterns and in our sense of self-worth. It is a past both invasive and lost to us. Addictions become attached to the management and expression of this mysterious pain.

I think that Rambo's model of temporal disjointing in trauma could also apply to other childhood attachment losses that break our sense of psychobiological cohesion. When we experience maltreatment, abandonment, or rejection as children, we enter into adulthood haphazardly, trying to organize the difficulties around a self and its relationships whose origins are partly mysterious to us. When we suffer so young, we do not have the conceptual ability to really understand why we are in pain. Substances keep us alive, but they do not give us the emotional space or safety we need to befriend our losses. When a preteen or teenager turns to early drug and alcohol use to manage that pain, the child has not lived enough to fully understand the extent of his attachment losses and integrate his past. He does not know what drives him to use and why it feels like a solution to him. As he begins using, he further damages his ability to see reality clearly, to examine his own feelings, or to learn new patterns of relating. He becomes a mystery to himself.

Resurrection is God's promise within the suffering of these kinds of deaths, but Rambo says that the pressure to get over, forget, or wipe away the past is often reinforced by reading Christian redemption as personal victory. A narrative of triumphant resurrection promises a radically new beginning to those who have experienced something devastating. The suffering will be wiped away and, behold, something new will arise. But if addictions have become tightly wound to survival and identity, on what foundation does one build this new life? Certainly, resurrection is the stubborn promise that our suffering matters and the subversive hope that new life can arise from death. But this promise and hope must indeed be stubborn and subversive, not an anxious desire to ignore the suffering that remains. Rambo encourages us not to be seduced by what appears to be a simple movement from cross to resurrection, from death to new life. Instead, trauma uncovers a middle ground in this narrative where death and life weave closely together.

Drawing from theologian Hans Urs von Balthasar's reflections on Holy Saturday, Rambo reminds us that Jesus walks a liminal place between death and life. In liturgical traditions, Holy Saturday is the time between Good Friday and Easter Sunday morning, between death by crucifixion and the new resurrection. Jesus descended to the dead. Some traditions say that he descended into hell. So Holy Saturday is the valley of the shadow of death, an ambivalent place where death and life combine for Jesus. While Jesus creates a bridge from death to life by journeying through this middle place, it is a tenuous bridge, a fragile thread. It is not a smooth passage from God-forsakenness to eternal life, nor a discrete transformation from one thing to the other.[61] Even in the resurrection, Rambo notes, Jesus's suffering is not neatly contained in the past. The witnesses see him through his recent history of trauma and loss, and he rises with his wounds intact. Therefore, "the rescue from the abyss is not being spared from the death; it is not escaping the experience of death's finality, but emerging out of it, knowing that this death is pulled into life as we know it."[62] Death still marks Jesus as a new creation. New life grows from his experience of forsakenness, from the wounds that remain.

When seeking change in trauma-informed addiction care, we must remember that chronic behaviors have helped the person to survive the pressing of these wounds. They provided a sense of identity, a relationship, and a way to manage the self. To lose the behavior is its own kind of death. When we have a short timeline for another person's resurrection, we miss the point that we can never completely cut the suffering threads that weave into our histories. Childhood suffering and adult behaviors intertwine, become part of ourselves, and carry our past suffering forward into the present. The recovering person grieves the death of her resistance to this wound, an identity that she has built from managing or escaping her suffering. It is within that woundedness, in the midst of death, that she must remain until she reweaves the threads that can lead her back into an integrated life.

When I teach courses on pastoral care and addictions, someone inevitably asks me about the timeline to recovery. When do people get to put it all behind them? Some addicts may do so quickly, depending on their score on the DSM-V and with the right personal and social resources. But for many people, recovery is a middle place where "getting over it" is not quite the answer. We should not try to cut off another's woundedness and leave it quickly behind on our path to progress. Instead, we are with people through the ambiguity of claiming a new life that feels like a death to them. We accompany them as they work to bring wounds forward into new ways of living their daily lives. For Jesus, the suffering of his passion was not erased, but was raised with him in those strange wounds that still punctured his hands and feet. Within his rising in the midst of death, we learn something mysterious about a new creation. It is not, after all, an erasure of the past, but is the past's incorporation into the present. We do not lose our wounds when we recover. But, with the passage of time, we can befriend them. They are not fully erased, but that's because redemption is not about escape. Our wounds are crucial to a future redemptive way of living compassionately with others.

Chapter Four

Addiction and Social Suffering

> Why would anybody who is not suffering from an agonizing lack of psychosocial integration ever devote his or her life to a narrow, dangerous, offensive lifestyle?
>
> —Bruce Alexander,
> *The Globalization of Addiction: A Study in Poverty of the Spirit*

> Drink, over-eating, sexualism, vanity, and idleness are still reliable standardized sins. But the exponent of gigantic evil on the upper ranges of sin, is the love of money and the love of power over men.
>
> —Walter Rauschenbusch,
> *A Theology for the Social Gospel*

While we begin with the bodies of our parents as our first secure environment, in the end we seek the body of the social to meet our needs for attunement, safety, and meaningful connections. We expand from the sphere of our first caregivers and begin to explore our world. We attempt relationships with more and more people and institutions. We find ourselves situated in broader systems of power. We take on increasingly complicated social roles via employment, education, or parenthood that influence the possibilities of our future emotional and physical health. We remain created to need each other. Our self-identity is always in reference to our position in relationship to the broader social body.

African American family therapist Nancy Boyd-Franklin provides the image of concentric circles drawn around the self, to resituate the individual within her expanding environment. Our relational dynamics ripple from the individual to the core family unit, to extended family and fictive kin, to neighborhood and church, to social institutions, and to broader social systems.[1] While we assume that our problems are individual and innate—I am naturally shy, angry, helpless, criminal, caretaking, or addicted—these are actually patterns of relating that arise from our position within these broader circles. The foundation is laid by our caregivers closest to our center, but we remain deeply influenced by others as we move within these overlapping circles. The problems, connections, blessings, and oppressions met throughout our widening interaction with people, social systems, and institutions profoundly affect our functioning, along with our mental and physical health.

Attachment experiences such as attunement, empathy, and mentalizing are important in each layer of social interaction. Throughout our lives, we need to feel securely and safely connected to a social group. We need to feel understood and have the needs of our bodies and emotions taken seriously. We need to be mentalized—to be treated as thinking and feeling selves in our own right. On the other hand, the abuse or lack of empathy across these concentric levels can cause their own stressors and leave an individual without a sense of connection to a relationship that is soothing and secure. Attachment theory reminds us that it is impossible for individuals to completely regulate their affective states alone.[2] Our central nervous system remains an open-feedback loop. This need for the other continues into adulthood. Without a secure base within the social body, we will struggle to find the flourishing life that a relational God intended for us.

As Christians, we know how important this is because there is no love of God without love of neighbor. The first sign of discord out of Paradise is Cain's murder of Abel because Cain's sacrifice to God was not accepted. Then comes the ironic question, "Am I my brother's keeper?" The answer is: Yes—actually you are. For God, the ground cries out against Cain for breaking his responsibility to care for the other, implying that this kind of keeping is the true sacrifice that is pleasing to God. There is no vertical relationship without the horizontal, no call to love God without the call to do so via our love for the other. This responsibility is attested in the commandments, where acting unjustly against the neighbor or oppressing the foreigner is a sin against God (Exod. 22:21). It is a sin judged by the prophets, who declared that economic and political injustice broke covenant with God (Isa. 1:1-17; Ezek. 22:29-30; Mic. 6:8-9). It is enshrined at the center of that greatest commandment, that is, to first love God and then others as we love ourselves. It seems that God knows all about Boyd-Franklin's concentric circles. On this side of paradise, we remain responsible for creating a social body that is attuned to the needs of others. The sin of this holy obligation to the other is discrimination, marginalization, and oppression—the unempathic and abusive social body.

I will talk about racism, homophobia, and socioeconomic insecurity throughout this chapter, but I am not trying to suggest that marginalized groups use more substances than privileged individuals. I am saying that those who experience marginalization may have particular sources of suffering that need to be addressed in our pastoral care. Studies show that discrimination causes distress and that socioeconomic insecurity leads to a proliferation of emotional and practical stressors. This is important for our work in addictions because people use drugs and alcohol to manage stress and negative affect. According to psychiatric researcher Marijn Lijffijt, human stress can trigger earlier experimentation with substances, increase the risk of transition into recreational use, increase the risk that use will escalate, and diminish the motivation to quit.[3] The experience of our environment is intimately related to our progression into addiction.

By claiming this place for social sin in the etiology of addictions, I am also trying to dislodge our tendency to individualize chronic behaviors in ways that flatten out the three-dimensional nature of suffering and in turn flatten our compassion. If we merely think of addiction as a personal problem, we will not be able to effectively address the different practical and social needs of those who come to us for care. Finally, an awareness of social sin also broadens our pastoral care into community resilience-building and political advocacy. It encourages us to consider the real contextual and practical challenges to recovery within these concentric circles that make up an addict's filial and social worlds.

Racism, Homophobia, and Distress

We take our seat at another circle of chairs. A woman tells her story about addiction, but it is also a story about how abuse extends from family, to society, and right up to God. She lived through the confusion of a physically abusive, alcoholic father and a devout but emotionally demanding Christian mother. She attended Sunday school, Wednesday choir, and weekly Bible study. Then she discovered alcohol at fourteen, and it helped obliterate her memories of violence and her dawning sense that she was attracted to other girls. When her family found out about her sexual identity, they totally rejected her. She said that they told her that "God hated me and I was going to hell." The church became a dangerous rather than a welcoming place. She felt rejected by her parents, by society, and by God. There was no individual or social place to go for an attuned, empathic environment.

Remember that addiction is an opportunistic infection. It organizes itself around a host of vulnerabilities, progressively infecting our souls until it takes on a life of its own. For this woman, her drinking careened throughout her twenties and thirties until it became the one consistent focus in an otherwise chaotic life. To her, it was as if God was already punishing her. God hated her, and she was not worth anything better. As she talked in the session about the consequences of addiction throughout her life, she punctuated her story over and over with the same refrain: "It didn't matter because God hated me." Her experience of homophobia in her family, church, and society seemed to pool together into her image of God. When she entered into recovery, she found a sense of security with the women in her 12-step meeting, but she struggled to overcome the message of hate that had encircled her life. Finally, she tried therapy. Her therapist told her to write down all the one-word attributes that she thought defined God. So she made a list: God was "hateful, punishing, vengeful, rejecting." Then the therapist told her to write down the opposite: the attributes of a higher power that she wanted instead. She wrote down "loving, friend, caring, helping." She had to give up the Christian God of her childhood to find one who would heal and love her as a lesbian woman recovering from addiction.

This recovering woman's life had foundered on a legion of suffering, including abuse and rejection in her home, in her church, and in the homophobia of her larger culture. By the time she was a teenager, alcohol seemed like a solution to the collapse of every layer of her concentric world. It helped her to escape an abusive home and to medicate trauma. It helped her numb the feelings of fear and vulnerability evoked by attacks on her sexual identity. It helped her to symbolically enact the punishment that she felt God and society were both eager to offer. Over time, she internalized alcohol into her sense of self-worth. She deserved nothing better, she thought, because God hated her, making her later addiction an intimate part of her theological worldview.

If we are relational beings at our core, marginalizing conditions such as racism and homophobia result in consequences that by now you should know by heart: higher negative affect and higher stress. Imagine all of the attachment losses that we covered in the last chapter and apply them to the experience of our social world. In these cases, the social body itself causes our stress without repair. Our needs are neglected or our efforts to gain connection are rejected. Our attempts to explore our environment are stymied through the impingement of stereotypes, subtle rejections, and experiences of violence. Our attempts to find attunement or empathy, to regulate our stress through connection to the social body, are denied by others. We are objectified—rather than mentalized—as thinking and feeling selves in our own right. Socioeconomic inequality, stigma, and stereotyping are pervasive throughout the dominant institutions and cultures that circle around the lives of sexual minorities and people of color. The social body does not mirror their reality, is not empathic concerning their humanity, and is not attuned to their basic human needs. Instead, it is often outwardly abusive to their bodies and souls.

The effects of racial discrimination on our mental health have been well researched. Daily experiences of racial discrimination are connected with heightened daily stress.[4] This stress is also internalized. For instance, a meta-analytic review of sixty-six studies about perceived discrimination and African American mental health found an overall connection between discrimination and psychological distress.[5] Perceived discrimination was also associated with feelings of depression and anxiety. Studies by sociologist Robert Carter on African Americans and discrimination further found that these experiences may lead to traumatic stress symptoms, such as intrusive memories and hypervigilance.[6] For Chinese and Taiwanese international students, discrimination also predicted symptoms of post-traumatic stress disorder (PTSD) beyond a general sense of life stress.[7] In another study, depression appeared at greater rates in Asian and Hispanic young women, highlighting the intersectionality of gender and ethnicity in relation to our mental health.[8]

If we use substances to manage stress and negative affect, and also to transform self and relationships, then discrimination and marginalization are among the factors that make us vulnerable to the solution that substances seem to bring. Racial discrimination is associated with distress, such as increased rage, anxiety, and depression, and these stressors are connected to drug or alcohol use throughout the life cycle.[9] For instance, according to one study, African American adolescents who experienced early cumulative discrimination and who used substances as a coping strategy had a significantly greater increase in substance use as adults.[10] In another study, youths' experiences of discrimination were correlated with depression and increased alcohol and marijuana use.[11] While studies show that an individual's experiences of racism affect mental health, the larger problem is that our social systems, institutions, and culture perpetuate racist environments from one generation to another, creating a pervasively painful context.[12] In this environment of pain, "anger appears to be the primary affective response that mediates the relationship that has been consistently found between discrimination and substance use."[13] It should be clear that this proposed link between anger and substance use is not the problem of minoritized people. The problem is systemic and institutional racism, against which minority groups—in order to survive—must find some coping strategies.

For sexual minorities, researchers use Ilan Meyer's theory of minority stress—the idea that excess stress is experienced by individuals from stigmatized social categories—to describe the experience of the unempathic social body.[14] Part of the theory brings us back to attunement: the minority person experiences emotional distress and practical conflicts because the dominant culture, social structures, and norms do not typically mirror those of the minority group. In the concentric circles that surround us, this means broad political discrimination, such as laws curtailing the rights of same-sex partners; personal discrimination, such as job loss or harassment at work; and abusive experiences, such as violence against transgender people.[15] The social body lacks attunement and empathy for LGBTQI identities as the culture enables, normalizes, and rewards traditional gender and sexual expressions. As for the woman whose story appears above, it is often true that faith communities anathematize sexual minorities and deny them the love and security of the religious body.

Use of substances among sexual minorities appears to be connected to this experience of hostility and rejection, from the core family unit all the way to the broader culture. According to the National Survey on Drug Use and Health, sexual minorities were more likely to be cigarette smokers and to have used alcohol and illicit drugs compared to their heterosexual counterparts. They were also more likely to have experienced harassment and violence due to their sexual identity. Finally, sexual minority adults were more likely to suffer from a substance use disorder.[16] In a survey of LGBTQI individuals, those who reported verbal and physical assaults because of their sexual minority status were more likely to have a lifetime substance use problem and to experience suicidal ideation than those who did not report these attacks.[17] Substance use as a coping response to homophobic verbal and physical attacks may also increase suicidal ideation and self-harming behaviors. LGBTQI young adults who reported high levels of family rejection when they were adolescents were 8.4 times more likely to report having attempted suicide, 5.9 times more likely to report high levels of depression, and 3.4 times more likely to use illegal drugs.[18]

Childhood trauma can combine with the social stress of marginalization, including multiple experiences of violence throughout the life cycle. A community study of nine public schools in socioeconomically disadvantaged neighborhoods (a total of 1,143 high-school seniors) found high levels of childhood adverse experiences, which included parental unemployment or substance use, abandonment, and witnessing or experiencing assault, sexual abuse, and rape.[19] Increasing frequency of these experiences was significantly associated with increasing depressive symptoms, drug use, and antisocial behavior. This effect was strengthened when a respondent had experienced multiple adverse childhood experiences. Research on poverty and African American youth further points to the complex intersection of racism, poverty, experiences of violence, and drug use.[20] In one study of urban African American and Puerto Rican men, those with the highest levels of violent victimization throughout their youth and young adulthood were also the highest frequency marijuana users and further suffered more problems with mental health and substance use disorders.[21] In another survey of sexual minority substance users, those who had experienced childhood interpersonal violence were more likely to struggle with substance use. The study suggested special concern for the combination of childhood abuse and adult relationship violence as a stress pathway toward substance use for sexual minority men.[22] These studies point to a complex trajectory into substance use, wrapped in a legion of childhood and adult suffering.

As I suggested in the preceding chapter, factors that make one vulnerable to addiction are mitigated by factors of resilience that help an individual develop coping skills and positive identity despite very painful life situations. It is this variability that makes it so difficult to draw a line and say that one or another experience of suffering is directly related to the development of addiction. With the cards that we are dealt, there are many hands played between vulnerability and resilience. Resilience can include personal traits such as hopefulness, humor, or mental flexibility.[23] Common relational resilience factors for youth include stable family structures, consistent and supportive parenting, and other adult attachment figures, such as mentors or teachers. For instance, in one community study, anger at discrimination was connected to a greater willingness to use substances.[24] But this connection between discrimination, anger, and substance use was buffered by the presence of supportive parenting.

As we span out from Boyd-Franklin's concentric circles, resilience can be found in positive school involvement and other expressions of talents, such as participation in sports or the arts. Within all racial/ethnic groups, young people for whom religion is more important—who attend religious services more frequently and who are affiliated with a religious denomination—are less likely to drink, smoke cigarettes, or use marijuana than their less religiously committed counterparts.[25] We have an important sense of belonging to offer our youth. Meyer also points to the importance of the wider minority group's ability to mount self-enhancing social structures that counteract discrimination's effects, such as LGBTQI centers or affirming churches. Those who suffer the mental health effects of the unempathic social body seek social groups that can help mirror back racial, ethnic, or queer identity and can encourage a sense of belonging to those considered "my people." This repairs social misattunement with mirroring, and repairs dehumanizing treatment with empathy. But the need for "resilience" itself reveals the effects of minority stress on one's mental and physical health.

Acculturation is another variable factor related to coping with marginalization. For instance, some minoritized individuals have a strong internalized sense of their racial identity, others do not see race as a problem, and some are in a stage of transition about how they see race influencing their lives.[26] It is interesting to note that one study suggested that people fared better in terms of substance use when their experience of discrimination confirmed the sense that their group was viewed negatively by the dominant culture.[27] Those who did not expect to experience racism felt more disappointment and distress at discrimination than those who assumed the realities of racism.

Finally, age and life-cycle development may make a difference in one's resilience. In one study, Asian immigrants thirty years and older experienced heightened discrimination distress. While the researchers had expected more distress in younger adults, they theorized that the life-cycle challenges of marriage and career stability are vulnerable times because we are trying to establish cultural norms of identity. These pursuits also increase our involvement in the dominant culture as we interact with employers, schools, and institutions. The need-to-achieve identity formation might intensify the mental-health effects of racist treatment at this life-cycle stage.[28] Thus, experiences of discrimination and marginalization don't affect every person in exactly the same way. They constitute a social stressor that people experience differently depending on their assimilation into dominant cultural norms, the support of loving relationships, socioeconomic stability, and the personal resources that they can access to manage this kind of suffering.

Social Stress and the Crossover Effect

In this chapter I am focusing on issues of marginalization because pastoral care must address the sources of suffering behind addictions, and we must be aware that these sources can be rooted in experiences of social oppression. Understanding the complexities of social stressors can help pastoral caregivers avoid universalizing or oversimplifying the experience of substance use and its progression into addiction. For instance, one dynamic of perceived discrimination and substance use is the "crossover effect" theorized concerning African American youth. African Americans do not use drugs and alcohol at drastically higher levels than their white counterparts. As a matter of fact, when it comes to alcohol, African American young people tend to start later and to average lower drinking throughout high school and young adulthood than do their white peers. Studies theorize that family respect and religious involvement help deter early use, and these are well-researched resilience factors for youth.

But for African Americans who do use substances, sometime in their mid- to late twenties the deficit in their use seems to reverse, and they move into addiction by middle age.[29] At the same time, while white users appear to peak in their twenties and thirties, many begin to lessen or stop heavy substance use as they move through the life cycle. So these demographics cross over at some point, with whites beginning to lessen use while African Americans begin to increase use. This crossover effect is also suggested in the Treatment Episode Data Set, the national statistics for substance treatment admissions. For instance, for their chart on alcohol admissions, white men have a high curve for treatment in their twenties, while the bigger bump for African American men comes in their fifties.[30] This could point to a later progression into addiction, though it may also reveal inequalities in access to affordable or culturally appropriate treatment for African Americans. These two dynamics may be related, since the progress of addiction may be exacerbated by a lack of appropriate treatment resources earlier in the life cycle.

What might the context of this crossover effect be? As many white youth traverse the bridge of emerging adulthood, they settle into new adult roles through socially sanctioned pursuits, such as marriage, higher education, or stable employment. They create pathways toward socioeconomic stability. They find that the social body generally mirrors their own, and it is attuned to their culture and concerns. As they create a sense of belonging for themselves in the wider environment of adulthood, they stop or moderate alcohol use. When African Americans enter more fully into the roles and institutions of adulthood, they may find more experiences of racism and fewer opportunities or rewards for the cultural trajectory into socioeconomic security. There are fewer incentives to moderate and more life stressors to manage. So young African American adults may continue using drugs and alcohol regularly—and they may thus progress into addiction later in the life cycle—just as their white counterparts begin to find the social avenues and sense of belonging in society that enable them to cut down their use.

Hispanic youth, in theory, have a different trajectory than African American teens do, and their risk factors include immigration, acculturation, discrimination, and lower socioeconomic status. According to data from the Monitoring the Future study, eighth-grade Hispanics were more likely to have used substances that year or consumed alcohol in the past month than either white or African American eighth-graders.[31] This is a concern because it suggests that these children suffer adverse childhood conditions, and they may be in danger of developing an addiction later in life. While national surveys suggest that Hispanics do not use more than do other groups in the general population, those born in the United States are more likely to use substances than those born in Mexico or Puerto Rico.[32] It is possible that oppressive material conditions may affect this next generation's drug and alcohol use: Latinos suffer greater poverty, have less education, and experience more social disadvantage than do their white counterparts.[33] Research also suggests that Mexican Americans who are more assimilated into American culture may be at greater risk for drug and alcohol problems.[34] In contrast, Latino immigrants who retain cultural identity and have a connection to family-centered values may be able to buffer against these adverse childhood experiences.

Finally, as I have mentioned above, sexual minority youth may have a trajectory into addiction marked by filial and social rejection and homophobic violence. Drug or alcohol use may be their way to cope with these stressors and losses, and substance use may also be normalized in their particular LGBTQI social community, such as gay-and-lesbian bar cultures where sexual minorities can socialize and find support.[35] Drinking cultures are not particular to sexual minorities, since there are fraternity and sorority drinking cultures or certain workplaces that encourage drinking as part of their socializing. The issue for the trajectory to addiction is how the legion of vulnerabilities might combine: how substance-use behaviors could develop into a repetitive response that they use to address stress relief and emotional regulation in the face of homophobia, while also becoming a source of socializing and support with fellow sexual minorities.

Sexual minority addicts also may avoid accessing treatment services for fear of experiencing further homophobia and discrimination in rehab. Treatment staff members may be uninformed about LGBTQI issues, or may be insensitive to or antagonistic toward sexual minority clients.[36] This does not provide a secure, attuned place to begin the work of healing. According to one interview with LGBT-identified addicts in treatment, hiding and secrecy about sexual orientation reinforced the denial that was part of their addiction.[37] Feelings of shame and guilt, low self-esteem, a sense of inauthenticity, and internalized oppression also impeded their choice to seek recovery.

Socioeconomic Insecurity

The third major social stressor that may affect substance-use trajectories is poverty or economic insecurity. In my course entitled "Pastoral Care of Women" at the seminary, we play an interactive computer game called SPENT, created by the Urban Ministries of Durham.[38] Since the majority of those in poverty are women (more than one in eight women, including 23.1 percent of African American women, 22.7 percent of Native American women, and 20.9 percent of Hispanic women[39]), SPENT helps students get a feel for the difficulties of balancing work, housing, children, and health needs on very little income. Rather than thinking of poverty as an abstract, unfortunate state of being, students look at the daily difficulties and realize the emotional and practical strain of a thousand small decisions. Along with racism and homophobia, economic insecurity is attached to increased stress across the course of life. In fact, poverty is probably the greatest stressor on physical and mental health—understood through what is called the stress-proliferation model. Stress proliferation is the idea that serious stressors tend to create symptoms or problems that are themselves stressful. These additional stressful problems and their symptoms have effects on one's functioning or environment, proliferating more stress.[40]

We often imagine that a person's physical and mental health is a personal problem related to biological functioning, genetics, or lifestyle choices. The building blocks of our genetics and our lifestyle choices certainly influence our wellness, but broader studies show that differences in people's health and well-being correspond to differences in their status within social systems.[41] The inequalities that are documented in physical and mental health across all kinds of social designations—from gender to race and ethnicity to lower social class— are produced by the different exposures to stressful experiences in those categories. Social stressors create changes in how our bodies and minds function, and chronic stressors can directly affect our physical and mental health.[42] In other words, if you wish to oppress a group of people, you do not need to do so directly. You just need to make them anxious, stressed out, afraid, and physically sick. You need to block a multitude of access points for basic health and socioeconomic stability—some subtle and some systemically obvious—that, over time, box in a person's options for economic and social resources, personal security, and agency.

According to the US Census Bureau, in 2015 there were 40.6 million people in poverty. While non-Hispanic whites make up a large majority of those living below the poverty line, the effects of historic and institutional racism are evident in the high percentage of people within minority groups living in poverty: the percentage for blacks was 22 percent (9.2 million), for Hispanics 19.4 percent (11.1 million), for Asians 10.1 percent (1.9 million), and for non-Hispanic whites 8.8 percent (17.3 million).[43] The poverty threshold in 2016 was $12,486 per year for a single individual and $24,339 for a family of two adults and two children. (These rates do not include the homeless.) Of course, the working-class poor and the working poor who live near this line can experience a lifetime of economic insecurity, and even households that are not officially identified as in poverty dip down below the poverty threshold for months at a time.

Designating what makes for poverty is only part of the picture of economic insecurity. Neoliberal economics—where individualism, competition, and free-market trade are the driving values, and corporations network labor, distribution, and sales across the world in a global economy—has led to a loss in America of skilled labor and working-class jobs that offer a living wage.[44] But dependable working-class jobs are only the beginning of financial stability, and they do not necessarily cover the cost of mortgages, childcare, college education, sick children, or the care of elderly parents. More education appears to be the answer because the more education one is able to achieve, the greater the chance is for stable employment. For instance, in 2016, 88 percent of those with college or advanced degrees were employed, as opposed to 69 percent of those who had completed high school.[45] However, the more education a person attains, the more lifetime debt he or she must manage. Holders of bachelor's degrees owed an average of $25,000, while postgraduate-degree holders owed an average of $45,000 in student loan debt. This means that one in five graduates between the ages of twenty-five and thirty-nine have to hold two jobs to manage their debt.[46]

The stressors of economic insecurity are themselves legion, and in the stress-proliferation model we can imagine them spinning out into a host of other stressors that undermine emotional and physical health. People may put off health care, patch together childcare, or have to choose between utility bills and car payments. I've certainly witnessed the mental and physical effects of these stressors in my work as a priest in a predominantly working-class congregation, where members suffered from toxic work environments, took on extra jobs to make ends meet, were forced into evenings or double shifts, or were disempowered by supervisors. They had little extra income for children's expenses, doctor's appointments, counseling needs, or even medicine for chronic health conditions. They were one crisis or hospital stay away from bankruptcy. And this group was not an isolated case. According to one review of the literature, lack of social and economic resources is associated with an inability to achieve goals, and this experience of powerlessness leads to heightened distress.[47] Our national conversation has started to make this connection, describing addiction in the context of the growing economic challenges in poor and working-class communities in the rural Midwest.[48]

The material conditions of economic insecurity proliferate over the course of life and across generations, widening health gaps between advantaged and disadvantaged groups.[49] This does not mean that one will inevitably respond to stress proliferation by abusing substances. But if substances regulate negative affect and transform our sense of self with others, then the greater the stress and sense of social exclusion, the greater the risk that substances will be used to manage these difficulties. For instance, involvement in gang activity—or the perceived need for toughness or emotional isolation in response to dangerous neighborhoods—may lead to a sense of hopelessness that heightens the likelihood of substance use.[50] In another study, white males who were less educated and living in poverty were more likely to suffer from co-occurring substance abuse and psychological distress than were their demographically similar counterparts.[51] In terms of resilience factors, marriage and religious practice both appeared to buffer this result. Our personal resources, social environment, and ability to build a meaningful and healthy life are intertwined.

Finally, those with less financial stability have fewer means to protect themselves from the harms of heavy substance use or addiction. Robin Room, director of the Centre for Alcohol Policy Research, asserts that lower social-class position is much more strongly related to adverse outcomes from heavy substance use than is the habit of the heavy use itself.[52] The poor have fewer resources with which to hide their use—less flexible jobs, fewer safe houses to use in, and less disposable income to buy and use in private. Poor access to nutritious food, medical care, and healthy living conditions can lead to greater physical and practical consequences from using substances. Furthermore, a greater exposure to others when intoxicated (using public transportation, walking home while intoxicated, gathering at strangers' houses, sleeping in public areas) can also lead to more experiences of victimization. So, while all social classes use alcohol and drugs, the poor may suffer more risk of further adult trauma, health problems, and challenges to life stability from the effects of their use.

While those with the fewest resources may have the most struggles, let me return briefly to the bigger picture of the neoliberal values undergirding global-market capitalism. According to pastoral theologian Ryan LaMothe, this dominant ideology is a pastoral issue, first, because its practices impoverish people and cause suffering; and second, because practices of care and community are influenced by the neoliberal philosophy of individualism and competition that drives this kind of economic structure. LaMothe claims that Judeo-Christian values "aspire to create a caring subject embedded in a community of faith and able to identify and respond to the needs and interests of Others."[53] In contrast, neoliberalism fosters "a narcissistic, atomized subject" who is isolated from community and from responsibility to others. It undermines practices that value "care, community, the common good, and relational justice."[54]

Addiction may be one of the symptoms of this broader existential and identity loss. According to Bruce Alexander in *The Globalization of Addiction: A Study in Poverty of the Spirit*, economic insecurity extends to a sense of alienation from self, place, and community.[55] He claims that addictive behaviors arise from the dislocation and lack of psychosocial integration that come with the cultural shifts of global-market capitalism. We are objectified, separated from meaningful labor, socially alienated, and transient in our search for socioeconomic security. Communities are no longer meaningful environments where we contribute to the welfare of others. Individualism and competition become the greatest goods, devaluing loyalties to family and friends or even the higher values of religion, culture, ethnic group, or nation. Alexander claims that dislocated people "struggle valiantly to establish or restore psychosocial integration," to try to create a sense of identity, of meaningful life, and of a relationship with the social body.[56] They attempt to manage dislocation by narrowing themselves into chronic habitual behaviors, from drug and alcohol use to the obsessive accumulation of goods, in an attempt to defend against this floating sense of loss and alienation.

To summarize, an individual becomes addicted in a personal and social context, and that context continues to matter when she tries to quit or moderate use. This does not mean that addicts are helpless in the face of their condition. Just as there are many factors that combine in the making of an addict, there are many that combine in the making of recovery. Gene Heyman, a psychology professor at Boston College, gives this review of why addicts choose to stop using substances:

> The correlates of quitting include the absence of additional psychiatric and medical problems, marital status (singles stay addicted longer), economic pressures, fear of judicial sanctions, concern about respect from children and other family members, worries about the many problems that attend regular involvement in illegal activities, more years spent in school, and higher income.[57]

Heyman is optimistic that people can choose to quit abusing substances, claiming that many people make this choice before the age of thirty by drawing on intrinsic motivators, such as wanting respect from family or a more economically secure life for themselves. He makes an important point for us to remember in our care: addiction is a learned behavior and many people have the individual or social resources needed to retrain their brains without extensive treatment. There is not one way to recover from substance abuse or addiction. But his list also summarizes why the most vulnerable people—those who are traumatized, socioeconomically marginalized, or suffer mental distress—might face different challenges when making the decision to change. Saying that "many do quit spontaneously and therefore everyone can" is like saying, "But some have money, education, housing, neighborhood resources, supportive families, and social attunement, and therefore everyone can." For many of the most vulnerable, life is much more complicated than that.

The War on Drugs

The other social side of addiction is its stigma and how public discourse concerning drugs further stigmatizes the vulnerable. This aspect of the abusive social body is called the war on drugs. For decades, the war on drugs has played a central role in America's "tough on crime" stance, justifying greater policing, search tactics, arrest and incarceration in communities of color.[58] By 2010, African American men were six times more likely than white men to be incarcerated in federal, state, and local jails.[59] This amounts to the public exile of one in ten African American men between the ages of twenty and thirty-nine and nearly a third of high-school dropouts aged twenty-five to twenty-nine.[60] Hispanics now constitute 35 percent of all federal prisoners, making them the largest ethnic or racial group in the federal prison system.[61] This is also connected to the criminalization of the undocumented, who are jailed or detained before they are deported. In New Jersey, where I live, 71 percent of jail inmates are reported to be either black or Hispanic.[62] Poor whites are also affected by this "tough on crime" stance: those having only a high-school education are twenty times more likely to be imprisoned than those with more education.[63] A stunning fact is that young African American men with no education beyond high school are more likely to be incarcerated than employed.[64]

The war on drugs and the pipeline from poverty to prison drives already vulnerable people even further from the social body. Drug offenders make up 18 percent of county jail inmates and about half of all federal prison inmates.[65] They become a particularly marginalized class of people who have missed life-cycle opportunities for education and skill-building, and at a young age have been denied the nurture of families and the development of identity. Due to criminal records, they are unable to vote or gain licensure in certain occupations. They experience job discrimination and they cannot receive public assistance or housing aid. And yet they are sent back to somehow survive in the midst of onerous probation regulations. People can continue under the discipline and surveillance of parole or probation for many years. There are currently more than eight million people in some form of punitive state control, such as prison, jail, probation, parole, community sanctions, drug court, and immigration detention.[66]

Incarceration is also a traumatizing experience. According to political theorist Marie Gottschalk, our prisons and jails are "exceptional for the extensive use of demeaning and degrading practices that would be considered flagrant human rights violations in most other industrialized countries."[67] Gottschalk further reminds us that women have been the fastest growing segment of the prison population, and they are much more likely than male inmates to be serving time for a drug offense.[68] Ending the war on drugs would largely reduce their numbers, especially those of African American women. If we are really concerned that illicit drugs are damaging people and thus must be illegal, then we might want to consider how much incarceration damages people. Imprisoning people with neurobiological problems neither solves their problems nor limits the market for addictive substances.

As the demographics of the incarcerated show, this war is applied more rigorously to certain populations and neighborhoods than to others—with clear racist implications. For instance, while whites use marijuana at rates similar to blacks, blacks make up the majority of arrests for marijuana. In my state of New Jersey, blacks are arrested at three times the rate of whites for marijuana possession.[69] In my former hometown of Pasadena, California, African Americans were arrested for marijuana at twelve and a half times the rate of whites.[70] While incarceration is a punishment that devalues and dehumanizes many people of color, the war on drugs has further encouraged pervasive policing practices that target African Americans and Hispanics, extending surveillance to their daily lives whether or not they use drugs. Inordinate policing creates a pervasively unempathic, dehumanizing, and often dangerous environment. So the whole picture of the war on drugs is the policing, the stop-and-search practices, the various levels of state control and surveillance, and the verbal and physical humiliations that African Americans and Hispanics experience under the auspices of our national crusade against drug addiction.[71]

Social Sin in Pastoral Care

I have been claiming throughout this chapter that our childhood need for the empathic body of our caregivers extends to the adult need for an empathic place in the body of the social community. A part of the church's call to the pastoral care of the addicted is to discern how to be this empathic body, a source of resilience-building and advocacy for those who suffer social sin. I am often asked to speak in church forums on the opiate epidemic. I can do so, and perhaps this increases awareness about the dangers of this class of drug. But a better topic would be: How can the culture and practices of this worshiping community promote lifelong resilience for both its youth and adult members? Resilience-building—and the connection between church involvement and delayed initiation into substance use—teaches us how important it is to have a place of mirroring and attunement, a sense of belonging, and a community that offers alternative practices to manage negative affect and stress. The church could be a place where people bring their social suffering and find themselves mentalized as thinking and feeling selves—as children of God—in their own right.

I am not suggesting that changing church culture is easy or that all congregations have a wealth of resources to address every issue they face. As a parish priest, I've seen how difficult it is for a small, struggling congregation to simply survive. But I suggest that church programming, small or large, could be discerned under some guiding assumptions: that Scripture matters to our well-being, that God knows the complexity of our personal and social struggles, and that practices of care should address the emotional and material conditions of the worshiping community and its surrounding neighborhood. We can also engage in preaching and teaching that breaks the stigma of chronic behavioral conditions. If we begin to preach and teach that addictions are simply solutions that have turned against us—ways of survival that are no longer useful to us—we can lessen the stigma and imagine new ways of solving and surviving our lives together.

The stigma of addictions brings us to the next move in the pastoral care of addictions: a political response. Pastoral care includes advocacy, adding our voice to the legislation debates concerning the war on drugs. We have a double-sided message about drugs based on what appeals to the emotions of the electorate, with national and local officials claiming that we need more compassionate care for the opiate addiction while at the same time supporting the arrest and maximum sentencing for individuals using those drugs. Pastoral care also includes advocacy about the health-care debate in America and the roadblocks to effective medical and mental-health treatment. Federal decisions about health care and criminal justice make a sometimes life-or-death difference to the people in our pews and in our neighborhoods who are using drugs and alcohol. There are many websites that offer opportunities for advocacy at the state level, and broader organizations, such as the Drug Policy Alliance or the American Public Health Association, that can help congregations get educated and involved in the decisions made at the national level.[72]

Furthermore, since policing and arrests for drug possession are so clearly racially biased, the pastoral care of addictions includes joining voices for racial justice and protesting the policing practices that are encouraged by the war on drugs. The deaths of African American men and women at the hands of police or vigilantes—including the debates on the news about whether or not the person was high or intoxicated and therefore at fault—are related to the long history of stigmatizing African Americans in the war on drugs.[73] As theologians Lee Butler, Kelly Brown-Douglass, and many others have contended, the shooting of African Americans is a continuation of the logic of lynching: that African Americans are physically dangerous to society, that they are associated with blackness and evil as whites are associated with whiteness and good, and hence their removal by arrest or death is for the public order and the safety of the innocent.[74] Currently the drug war rhetoric is shifting to Hispanics and to politics around securing America's southern border. Language eerily familiar to the Chinese Exclusion Act (see chap 1) is now set against Hispanics who are vilified as the cause of drugs and crime, crossing the border to poison our innocent youth.[75] Finally, for me, as a white pastoral caregiver, knowing about the history of racist abuse in this country further means learning how my central cultural position as a white person dulls my compassion for others and limits my imagination. I need to remain teachable about my own racism, and I have to teach against the stigma of addiction that so often fuels racial marginalization.

Issues of class and economic insecurity also require a systemically curious pastoral care. In his book on mental health and class oppression, *Pastoral Power,* Philip Helsel encourages pastoral caregivers to resist individualizing experiences of mental distress and to think more systemically about their socioeconomic causes. A mental-health diagnosis, which includes the DSM-V symptom list for addictions, labels the individual as a problem and suggests that his symptoms of suffering are internal to his functioning, rather than a result of the material conditions within which he lives. Helsel reminds us that, by "envisioning the entire person-in-context, one can exercise a pastoral imagination that sees the real extent of social suffering brought about by oppression, and how this has an impact on the minds and bodies of individuals in communities."[76]

Remember that substances first seem like solutions. So we ask more questions, with Nancy Boyd-Franklin's broader understanding of what might be the problem. We note the signs of stress proliferation on those who are struggling to make ends meet. We pay critical attention to how personal problems are actually the effects of economic struggles and their broader context in global-market capitalism. Helsel further suggests a solidarity model for pastoral care in economic suffering, "working to change the conditions of work, what one has to do to survive, and also foregrounding the *voice* of those who are in working-class positions."[77] We seek to resist the shame of not living up to the "American Dream." We advocate and support working-class rights.

Finally, differences in class, culture, and sexual identity should be considered in recovery. There is more than one way to develop an addiction, and so there is more than one way of seeking its healing. LGBTQI advocates ask if the usual rehab treatment model is really a safe place for queer addicts, or if it will just be one more experience of homophobia, discrimination, and heterosexism for those trying to seek recovery.[78] African American advocates ask: What about the importance of racial pride in these colorblind recovery models? What about accessing better Christian resources in recovery for those inspired by the black church tradition?[79] We also assume that addictions are easily addressed by going to rehab, taking the treatment (however we conceive of this), and getting better. But these programs cost money and time. Knowing about a person's resources, insurance coverage, employment situation, parenting responsibilities, and other limitations is obviously crucial when one speaks of recovery.[80] We might send someone out of the office with a referral to a rehab without considering that she doesn't really understand her insurance plan, she hasn't asked her employer if she can take the time off, and her ex-partner has sometimes refused to watch their child. What can seem like resistance to change may be the burden of multiple practical responsibilities or limitations that the individual will not share with us unless we broach the subject.

If all this advice is a little overwhelming, let me conclude by going back to the beginning. We are created for an environment. We are entrusted within the circling of others' bodies, from the body of our first caregivers, to the body of the social, and finally to the body of God who became flesh for us. We are never a self outside the compass of the other. The Fall is an account of the fragility of these connections. It ended our primal union with all of creation and covered us with shame and conflict with the other. It speaks to a thoroughly relational loss. We leave Paradise. We commit violence like Cain and are violated like Abel. We take part in systems of power that oppress and traumatize others, and we push away the stranger, the poor, and the outcast in our midst. We long for a new creation. Addiction is a symptom of this brokenness, an infection within the wound of our relational fragility. And the stigma of addiction is a part of the cycle that continues to break individuals and communities in the war on drugs.

Jesus is the embodiment of God into the center of those circles of personal and social suffering. He is God with us, God in relationship to us. He ministers particularly to the sick, the impoverished, the demonized, and the marginalized. He comes for those who are separated from the social body. It is through his physical proximity to the least of these that Jesus is revealed as Messiah, the Son of God. This Messiah is ultimately imprisoned and tortured. He dies a political execution on the cross, an execution meant to terrorize others seeking liberation.[81] Jesus truly takes on our sins—our betrayal, violence, oppression, and hunger for power—those worst moments of our fallenness, when we violate our created purpose to love God and love the neighbor as ourselves. But Jesus is raised from the dead, overcoming the sin of this world. He is the first-fruits of a new creation, yet oddly a body still wounded by trauma and betrayal. He once again draws close to his disciples, sending them back out through the circles of their world to spread the story of a new kind of savior whose power takes root in the middle of oppression and death.

As pastoral caregivers, we are still humbled by the mystery of life's slow, troubled emergence from centers of death. We see it in the ambivalence of individuals as they struggle with their personal demons of addiction. But perhaps we are too apt to take this broad breakage and stuff it into each individual encapsulated soul. Our concern must also extend to what is death-dealing in the social world. We are asked who we will be as followers of Jesus in this tangle of life in the midst of death, survival in the midst of oppression. If this is our perspective, we can work for addictions care as a kind of political care, a care that is built from the circles that ripple out of our old longing for Paradise. We can continue to advocate for the place of all God's children within the suffering of their own bodies, the social body, and the whole of creation. Our job is to stay with that suffering, responding faithfully to its personal and social manifestations as we accompany others into recovery.

Chapter Five

Soul-Sickness and the Legion

The man lived among the tombs;
And no one could restrain him any more
Even with a chain,
For he had been restrained with shackles and chains.
But the chains he wrenched apart
And the shackles he broke in pieces
And no one had the strength to subdue him.
Night and day among the tombs and on the mountains,
He was always howling and bruising himself with stones.
When he saw Jesus from a distance, he ran and bowed down before him.
And he shouted at the top of his voice,
"What have you to do with me, Jesus, Son of the Most High God?
I adjure you by God, do not torment me."
For he had said to him, "Come out of the man, you unclean spirit!"
Then Jesus asked him, "What is your name?"
He replied, "My name is Legion; for we are many."
He begged him earnestly not to send them out of the country.
Now there on the hillside a great herd of swine was feeding;
and the unclean spirits begged him, "Send us into the swine, let us
enter them."
So he gave them permission.
And the unclean spirits came out and entered the swine;
and the herd, numbering about two thousand,
rushed down the steep bank into the sea, and were drowned in the sea.

—Mark 5:3–13

Mark's Gospel is about Jesus's minstry to people in conditions of pain. Exorcism and healing formed a couplet in his ministry, and represented his authority over both the spiritual and physical realm. Jesus's first miracle was the exorcism of an unclean spirit in the synagogue (Mark 1:21–27). He then healed Peter's mother-in-law. By the evening, all who were sick or possessed of demons were brought to Simon and Andrew's door (1:32). Jesus continued to "heal and cast out their demons," and Mark reminds us that he silenced the demons because they knew who he was (1:34). He then traveled from town to town, "teaching in the synagogues and casting out demons" throughout Galilee (1:39). Exorcism, healing, and controversy tumble over one another in Mark's hurried account, and by the third chapter we are reminded that "he had cured many, so that all who had diseases pressed upon him to touch him. Whenever the unclean spirits saw him, they fell down before him and shouted, 'You are the son of God!'" (3:11).

Mark is not one to mince words, and Jesus's ministry to our need explodes among Mark's clipped accounts, quickly building suffering upon suffering, setting the wonder-working Jesus apart from the religious leaders of his day. There is no time for long stories when we are scrambling for healing, caught in a swirl of desperation and hope. People came in droves to Jesus because they longed to be transformed in body and spirit. But as Jesus began to sail across the sea to the land of the Gerasenes, Mark's narrative suddenly slows down. He tells us about the storm ready to capsize the boat. He allows us into the fear of the disciples, who asked whether Jesus really cared that they were perishing. He describes how Jesus cast out the wild storm using the same words that he used to cast out demons.[1] Jesus claimed authority over the chaos of the sea and the chaos of our doubt, as we make our way across the quieted water to the land of the Gerasenes.

When we arrive on the shore, we find a man caught in the throes of a soul-sickness. He is the embodiment of that stormy sea and he is perishing. He is restless and sleepless. He bruises himself on the rocks without seeming to notice. He moves at the impulse of an inner violent force. No one can control him, though many have tried, using shackles and chains, imprisonment and rejection. He is rejected by those who might once have cared for him. He is estranged from himself, yet, at the same time, he has been grafted upon the agent of his own destruction. He has been left to deteriorate at the edge of his society, roaming the tombs as if he no longer cares whether he is alive or dead. The frenzied death of the pigs suggests that this possession is powerful, malevolent, and actively damaging.[2] It is a destructive and progressive condition that eventually would lead to his death.

The Gerasene's possession helps us to better imagine the suffering of the addict's soul in distress. In this soul-sickness the addict is possessed by his behavior. His actions are not completely his own. He can no longer access the beauty of God's creation or his own belovedness as a child of God. He is dulled to reality, lost in a kind of twilight at the edges of civilization. In the divided mind that now infects him, he is strangely incapable of feeling the consequences of his behavior deeply enough to make a change. What is most compelling to the addict is the storm in his own head—a tightening cycle of stress, mental struggle, and self-involvement. He is stuck in a condition of pain, a state of being that has emerged over his continued substance use and has locked into place. It is a spiritual state that estranges him from self, others, and God.

The image of the legion illustrates the multiplicity and emergence that is characteristic of this condition. As this wild figure rushes to meet Jesus, it first appears that the man is the one begging Jesus not to torment him. Then we realize that it is the demon who is speaking. Soon it becomes clear that it is not one demon but many demons that have taken up residence inside of the man and organized into one voice. Who is actually doing the talking? We were introduced to this strange emergence from many into one in Jesus's first exorcism in the synagogue, when the man with the unclean spirit cried out, "What have you to do with *us*, Jesus of Nazareth?"(1:24). This combination continues in the Gerasene, when his many demons cried with one voice, "Do not torment *me*." Is it the voice of the man, or the demons in concert, or the legion as a single entity? Perhaps it is all of them combined, controlled by the singular will of the possession. In the same way, it is difficult to pin down a single cause or motivation for an addiction. The many threads of this self-regulatory need are now drawn together into a singular compulsion.

The Gerasene's sickness further blurs the lines between agency and possession, action and identity. We could say that the Gerasene is no longer himself, but perhaps it is more accurate to say that the Gerasene no longer knows himself apart from his demons. The translation of the Greek phrase in Mark, "a man in an unclean spirit," suggests that the Gerasene has been swallowed up in the demon's identity, as if an independent agent is operating outside of the man's will.[3] The needs of the possession are prioritized and they motivate his actions. The Gerasene moves where the demon takes him and speaks through its voice. This points to that strange feeling that we can get when talking to addicts who are in the storm of their condition. They can speak with passion and emotion—even with conviction to change—and yet feel somehow absent, as if someone else is actually doing the talking. There is a sense of disjunction to the rationalizations given for their behavior, a feeling that a force of will beyond the person is now in charge.

While the possession controls his body, it also seeks his harm. This is a characteristic spiritual evil of addictions, and one of the hardest for loved ones to watch unfold. The Greek text suggests that the Gerasene demoniac does not bruise himself against the rocks as if by accident. He is continuously cutting himself with stones. He is restless, howling across the countryside, unable to find peace. A soul-sickness is at its heart a condition of self-harm, and addictions are rife with physical and psychic injury. Yet the Gerasene also has a perverse freedom: his possession makes him preternaturally strong as he breaks the chains with which people have bound him. He does not fear the death that surrounds him in his uncanny home in the tombs. He seems oblivious to consequences. His legion makes him larger than he was without it, while it imprisons him within his own uncontrollable body.

How do we ever survive such a sickness? It makes us invincible while it tears us apart. Addicts appear inured to the danger that they repeatedly confront. Over and over, recovering people say that they eventually crossed the "I'll never do *that*" line-in-the-sand list of actions as the possession increased. Driving drunk. Leaving young children alone without a babysitter. Embarrassing themselves at business dinners and family weddings. Being high and lost in dangerous neighborhoods. Finding one too many strangers in their bed. Dating the drug dealer or taking any pill that a stranger might hand them. Getting arrested. Engaging in sex for money. Multiple overdoses. Accidents and injuries. Showing up drunk to work. Abandoning sick parents. Ignoring spouses. Finding themselves homeless—and so on. It is significant that the Greek word *diabollos* in this passage suggests being thrown apart or broken in two.[4] In the midst of this demonlike possession, the divided mind seems to further unhinge. As in Proverbs 23, none of it feels entirely real. The addict is in a fog of denial. She makes up excuses to try to make sense of it: it is some other person's fault, or fate, or bad luck. But deep down, even these harmful consequences become part of the addict's self-identity. "This is who I am" is what I hear over and over again: "I'm bad, worthless, unlovable, punished. I am my own demon."

In this consuming force, a soul-sickness defends itself from change. It is a supremely self-protective condition. It is this ambivalence and resistance that first struck me about the Gerasene and his legion. When Jesus stepped onto the shore, the Gerasene was not happy that this wonder-worker had come there, trying to heal him. He rushed to Jesus, fell at his feet, and begged to be left alone. The demon called Jesus the Son of God and Jesus responded by demanding his name. In ancient magic, knowing the name of a god or demon grants one power over it.[5] So we can imagine that sickness and healing are in a duel as they each try to gain knowledge and power over the other. The legion fights to avoid the pain of its dissolution. It makes a plea that Jesus allow it to survive in the country by residing in the herd of pigs nearby, even after the man's healing takes place. It bargains with Jesus and tries to manipulate him. Healing is full of ambivalence. This is understandable when we remember that being healed from a demon is an experience of torment. It appears to first cause *more* distress to the body and soul of the possessed (e.g., Mark 1:26; 9:26). Indeed, so does recovery. The addict is not willing to completely lose this legion that is so central to his functioning. It's good to keep the demons close—just in case.

Finally, a soul-sickness separates us from our connections to others. Possession is similarly a condition that causes physical and emotional suffering, while also placing the demoniac outside of religious and social belonging. We know that the possessed were ritually separated from regular communities, since they were infected with an unclean spirit. But Mark, never one to be subtle, wants to pile on the signs of separation. The Gerasene is obviously separated from civilization, living among the dead. Attempts have been made to chain him down and thus to control him. Tombs are unclean because corpses are unclean (Num. 19:11; 19:16). Pigs are also unclean (Lev. 11:1-8; Deut. 14:8). The idea of Gentile territory further suggests social and ritual uncleanness. Unlike Mark's earlier reports of Jesus's exorcisms in the region of Galilee, this possessed man is multiply separated from the disciples who are watching this duel, making any identification with him nearly impossible. Mark makes sure to outline a picture beyond possession and into abjection.

While we might have compassion for the Gerasene because of his exiled state, we can also be wise enough to imagine that he might not have been the best person to have around the house. With his history of violent possession, we can assume that he had done some damage in his community. He was not only a victim but also a victimizer who had probably caused a portion of suffering within his family and town. So when Jesus restored the Gerasene to his right mind, it is not surprising that the man wished to escape all of this separation and return with Jesus to be his disciple. We can imagine that he begged to follow Jesus out of gratitude—but also because he had nowhere else to go. He wanted to start a new life in a new land. This is the immediate conversion, or the early recovery. The addict is clothed and in his right mind. But perhaps he would like to walk away from the damage and the consequences that remain littered across his life.

Jesus refused the man's plea to travel with him and to thus escape this country, where his own stigma was still fresh in the minds of the community. Instead, Jesus returned him to his hometown, back into the middle of those who had rejected him and who had left him at the edges of their social reality. We can imagine that he also sent the Gerasene back to those whom he had hurt. This return is not nostalgic or romantic. In facing these others, he had to face his own past actions, as well as facing those who rejected and injured him. There are no guarantees that his miraculous healing will redeem or restore that past. The healing of a soul-sickness takes a similarly difficult route. Even when Jesus removes the mental anguish of addiction, deep healing does not happen immediately. We need to learn how to reconnect with the land of the living and negotiate new relationships with the families and communities that we have lost.

The Social Demoniac

Mark's Gerasene also has particular social implications that can help broaden our compassion for the soul in distress. The demons offer their name as "many," but the word "legion" had a particular connotation in the ancient world. It was a Latinism that denoted a Roman military unit of 6,000 soldiers on foot and 120 on horseback.[6] The tenth Roman legion was stationed in the Decapolis at the time Mark wrote his Gospel. Their military ensign was a boar, and Mark's use of the pigs and their fate in this story is probably an ironic gesture to the Roman presence in the land.[7] The Roman forces in the Decapolis established outposts in the region and were involved in troop movements and increasing encroachments in the area.[8] And they were not an innocent presence: they posed an active threat of violence and oppression, perhaps even keeping people like the Gerasene "in line." Postcolonial scholars remind us that hatred and fear of the Romans would be symbolized in the violent, organized power of the demons.[9]

Paul Hollenbach inaugurated a sociopsychological reading of the demoniac in the Gospel of Mark by drawing on the work of the psychiatrist and race theorist Frantz Fanon.[10] Hollenbach claims that mental illness, manifest as demon possession, was caused—or at least exacerbated—by social oppression. The Gerasene's condition exemplified the mental-health crises brought about by the dehumanization of colonialism and the pathology of its violent atmosphere. Fanon's *The Wretched of the Earth* focuses on colonial Algeria on the verge of revolution, and he reminds us that it was the whole environment, the "bloody, pitiless atmosphere" of colonialism, that broke human bodies and spirits.[11] The psyche reacts to the "running sore" of colonization with muscular spasms, overexcited affectivity, and ultimately in experiences of the demonic that express psychic disintegration and the splitting of the personality. The wound of trauma pushes powerfully into the present.

Fanon theorized that the ecstatic rituals of possession and exorcism acted like a coping mechanism to release the psychic pressures of colonialism, and thus helped people survive oppression rather than fight against it. But he also expanded our ideas of mental health, helping to contextualize the strain on the psyche within the unempathic and abusive social body. Socioeconomic exploitation, racist practices, and physical atrocities traumatize the mind, body, and spirit, manifested clearly in the mental and physical health of those who carry the load of an oppressed group's pain and anxiety.[12] In this reading, the Gerasene is not only himself but also a symbol for his people. This returns us to Robert Carter's work on racism and post-traumatic stress. It is important for Carter to make clear that depression, anxiety, hypervigilance, and intrusive memories are not the inner "problem" of minority people. The problem is the pervasive environment of racism that evokes them.[13]

For the Gerasene, the legion inside him is an allusion to the evils of Roman occupation and it complicates how we understand spiritual disease. It reminds us that our mental and spiritual health is deeply interconnected with others. When our environments are oppressive, violent, or traumatizing, our souls suffer. It also reminds us to avoid assuming simple characterological reasons for why people develop chronic conditions. As I have elaborated in the last two chapters, it is crucial for our compassion to understand that addictions are not caused by certain types of people. They are caused by certain types of pitiless situations. Sometimes that pitilessness may grow solely within the individual, but more often it is the result of our interaction with the relational or social realm.

If the Gerasene is expressing the psychically disorganizing weight of an oppressive environment, he is then doubly oppressed by the stigma of his condition. Shackles and chains were used to restrain prisoners, so he is not simply restrained for his own good or the safety of the people, but imprisoned or punished for his condition.[14] At the end, he is abandoned at the edges of civilization. The Gerasene's chains follow an ancient trend in magic practices, where it was believed that harsh punishments like chaining or wounding the possessed would free them of their demon.[15] In the same way, the war on drugs attempts to cleanse the anxieties of the social body by punishing people for addictions. As I mentioned in the preceding chapter, the war on drugs has justified greater policing, search tactics, arrests, and incarceration, especially in communities of color.[16] To be policed, incarcerated, then controlled through probation and parole—these make up the contemporary form of uncleanness. It constitutes a new class of half-citizens who are pushed to the edges of the social body. The Gerasene's legion also grows from the wound of an oppressive empire—a violent and pitiless environment—and he then experiences further violence and rejection from others because of his demon possession.

This brings us to another key insight that the legion offers for the pastoral care of addictions. The Gerasene is a survivor. When we work with self-destructive people, we must begin with the assumption that their behaviors once helped them to survive. For addicts, substance use helped them manage situations for which they did not have the mental and emotional resources. It helped individuals to escape, as one alcoholic put it, to "get to the other side" of her suffering, to be anywhere else than where her body was. If we listen closely, we will find that the unmanageability or insanity surrounding substances is symbolic communication of that survival. Again, suffering insists on telling its story. People tell their history, how they have been hurt, what they think they deserve, and how they relate to the world by reenacting a pattern with substances. They express their anger or rebellion, claim power or avoid consciousness. They have stayed alive by means of the substances that later try to kill them. This perspective garners the respect for the person who is so often lost in assumptions of moral weakness, poor self-control, or criminality.

We can further notice the political implications of this wonder-worker and his deliverance ministry as Jesus—not the emperor—is proclaimed the Son of God. In the preceding chapter, I mentioned that stratifications in social class produce stratifications in mental and physical suffering. If society oppresses people via a thousand roadblocks to mental and physical flourishing, then Jesus's healing ministry is a fundamentally subversive, creative act, preparing a people toward resistance. Through his healing and deliverance ministry, Jesus tied up the "strong man" and was pilfering his house (Mark 3:27). At one level, we can consider this strong man to be Beelzebul, the prince of demons—the sickness and the possession of the people. But in its context, the demonic kingdom is also the Roman Empire and those religious leaders who colluded with it. It is the death-dealing strong man of occupation and oppression. Jesus's deliverance ministry, including the Gerasene's healing, was a form of creative resistance to the wounds of power upon bodies and souls.[17] According to Mark 3, people from all around, from Galilee to Jerusalem to Tyre and Sidon, were coming to him because of all the work that he was doing (Mark 3:7–8). Those on the margins became the center as Jesus removed the spirit of sickness and oppression that was on the people, empowering them for the new reign of God.

Bargaining with a Demon

Mark's Gerasene helps us to imagine how the complex personal and social causes of addiction organize and emerge into a singular possession. It also captures a sense of the challenge we might face when offering pastoral care to a legion. I was first drawn to the Gerasene because he didn't make healing easy for Jesus. His first attempt to exorcise the demon failed. Then Jesus had a screaming man bowing before him in a pantomime of submission. He prostrated himself at Jesus's feet as if in worship, but it was really an effort to avoid him. He adjures "by God," even though his legion is of the devil. He begs for an end to Jesus's torment, when he is most obviously tormented by his possession. There is something disorienting about working with a soul-sickness, because it is hard to know who is doing the talking. Finally, his demons bargain to stay in the country, as if they could convince Jesus to keep them alive and waiting to return. Jesus has to manage ambivalence and resistance in removing these demons. In the end, he works with the legion, making a compromise by granting the demons' request, until the frenzy of the pigs cleans them out for good.

Many addicts also protect their legion. Remember (from chapter 2 above) that the instinctual brain creates the cravings and the executive brain furnishes the excuses. Minimizing, rationalizing, or denying the problem is a way to resolve what is irrational about the behavior. It is an attempt to make the inner and outer world of the addict make sense. In pastoral care we hear the legion's self-protective voice when addicts try to make excuses, blame someone else, or try to avoid conversation about their use. They may take on a cheerful wall of denial, a rebel's disdain for authority, or a simple resignation to their fate.[18] They might even eagerly talk about change, only partially aware that they have no intention of following through with it. They can be confusing for pastoral caregivers because we find it difficult to speak into such cognitive distortions. We also sometimes confuse the neurobiological compulsion to relapse with a resistance to change. We forget that, in the divided mind of the condition, the person can both want to change and use substances at exactly the same time.

Two particular conversation challenges characteristic of addiction are deflection and disconnection.[19] Deflection is when we look at the negative consequences of our behavior and blame a technicality surrounding that consequence for the problem. For example, one loses one's license for drunk driving and blames it on the cops trying to meet their ticket quotas. It's not a problem with the drinking behavior. Disconnection—or denial— is when we pretend that consequences are not related to the behavior at all. It means blaming another factor for one's problems or deciding that the source of one's pain is unrelated or minimally related to the substance use. For instance, the real problem causing one's emotional stress is a demanding partner or unfair treatment at work rather than drinking. Finally, there can be a slippery lack of consciousness about addicts, as if they cannot quite grasp the seriousness of their situation. Even when they talk incessantly about their behaviors or ruminate about their need to change, something about the reality of the situation does not seem to stick. They seem, like the Gerasene, to be controlled by the force of the addiction outside of their own functioning.

My favorite story of the legion's self-protection is from a man who drove to a local bar one night and woke up the next morning in his home after a blackout. A blackout is a common sign of a drinking problem. You appear awake and yet you are no longer actually consciously aware of your functioning. Your brain is no longer processing your experience into memories, and so you lose hours because you cannot remember what happened. The next morning, my friend walked out of his house with a huge hangover and realized that his car was not in his driveway. He felt complete dread and shame. He was absolutely sure that he had killed someone or crashed his car and left it by the side of the road somewhere. He walked up and down the neighborhood looking for it. He turned on the TV expecting to hear a story about an accident. After a few hair-pulling days, one of his friends told him that he should pick up his car because it was accumulating a pile of parking tickets. He found out that he had left it parked on a side street next to his final bar of that evening—a bar that he did not even remember entering. He had then walked home two miles in a blackout. He had not killed anyone, and the cops were not after him. His conclusion? "Well," he said, "obviously the *car* was the problem: I should drink at home from now on." That is major deflection!

These self-protective tactics are symptoms of the soul-sickness and thus are grounded in suffering. They are a part of the disconnection from reality and the estrangement from others that mark this condition. They are a result of the brain's reward center moving thoughtlessly toward its tunnel-visioned goal. It is also common for people to protect their addiction because losing the habit feels like an attack on the self. It is hard to let go of something that feels like a source of survival and identity. For those who began to use when they were essentially children, they have known no other way to live their lives. For those who have been functional and even successful while spending years abusing substances, their sense of self-identity is threatened by the idea that they are now really out of control. When we as pastoral caregivers see distancing, deflection, or denial, it further reminds us that we are getting close to something that is important to that person. Motivational Interviewing suggests that it is best not to confront resistance head-on or get into an argument. Pushing back on minimizations and excuses, or trying to argue someone into sobriety, usually ends up in a power play rather than a fruitful conversation.

Jesus can teach us something about how to work with this sense of possession. He does not blame the man or give up on him. He does not demand that he be aware of his problem or come to consciousness about his condition. He does not disparage his abjection, forgotten in the tombs and howling across the hilltops. Instead, Jesus gets to know the voice of this particular demon. He works with these multiple challenges until the hold of the possession can be broken. My last two chapters will help develop the skills behind this work, but before we acquire practical skills, we pastoral caregivers must have Jesus's vision of the person within the possession. We must respect how change can be viewed as a threat or a torment for many individuals who are struggling with addiction. When the addict's survival or identity is wrapped up into a legion, that person can be ambivalent about change—and for good reason. Jesus figures out what will work with this particular possession, and we can take the same time and compassion with those we serve.

Healing and Restoration

Speaking of time, I also like the story of the Gerasene because there is a hint that a longer work of healing is still to come. Jesus returns the Gerasene to his right mind, but we are left with the question, What will the man do next to restore all that he has lost? How will he seek forgiveness for his sins or heal from the sins done to him? How will he recover from the chains and exile that traumatized him in the midst of his illness? He wants to follow Jesus to be his disciple. Instead, his own pathway to discipleship is to return and find a new life among the old wounds of his hometown.

Pastoral caregivers must also consider this longer work of recovery. It begins with addicts being returned to their right mind: detoxing, entering into treatment or therapy, and seeking to recover from the immensity of the possession. It then includes surviving the storms of affect or stress, as the recovering addict begins living with new coping skills one day at a time. It means grieving an old identity and beginning to find a new life in the midst of that death. As people in recovery gain stability and spiritual balance, they also need pastoral caregivers to help them think through the implications of guilt and forgiveness, including how best to forgive themselves and to seek forgiveness from others.[20] They may need pastoral support as they work to reconcile their sense of guilt or self-loathing with the mercy and love of God. Over time, some people need to face the grief of leaving abusive relationships or challenging difficult social realities that have fueled their substance use. They will need further spiritual guidance as they grow from these old wounds to new life.

So the legion reminds pastoral caregivers of the more complicated work of spiritual healing over time with addictions. Jesus begins the healing that the Gerasene himself will need to complete. This lens is useful for pastoral caregivers, because both we and the addict can harbor expectations for a quick recovery. It is true that some people can choose abstinence and recover without treatment. But others get caught up in the dream of a quick solution—whether a stint in rehab or a conversion experience—and then find themselves relapsing into the cycle of addiction. Some people may struggle with emotional ups and downs—and small lapses into using—as they attempt to replace old behaviors with a new way of life. Others might stay on the border of change for many years, wrestling with their demons. These are very common experiences and do not mean that the addict is fated to this life or has no hope for a different future. It means that recovery is a process, and an individual slowly learns what she needs to sustain it. Some find that they need counseling resources while others need more practical help to gain life stability. Some also need assistance to address co-occurring disorders that have been covered up by the haze of the substances, such as behavioral addictions or mental health conditions. Others come in and out of rehab or 12-step programs until they find a program that can help them manage the torments of this loss.

As pastoral caregivers, we have the opportunity to encourage hope during these many paths to healing. A lapse into a day of use or a full relapse into the cycle of behaviors does not mean that the person has failed. We can examine these experiences for what they can teach us about the individual's recovery needs. Similarly, the problems and losses that scatter across past and present will take time to heal. Building a person's self-efficacy means celebrating his good intentions and daily efforts at recovery, noticing his strengths, and reminding him of how far he has come. Every day's small effort begins to build whole relationships, restored identity, and the life of nourishing discipleship promised to God's children. The long-term goal is not just about stopping a behavior; it is about God's hopes for the wholeness of God's beloved child. We accompany those seeking recovery in this tenuous work of restoration.

In summary, there is spiritual resonance between the story of the Gerasene and the experience of addiction as a kind of soul-sickness. The legion of addiction emerges from many causes into one organized force that overtakes the will. It is fundamentally self-harming, yet it becomes central to our identity and we protect it from any threat of change. Between our voice and that of the legion, it is difficult to tell who is doing the talking. It divides the mind, so that our actions seem strangely disconnected from reality. It also divides us from others. It grows from the breakage of personal and social relationships, and further estranges us from them. The Gerasene's meeting with Jesus finally illustrates the challenge of untangling the individual from the illness. It represents the ambivalence and bargaining, the efforts to keep close to the addiction with which we now identify. It is interesting that, even after the Gerasene is healed, Mark calls him the "the demonized one" (instead of a past perfect construction: "the one who *had been* demonized").[21] We do not quickly slough off the effects of such a physical and spiritual sickness.

The Soul in Soul-Sickness

We take our seats around another circle of chairs, and the subject for discussion is how to make amends to those whom we have harmed. Some talk about how they never considered the feelings of others in their addiction: full of self-pity, they felt that whatever happened only happened to them. One woman talked about how everything was someone else's fault. The divorce, the DUI, the loss of her children—all of these filled her with resentment instead of remorse. They were not wake-up calls about her use. Instead, they were an excuse to use more because everyone was against her. Another woman said that she knew she was hurting her spouse and children, but at first she didn't care. When she started to care, she just drank more to stop feeling anything. Years later, she still finds herself suddenly startled into painful memories—"cringe-worthy" she calls them—about the selfish things she said or did while drunk at office parties, family gatherings, or even at home with her children. Another woman described the guilt and shame she carried with her for losing custody of her children. In the midst of her condition, she thought that her inability to stop drinking was God's punishment for her sins, her own purgatory here on earth. The more she drank, the more unworthy she felt of any better kind of life.

These women's stories illustrate the everyday experience of a soul-sickness. If we are created for union with our environment, with each other, and with the God who became flesh for us, then soul-sickness is a progressive loss of God's intentions for our lives. The addict becomes disconnected from her deep need for others and God. She loses her ability to perceive reality clearly and respond to it rationally. She becomes less and less able to make considered moral choices. Her responsibilities to others become blurred, and she lies to protect her legion. She loses empathy. As one person in recovery said, "We feel isolated, as if we were in a ship caught in a storm, constantly pummeled by fear and shame." In other words, we feel estranged from ourselves, others, and God. And yet, part of the divided mind just doesn't care. The addict loses her ability to see the good in herself and in God's good creation.

Addiction is not a sin, but it is a corrosive evil on the soul that progresses as the addiction takes hold. Theology imagines evil as a privation of the good, and we know that addictions are evil because they whittle away the signs of the good in our lives. Perhaps foremost is a loss of hope or of any ability to imagine a different way of life. Just the other day, I asked a group in a rehab to tell me what they gained from using drugs and alcohol. We found the usual suspects: "It made me feel better." "It took away stress." "It numbed painful memories." "It shut down my body." "It connected me to others." "It gave me excitement." "It helped me get through the day." These desires, many of them survival needs, are not evil in themselves. But meeting them via addictive behaviors was a tragic mistake, and as the addiction progressed a corrosive evil was bred into their lives. A cycle of pain developed, which was tied into the cycle of withdrawal, craving, and use. As one man explained, he later used substances just to feel normal. Addicts are focused only on managing the pain of the addiction's possessive force.

When we are so intent on escaping pain in the present, we are oddly deprived of our future. The legion emerges differently for each person, but as it comes into being, the addict falls deeper into possession's grip, stripped of a larger vision for her life. Some people are highly functional in their abuse of substances—they have successful careers, families, achievements—but they become isolated emotionally, or their lives are littered with resentments and fears that strangle the kind of healing God wants for them. Others become stuck in Holy Saturday, with shame or rage about their past while at the same time seeking to numb the symptoms of trauma that flood into the present moment. Time collapses. They lose hope that they have the capacity to respond differently to the ambiguous pushing of past into present in order to imagine a changed future. Those who began to use drugs or alcohol to connect with others later find themselves isolated and alone, stuck on a continuous wheel of craving and use. There is no personal growth. Substances change our perception, and so they strip us of reality, making it difficult for us to take in new information and learn from it for future change. We become stuck in this moment and its immediate withdrawal-induced sufferings.

It is not surprising that this corrosion of hope leads to a high suicide risk among addicts, especially those with co-occurring mental health issues. If we imagine that evil is a parasite on the good, then evil's flourishing slowly destroys the reasons for living into our own futures. As one literature review summed up the legion, disruptions in intimate relationships, employment and financial stressors, childhood maltreatment and sexual abuse history, previous suicide attempts, and heavy substance use "combine in an additive fashion" with personality traits and mental illnesses, placing addicts at greater risk of suicidal behavior.[22] According to the World Health Organization, alcohol and other substance-use disorders are found in 25 to 50 percent of all suicides around the world. Of all deaths from suicide, 22 percent can be attributed to the use of alcohol alone: this means that every fifth suicide would not have occurred if alcohol had not been consumed.[23] In another meta-analysis of alcohol use and suicidal ideation, the higher the amount of alcohol, the greater the risk that depression, impulsivity, and suicidal ideation would overtake future-focused thinking.[24]

The second evil of a soul-sickness is that it destroys the good in our relationships. All addictive behaviors loop the individual tighter into the management of the addiction. The brain becomes less able to perceive and respond to reality, including responding appropriately to the people who surround her. Over time, she can find herself ignoring her responsibilities to others as the cycle of intoxication, withdrawal, and craving narrow her world. We cannot mentalize or attune to others if we are preoccupied with ourselves, and so the addict loses empathy. In the divided mind, she can both use substances and simultaneously be aware that this use is hurting those she loves. This is where moral sin becomes involved, manifesting itself in everything from ignoring loved ones' needs, to being an irresponsible friend or employee, to the outward abuse of partners or children. It includes sins such as driving while intoxicated, abusing drugs in front of children, stealing from others, or being cruel or manipulative to co-workers or neighbors.

Loved ones often struggle with the feeling that the drug is more important to the addict than they are. And in some sense this is true, but the addict is not evaluating reality or prioritizing action in the way that a normal person would. As one man said, with the purposeful irony that often marks a recovery story: "They told me I was a bad example to my little sister, and that really got to me. Because I loved that girl. It didn't stop me from robbing her blind, of course. But I loved her unconditionally." This isn't something that would make your congregation laugh, but an AA or NA meeting finds a lesson in these ironic parables that reveal "sick thinking," an attribute that they consider a typical sign of the disease of alcoholism. The divided mind falls further into progressively poorer moral decisions. Addicts become estranged from their best selves, while their sins estrange them from others.

Along with these obvious sins, the evil of addiction further unravels an individual's ability to create or sustain mutual relationships. If we were created to need others and be needed in turn, then addiction draws our souls into the evil of a deep isolation. For many addicts, childhood attachment relationships were such that they did not learn these healthy relational skills in their youth. Addictions further cut off their chance to learn how to have the life-giving relationships as they grew up. Childhood maltreatment may have left them with stubborn images of themselves as worthless and the world as dangerous. For others, the capacity to give and receive love was diminished as the brain focused its efforts more and more on the addiction. Addicts begin to turn inward as they refer to the inner realities—the impulsivity of hypofrontality and the cravings of an unbalanced reward system—becoming cut off from real relationships with others.

In this turn inward, fear and resentment can begin to dominate an addict's inner world, making it difficult to act in mature and responsible ways toward others. I was recently with a group who were talking about the topic of resentments. One person took on every neighborhood association rule violation as if it were a personal vendetta, another relapsed from anger at a sibling, while another waited for a special family dinner to instigate a fight. Another talked about how resentment against a family member left him ruminating for years on fantasy confrontations that would never actually happen. Of course, many people exhibit immaturity in these ways, even without addiction. But these recovering addicts were aware of how their emotional state was wrapped up into their substance use. Stress rose, anger seethed, drinking increased. The lack of connection between the instinctual and executive functions of the brain led to more imagined slights, misperceived dangers, and impulsive fights. More drinking and drugs seemed to solve the problems that had been made worse by their drinking and drug use in the first place. In the neurobiological condition, the addict's emotional volatility expands. In the soul-sickness, generosity and forgiveness are unthinkable.

This tightening self-involvement often hides the third form of a soul-sickness, which is an intense self-loathing and shame. I was with another group of women who were talking about the defensiveness that surrounded their addiction, which kept them blocked from honest and nourishing contact with others. One said: "I never asked for help even when my life was a mess in drugs and alcohol. I was always afraid of what you thought of me. I had no other emotions except pride, hurt, or fear." Another described how she appeared to be self-giving, but life was really about competition: "I was either better than you or worse than you, but never just okay in my own skin. I lied constantly—so you couldn't know who I really was." Another described how she used alcohol to cover her social anxiety and make friends. But as her condition developed into addiction, the benefits reversed. She became paranoid and isolated, afraid even to say hello to her neighbors in passing, lest they could tell that she had been drinking. "So I had to hide from everyone," she said. "After all, I had always been drinking." These women were protecting their habit and also protecting themselves from relationships with others, too full of shame to be vulnerable and thus unable to be present to the people around them. While this turning inward is a sign of soul-sickness, it is a result and not a cause of the spiritual malady.[25] As these women gained time in sobriety, they were able to rediscover new ways of being vulnerable and trusting in their relationships.

As I have been suggesting in the last three chapters, the spiritual cause of addiction is our human fragility. It is our created interdependence and the evil that grows in the wounds of that primary relational need. Remember that chronic behavioral conditions arise from a thousand small attempts to manage a lack that often arises from our relationship with others. So they are not a prideful replacement of God with a substance, or a turning away from God toward pleasure, but ultimately a turning inward into a self-harming cycle of suffering. The effects of self-centeredness and self-negation may also be two sides of the same coin. One woman described it this way: "I was the center of the universe and yet the worst person at the bottom of the garbage pail. I hated myself, but *I* was all I thought about." Shame and guilt tend to make us self-involved, and it is the character of chronic conditions that they end up further eroding our self-worth. The addict's identity often becomes fixed on the totality of self-loathing, shame, and guilt, sometimes hidden in a veneer of defensive pride or strength. As one addict profoundly put it, "Shame was my master."

Untangling the Demoniac from God

Our particular vocation as pastoral caregivers leads us to the next symptom of soul-sickness: an understanding of God that has become fixed on punishment or abandonment. Many addicts whom I meet have rejected religious upbringings because they believe that God is a God of punishment and judgment. Religious belief draws from an individual's self-perception and from the teachings of his faith community, and so not every addict has one simple view of God. Some people have a very positive image of God and draw from it as they seek recovery. But judgmental or punitive images of God are a common enough spiritual issue in addiction to warrant our awareness and care. They can become wrapped into the drama of addiction as people imagine that the condition itself is fated by God or a part of how God is punishing them for their sins.

Pastoral caregivers might feel strongly that God is love: all-embracing, merciful, and forgiving. But it is not too difficult for someone to arrive at the idea of a punishing God, since the threat of punishment is the premise upon which our need for salvation is built. We are saved, it is commonly taught, because Jesus paid the price for our sins on the cross, taking on our punishment and thus "turning away God's hostility from us."[26] We are not just saved from bondage to sin, but from the requirement of God's punishment. So the connection between sin and punishment remains the condition behind our need for forgiveness. We have still assumed that sin, by logical necessity, must be punished. It must separate us from God. There appears to be no other possible initial response that God could make to our failings. This necessity remains fundamental, even if the solution is Christ's self-giving love on the cross. In order to avoid this punishment, one must return and repent. But this ability to choose a new life is exactly what is compromised in addiction. If an addict grows up believing that God must punish sins, then the suffering of addiction may provide both proof of his worthlessness and the holy punishment he thinks he deserves.

A soul-sickness is a condition often replete with shame and guilt. The more acutely one feels self-loathing, the more likely he might focus on the punishing aspect of God. Let me give you an example of a pastoral care conversation I had with someone after about a week of sobriety. The man told me that he had done some very bad things, things that made him "feel like a scumbag," and he did not believe that God could forgive him. He wanted me to explain something to him. He said that he had spent seven years of his childhood in Christian schools, and they had told him that God was going to send him to hell for his sins. Now, he said, there's "this new idea of God" as forgiving, and now everything's supposed to be alright. He said that he didn't get it. I asked him, "What would be different in your life if God had really forgiven you?"

"Well, it would change everything," he said. "But it's not like that."

He was going to hell, just as he had been taught. It is not useful to try to fix this quickly with simple assurances of grace. It is not like this man had missed Easter celebrations or had never heard about the forgiveness of sins through the blood of the cross. But in the end, this hope was overshadowed by the much-repeated theme of his Christian education: he was a sinner, and sin had to be punished. This message is hard to change because it now makes sense of how he feels about himself. The man cannot forgive himself, and the order of his universe does not make sense if his violence and wrongdoing can be simply brushed away. This is actually a moral stance, becuase this man is not laissez-faire about his past. It invites a longer conversation about his theological resources, the depth of his relationship with God, and his own feelings about his sin. It might take a long time of experiencing life as a sober person before he can begin to find different images of God or distinguish the signs of God's love and mercy in his life. A soul-sickness often weaves together self-worth, sin, and punishment into a theological corner that is hard to escape.

In another conversation, a man who had thirty days of sobriety told me that his higher power was Jesus, but he had a hard time returning to the faith because he felt so ashamed for what he had done. How could he be forgiven for the really bad things? Compared to the man in the above paragraph, his theology was at least a little less focused on punishment. But salvation still rested on his ability to repent and sin no more, and that meant giving up his behavior. He had relapsed enough times to doubt that he could return to Jesus *and* remain clean. Even friends have their limits, and the man was worried that he had long passed the limits of Jesus's patience and forgiveness. He needed some help talking through his shame and articulating what he already knew about Jesus's love and mercy. In both of these examples, I would advise pastoral caregivers to avoid the temptation to fix the guilt. Go into it and explore it. We can ask open-ended questions about recovering addicts' relationships with God to get to know what is behind these concerns rather than trying to change them with our theological counterpoints.[27] The issue is usually not simply how they feel about God or how they feel about themselves; it is about how those two sides interact in a relationship.

The treatment that an addict receives as a child can also get tangled into his image of God. One man tells a fairly common story of how his abusive parents left him feeling separated or abandoned by God. He did not deserve a connection to God and never sought it in his adulthood. He said, "I was worthless, a loser, and a bum, and I set out to prove it." His addiction was tied into the pain caused by the sins of his parents. In other cases, a church or institution has told people that they are worthless, unforgivable, and unloved by God. As one man said, "As a gay man, I grew up in a church with a God who hated me. So in recovery I had to create my own loving higher power—the kind of God who would have a picture of me on his refrigerator." Since AA and NA programs include the idea of a higher power, there is often talk about resisting organized religion because it is seen as more hurtful than helpful. As with the lesbian woman in the preceding chapter, some people speak about how they had to give up the Christian God of their youth in order to create their own higher power who was loving, forgiving, and a friend. Since I am a member of the clergy, the irony of this need regularly convicts me.

As we enter into pastoral care with those in recovery, we have to untangle this knot of self-hate and religious teaching with slow respect. We know that the word "God" is as multivalent as the word "addiction." A performative statement like "God will never forgive me" could mean "I can never forgive myself" or "I feel like a social reject." It could actually mean "I fear for my soul because I have sinned." Or it could just mean "You are a pastor, so I need to say this to appease you, even though I don't really feel that bad about what I've done." Again, I try not to get stuck on the immediate content of a statement ("God hates me"), but I try to find out first what that means for this person ("I hate myself," "I hate God," "I was victimized and God abandoned me," or "I did something that is unforgivable"). We can take some time to flesh out the picture from the person's point of view. I find that these conversations first make me anxious— I am afraid of saying the wrong thing. These can be difficult, freighted conversations because so much pain can be lodged in the question of God's love for us. But if I pause and ask some more questions, I get to relax a little and enjoy some holy curiosity about the child of God before me. Sometimes I do ask what she is hoping for from the conversation or what would be helpful for her to talk about regarding God. Usually, I want to keep her talking so that I can get a feel for the metaphors, the images, or the relationship with God that is resonant to her.

Meaning-Making through Moral Complexity

It would be outside of the scope of this work to tackle the many reasons why we decide God cannot forgive our sins, but I do want to briefly suggest that people who suffer don't always know how to make their faith meaningful to that suffering. Addiction compels behavior in a manner that feels both intensely inside but also curiously outside of the self. People often describe having a sense of not knowing what is happening to them. They describe it as a feeling of being trapped under water, in a daze, a kind of craziness, and even as a demon. In the meaninglessness of this compulsion, some kind of meaning must be made from the bits and pieces of theology that seem most significant to the individual. If these symbols are rigid, sparse, or formulaic, our options become limited, and the complexity of life and our efforts to survive it can exceed our theological resources. We have even less recourse if these images are wrathful or punitive.

Kenneth Pargament's work on spirituality and coping can help us with this idea. He says that we all possess an orienting system that we draw on to make sense of life events and to make meaning during crises.[28] Our orienting system includes our goals and values, our cultural and communal identities, our assumptions about how the world should work, and our religious and spiritual resources. Spirituality—or beliefs about what is sacred in one's life—can become an organizing value: it can help to integrate one's aspirations and goals into a coherent life-plan, providing daily direction and guidance.[29] People seek significance through their orienting system. They will interpret life events through the resources that they possess in as much consistency as possible with what already gives their lives meaning. When a crisis occurs, they will do their best to draw on this pool of resources to make sense of the difficult event and to fold it into their understanding of self, other, and the world.

So individuals translate their orienting system into methods of coping, including creating a story about what happened and why it happened, engaging meaningful practices to address it, and accessing outside support to better cope with it. Religious groups are a big part of our orienting system because they provide self-definition. We ask: Who am I in relation to this faith story? Where do I fit into my faith community's story? We take our self-understanding along with our resources for meaning and fold them into the experiences we have in our lives.

Those who cope positively look for some kind of benevolent meaning or possibility for growth in crises.[30] They seek spiritual support and connection with others, and they partner with God to address their difficulties. They also engage in practices such as prayer, confession, and rituals of healing or spiritual purification. Their relationship with God is consistent and safe enough so that God can remain a secure attachment figure in the midst of difficult emotions or morally complex experiences. Or their understanding of God is flexible enough to ultimately adjust when a crisis calls into question their most deeply held beliefs about God's work in the world. In contrast, when our symbolic resources are scarce or our image of God too inflexible, we have a harder time developing a theology that can make sense of our lived experience. For instance, problems with spirituality and coping include "small gods," whose character is weak, one-dimensional, or underdeveloped.[31] These are images of the divine that appear limited, judgmental, distanced, or punishing. We are unable to seek benevolent spiritual meaning in our crises, turn to these gods in times of need, or harness prayer and religious practices to help support us in our crises. Our faith formation is too narrow to hold what is difficult, painful, or confusing in human experiencing.

So perhaps the first part of the problem is that our theological resources are not always sufficient to the challenge of this suffering life. Pastoral caregivers who serve in preaching and teaching roles can offer more diverse images and metaphors of the Christian life to help deepen this meaning-making work. For instance, there are many ways to reflect on Christ's work on the cross, and a multitude of perspectives can expand our relationship with Jesus beyond a sole focus on salvation from punishment.[32] While this theory of atonement may be very meaningful to our tradition, if people leave our church believing that God's core instinct is to *not* forgive us, then something is going wrong with how we communicate the cross to our people. We need to educate on richer theologies of God's love and grace and to help people to identify the signs of God's presence in their lives. Part of our preaching and teaching work is to help individuals build an orienting system that can offer more complex and flexible responses to the dilemmas of life.

The second part of the problem might be how to harness this spiritual worldview for new meaning in times of crisis. In a post-Christian culture, we no longer have the luxury to imagine that this ability to connect faith with life is already present. People do not intuitively know how to take what they learn on Sunday and apply it to their daily lives, let alone their most vulnerable or confusing experiences. They need to practice the work of theological reflection—connecting lived experience to the scriptural and theological resources of our faith—in order to have some sense of how to make meaning in complex or morally ambiguous human situations.[33] If we are not taught how to reflect on our lives theologically, or we have never been affirmed in what was already spiritually significant in our point of view, it will be harder for us to embrace these resources for new meaning when we need them.

We can also help people draw from their own set of symbols and metaphors for their faith. Pastoral theologian Kathleen Greider has a lovely example of this kind of theological reflection in pastoral counseling as she responds to a case study of a pornography addict.[34] She suggests a three-part model for reflection within the counseling moment. The first step involves developing an understanding of the individual's addiction and relationship with God from his point of view. Second, we "amplify meaning and crystalize values" that we hear in the conversation, as we seek to see the addiction from his spiritual perspective. Third, we discern a response or action together. This sounds simple enough, but in her interpretation of the case, she is able to pause and see themes of theological significance from the person's own words that one could easily miss. She is able to use her own theological imagination to look for important disclosures regarding the man's spiritual understanding. His description of his addiction includes "underground despair," "ugly hurt," "evil force," and how "time seems to stop" when he engages in the behavior. He also expresses some feelings about religion, including an expression Greider particularly enjoys: "Face it, biblical faith is a paradox." He also says that healing would be freedom, but then adds "at least in part."

These themes are his spiritual language of addiction because they all point to ultimate concerns: they ask questions about existence, meaning, faith, and transcendence within his experience of addiction. Greider finds some theological points to explore, including the need for transcendence (time seems to stop), questions around biblical faith, the struggle with evil, and a loss of hope. As she seeks to crystalize values, she can explore what might give him hope in his efforts at recovery. Greider also considers her own perspective, wondering if defining the evil of pornography as systemic—an industry that preys on vulnerable people both in its creation and its marketing—might be a useful reframing of the problem. The man expresses anger about his entrapment, and she wonders if this can be related to how systemic rather than personal evil is at work in his addiction. Furthermore, the man wants freedom from his addiction "at least in part," hinting that there may be other counseling goals to explore.

In this way, Greider's own theological interests and insight play a part in this co-created conversation, but it is first a process of surfacing the spirituality already present in the person's point of view. We engage in a holy curiosity that delights in getting to know the people before us as children of God. We try to get to know what their words about God mean from their experience. As we get to know the spiritual landscape and concerns of individuals, we can imagine what theological and practical resources seem to resonate between us. We offer our own ideas respectfully in the mutual give-and-take of a conversation with another child of God. We co-create interpretation and meaning together, as we plan for spiritual renewal. At the most basic level, we can communicate Christian love by being an attuned listener, not shocked by these stories of moral failure, and consistent in our assurance of God's loving presence.

Incarnational Grace

Addiction is a condition of spiritual bondage, a state of the soul in distress. This doesn't mean that people are freed from the responsibility to address their soul-sickness or that they do not commit moral sin in the context of that spiritual oppression. It is clear that human beings engage in actions for which they are morally culpable. But I would like to mitigate the sense that the chasm between God and our brokenness is infinitely great. I would like to trouble the idea that the sicknesses that grow from the wound of our finitude separate us from God, or that moral sin leads inevitably to God's rejection and punishment.

This pattern of cause and effect assumes a kind of weakness in God, who must by necessity respond to human finitude with rejection lest it compromise God's holiness. We know that this is not the case because God walked among us in Jesus. In the incarnation, Jesus is the Word made flesh drawing close to us, which means that God is not prevented from a relationship with us even when we are in our sins, even before there is any act of sacrifice. It is God's first act of grace to break into human history as fully God and fully human. Through it, the Holy touched sick and sinful flesh. It is this reaching and touching, this active love in the incarnation, that points to an indissoluble closeness between humanity and God. If the work of redemption begins in the incarnation, and if the healing work of Jesus in the Gospels manifests the revelation of Jesus as the son of God, then God is not separated from us by the power of our sin or sickness. God comes to us in the flesh to heal, restore, forgive, and cleanse. Thus God's compassionate closeness has a more logical connection to our disease, shame, and guilt than do discourses that focus on distance, rejection, or punishment.

For our pastoral care, this means that human beings are sacred even in their deepest sicknesses. They do not become sacred when they get sober, or realize their human potential, or confess their sins. They are sacred because their suffering is sacred. It is not sacred in expiation offered, in penance paid, or in any kind of exchange between sacrifice and grace. It is not sacred as a kind of romantic ideal about the specialness of the poor and the outcast. Suffering at its base level is horrendous and should motivate justice. But suffering is sacred theologically because it is what touches the heart of God. Human fragility touches God so deeply that only God's presence standing in the midst of it is sufficient response to satiate God's great compassion for us. God moves toward us, not away from us, because of our suffering. So when we witness another person's pain and her attempts at survival, we are seeing what moved the Godhead to walk among us in Jesus. If we understand this, we will realize that we are allowed into the presence of the holy whenever a human being lets us into her most guilt-filled and out-of-control places. We are seeing what breaks the heart of God.

The Gerasene teaches us about God's compassion in addiction because Jesus meets the demon-possessed man before he can change himself. There is no need for him to come to consciousness about his spiritual sickness or to repent of his sins before he can draw near to Jesus. There are no plans to punish him, and Mark is careful to tell us that punishment and control have not worked for this man in the past. Instead, Jesus meets him as he is. He cares for the Gerasene in his abject state. Jesus meets him on the shore before he changes, because the Gerasene cannot change his possession alone. It is only through the experience of a healing connection with Jesus that the man comes to his right mind and comes to believe.

This is what the disciples surely witnessed. On the way to the land of the Gerasenes, as the storm threatened to sink the boat, the disciples gathered around Jesus in fear. They asked if he cared that they were perishing. When the Gerasene falls at Jesus's feet on the shore, they find the answer to that question. Jesus cares deeply that we are perishing. Not just our souls in some future life, but right now—here in the tombs, within the bounds of our aberrant and impossible possessions. As Jesus's disciples, they feel for the plight of the man as he protects what is trying to kill him. They see his desperation and his need. They feel the estrangement of a divided mind cracked by a pitiless environment. But perhaps most profoundly, they see Jesus there in the middle of that complexity. They see the one at the center of all the concentric circles of their lives, who is meeting suffering with mercy and grace. This is the healing that we still seek. It is surrounded by our immediacy, in the midst of chaos, at the center of our need. Since we are his disciples, the conditions of suffering that drew Jesus close are now ours to touch. "Don't you care that we are perishing?" is the question now addressed to us.

Chapter Six

Motivational Interviewing and Change

> Our admissions of personal powerlessness finally turn out to be the firm bedrock upon which happy and purposeful lives may be built.
>
> —Anonymous, *12 Steps and 12 Traditions*

> Lord, make me pure—but not yet.
>
> —St. Augustine, *Confessions*

As I begin this chapter on Motivational Interviewing, New Year's Eve approaches with all of its promise of new beginnings and lifestyle resolutions. Sometimes I have made resolutions half-heartedly, just to have something to discuss at a New Year's Eve party. At other times I have given serious thought to lifestyle changes. I have contemplated the physical and spiritual benefits of healthy eating and exercise, usually when lying semicomatose on the couch recovering from too many Christmas cookies. Sometimes I have even made a choice to change my ways and have contacted a fitness studio or signed up for the latest trendy workout. I have sustained that change for several months. Well, maybe weeks. But then life gets busy, the old rewards of chocolate and couch-sitting grow in appeal, and I celebrate my week of success by engaging in high-caloric self-sabotage.

If you asked me, I would not say that my sense of identity is related to chocolate and couches. I prefer to talk out loud about the part of me that likes vegetables and sees herself as an active person. (I just dug into a large holiday tin of caramel popcorn while writing that sentence.) If you asked me about my poor holiday eating habits, I would probably blame anxious family dynamics, or the stress of being a pastor, or the stress of being a teacher. I would blame pretty much anything before taking a good look at what psychoanalysts might call this "split off" part of myself and the emotions contained in her bad habits. If I could be honest about it, a part of my own legion gets to stay alive through this progression of eating into the holiday season. Indeed, it lives as a partial secret even from myself as I think about broccoli while eating chocolate. This temptation does not make me a chocolate addict. But we can gain some compassion when we consider that changing our way of life, even at its most basic, nonaddictive level, is surprisingly difficult.

The way the legion infiltrates into a person's voice and identity is significant for pastoral care because it helps us understand the resistance to change that so often accompanies chronic behavioral conditions. Addicts resist healing partly because they have developed a relationship concerning their use of substances. It is a conditioned behavior, knit into their daily rituals and triggered by a host of inner and outer cues. They do not know who they would be without the substance and its ritual, and their stress system is telling them that they need this habit to survive. Addicts have also developed an identity or a story about themselves associated with their use. They have created a rationale for why they are cycling through withdrawal, craving, and intoxication. They are strong and in control of their use, or they are deviant and worthless. They are wedged right between their divided minds, speaking of recovery from one side while fully intending to use again with the other. It is in the midst of this threatened loss, surrounded by these distancings, deflections, and denials, that the pastoral caregiver applies particular listening skills and strategies toward change.

Foundations of a Motivational Interviewing (MI) Conversation

Unconditional positive regard
Active Listening
Guiding
Avoiding the righting reflex

Motivational Interviewing (MI) was developed from counseling work with addicts to address the ambivalence so often manifested in the change process. In the next chapter, I will apply these skills to the Stages of Change, which is a model that can help us organize the goals of our care with respect to the addict's readiness for change. We are reviewing MI skills first because how we enter into the goals of change depends on our counseling commitments and the way we engage our listening skills. Below are the basic principles of MI that will continue into the next chapter.

Basic Principles of Motivational Interviewing

1. Express empathy for the individual's point of view.
2. Avoid arguments about whether or not they have a substance abuse problem or what they should do about it.
3. Roll with resistance. Resistance is a sign that what you are doing isn't working, so you might as well stop and try something else.
4. Avoid coercive or pressuring tactics.
5. Start where the person is, not where you want her to be.
6. Be positive and reassuring. The addict has a condition that can be treated.
7. Express interest, concern, and curiosity. Build trust and be on the individual's side.
8. Use "OARS": open-ended questions, affirmations, reflections, summaries.[1]

Let me start with the foundational attitude behind Motivational Interviewing. MI is based on a commitment to unconditional positive regard, including warmth, empathy, genuineness, and respect. This is drawn from the work of Carl Rogers and his client-centered perspective. It includes the belief that the person is the expert on her own life and can come to insight about what to do with her own problems. The listener attempts an empathic understanding of the speaker's internal frame of reference and endeavors to communicate this understanding back to the speaker.[2] In other words, we practice those old gifts of attunement and mentalizing. It is important that we be genuine in this process. Being genuine does not mean that we inflict our emotional states on people or tell them what we think they should do about their problems. Instead, we need to genuinely cultivate our own humanity so that we do not feel fake or withholding to the person. We also need to cultivate our compassion and love for the other, so that our warmth and respect feels real to her.

As pastoral caregivers, we might frame unconditional positive regard as a healthy respect for the sovereignty of God. We first need to know that God is in charge of this person and that we are always privileged to be in the presence of another child of God. My role as pastoral caregiver must not be to play God, whether I feel like saving, healing, correcting, or even punishing the person before me. That would be taking power that doesn't belong to me, placing myself above the other instead of alongside the other. It must be clear to me that the other person and I are both under the mantle of God's love and mercy. This person does not belong to me and I have no real power over the shape of her future. I can accompany and encourage the other, and together our mutual conversation co-creates perspectives and possibilities that neither she nor I could create on our own. I can give feedback and education, and offer a new perspective on a problem, but I cannot control the other. I also must remember that no diagnosis, no label, no stigma, and no sin can separate this person from the love of God. There is no shade or gradation to that love, and so this person before me is extraordinarily beloved.

This posture should help us avoid what MI calls the *righting reflex*. The righting reflex is the desire to fix, change, argue, or exhort clients into the behaviors that we think are right for them.[3] In the dark ages of the 1980s, it was popular to try to harangue someone into the realization that they needed change. Over the years, studies have found that this confrontational style does not tend to support long-term change.[4] Trying to argue someone into recovery can end in a power struggle. Rather than your helping the person to think through his addiction and its effects, the focus shifts to you and your need for the person to do something to please you. I know that I am ready to flex my righting reflex when I stop listening closely and instead start thinking up solutions for—or arguments against—what I am hearing. It is a sign that I need to correct my own spiritual discipline and return the person back to God.

The Balancing Act of Change

While the posture of unconditional regard draws from Rogers's client-centered approach, the strategies of MI are different from that approach because they assume that there is a specific direction or goal for behavioral change that the listener is working toward.[5] MI is not a purely "following" style. In other words, we are not simply going wherever the addict takes us, or we would end up winding further down into the distancing, deflection, and denial of the self-protective legion. Instead, MI calls for a guiding style of care.[6] We understand that the individual's behaviors are important to him, but we have optimism that he can change over time. We seek to evoke that commitment to change from his perspective. We encourage him to enter into an evaluation about his life because only he can make a sustained decision to change.

There are two major change dynamics that we can shepherd throughout this guiding process. One is called the *decisional balance,* where one vacillates for or against a decision to change the behavior. As we pile up reasons to change, the balance shifts toward making a decision for change. If we begin to have doubts the next day and start piling up reasons to use substances, the balance starts to shift toward avoiding change. For instance, every time I think, "Surely this chocolate is good for me. It's full of antioxidants!"—that is the swing of the decisional balance against changing and toward sustaining my behaviors.The second dynamic is the struggle of *self-efficacy versus temptation*. If you, like me, have started one of those New Year's Eve-inspired exercise programs and suddenly felt too stressed, tired, or angry to follow through, you know how quickly our self-efficacy can fade into a temptation to take back the couch. Quitting can almost seem like a reward for our tired and stressed-out selves.

The balancing act between changing/sustaining and self-efficacy/temptation can shift over time or even in the course of a single conversation. These dynamics can even appear when a person is maintaining a strong recovery. Our role is to help build up the changing and self-efficacy sides while also honoring the realities of the sustaining and temptation sides. It's good for us as pastoral caregivers to keep an eye on signs that attention is shifting back to sustaining the behavior, or if someone is tired and feels like giving up the work of recovery. We can invite a conversation about these challenges, and it can be a relief for those in early recovery to express doubts, frustrations, and temptations with a pastoral presence who is not shocked by their ambivalence. If an individual is able to admit that he is swinging into the sustaining/temptation side, we can problem-solve what he might need (often self-care and stress relief) to help him recommit to change.

Motivational Interviewing Listening Skills
Open-ended questions
Affirmations
Reflections
Summaries

MI refers to the counselor's basic listening toolbox by the acronym OARS: open-ended questions, affirmations, reflections, and summaries. Instead of appearing to be experts or adversaries on the outside, we want to come close to the other person for a rather gentle game of catch. We want the conversation to flow between us in a respectful back-and-forth style that focuses on our holy curiosity about the person as a fellow child of God. Most of this back-and-forth is the addict talking and we as pastoral caregivers reflecting back what we hear. We can then supplement that back-and-forth movement with open-ended questions to help keep the exploration moving, noticing points of dissonance and affirming glimpses of change. Affirmations of the person's strengths and efforts to change are also a way to throw the ball back in this game of catch. The affirmations keep the conversation hopeful and encourage the other's self-efficacy. We use reflections and summaries to get further attuned to the other, to faithfully try to imagine the addict's life experience, and to gently guide the conversation. Through these active listening skills, caregivers catch the ball of what we hear them saying and then throw it back by reflecting and summarizing their conversation.

First, we ask *open-ended questions* and try to avoid too many closed questions. Closed questions are ones that can be answered by one or two words or a yes-or-no response, for instance, "How much are you drinking every night?" "Does your spouse know?" "Have you tried to stop?" We might find that we ask a few closed questions just to get oriented, but it is better to ask open-ended questions because we will learn more about the person and often learn something that we would not have thought to ask about. Of course, closed statements meant to evoke guilt are also unhelpful. Telling someone that they are breaking their mother's heart or that they are throwing their lives away is not useful. First of all, these statements are hardly a revelation to the addict. Second, shame does not lead to sustained change and may actually feed more self-destructive use. Asking closed questions is certainly better than making closed statements, but they can start to sound like an interrogation from the outside, as though the caregiver were throwing the ball hard at someone's head rather than entering into a mutual relationship.

Open-ended questions are broad enough to allow for the individual to respond in more than one direction. They show a caregiver's interest in what they think and feel. Simple statements and questions like "Tell me more," or "What happened then?" or "Tell me about the day after," or "What does your family think?" or "What about that bothered you?" show interest in the conversation and keep it open for a free flow of information. If we listen closely, these seemingly vague questions will elicit more about their goals, about a relationship with a loved one, about their problems, about a usual day with the kids, about their families, and also their histories of substance use and abuse. My favorite conversation was with a particularly extroverted processor, where the only thing I did was pause for a good thirty seconds before reflecting back to her what she had said, and then asking, "Is there anything else?" I think I said, "Is there anything else" about five times between her answers (maybe also "Wow!" and "That's hard!" twice). By the end of our game of catch, she had worked out her problem on her own. Perhaps she is a rare case. But it certainly reminded me that I can be of much more use if I take time to get to know the other, rather than getting caught up in my own need to solve their problems.

Second, we are *affirming* throughout the process. We are affirming in the sense that we honor the person's perspective and don't try to convince, preach, or shame him into a different one. We also can be verbally affirming as we seek to build the person's sense of hope and self-efficacy. We can thank him for meeting with us, reflect back the strengths that we see in him, note how well he manages his difficulties, and show our appreciation for him as a human being. We have to be a bit careful about this, because we can seem condescending or minimizing from our places of authority if we overdo affirmations. Don't eagerly give someone "atta-boy" kind of statements. That's annoying. But, after listening well to the perspective of the other, we do have an opportunity to notice his strengths with respect. In these ways, we try to break the sense that addicts are worthless or are failures.

Third, *reflections* are a central listening tool used to throw the ball back and also to gently direct the conversation. At its simplest, we can repeat key words, ideas, or feelings so that the speaker hears what she is communicating more clearly. A more complex way to do reflections is to guess at the thought, feeling, or intention *behind* what someone is saying. We then make our guess in the form of a statement, not a question. So reflections can also help to identify thoughts or emotions that aren't obvious but are embedded in a person's conversation. In chapter 3, this was the skill I used to help Kim observe her emotional storm. Reflections are not passive. The listener still chooses to repeat the part of the conversation that captures important thoughts and feelings about the speaker's current situation. As the speaker confirms, corrects, or builds upon the listener's reflection, certain storylines are emphasized and developed while other plotlines are left fallow or visited later. For MI, reflections try to capture the speaker's implicit goals and values, her evaluation of her current situation, and her thoughts about change.

Reflections can also be a way to evoke values or goals that might be motivators to change. A long conversation about someone's troubles at work can lead to the reflection "your job is very important to you," or "it's really important to you to provide for your family." This is a value embedded within the concrete details of his troubles, and it could be a jumping-off point from complaining to reflecting upon what is important in his life. I just saw a lovely example of this in a training recently. It was a role-play of a nineteen-year-old pot-smoker who had gotten caught at college and suspended. After a few sentences, the therapist understood that "life sucked," "now I'm going to get kicked out of school" and "I need to get a job or something because I can't stand living at home." He affirmed that his client had a lot of impressive goals: he wants to finish school, get a job, find a new place to live—all of which will improve his life. That is an affirming way to reframe the conversation, and it is also true.

There are more complicated reflections that are particularly helpful in working with the ambivalence that we find in changing chronic behaviors. My favorite is the "double-sided" reflection, which presents a discrepancy back to a person in a nonjudgmental way. For instance, someone says that drinking relaxes her at the end of the day, but then later describes how she mostly drinks alone. We can say, "So drinking helps you relax *and* also has isolated you a little from the outside world." If there is tension in the family, we might say, "You deserve to relax in the evening, *and* the drinking is also making your kids angry." Reflections are also a useful way to get out of a sticky argument, not because we are afraid of conflict, but because arguments usually shut the work of self-reflection down. If someone says, defensively, "My drinking is just fine!" then a reflection back could be, "You're happy with your drinking" or "It's annoying you that people keep saying that you have a problem." These reflections respect the person's perspective but also help her to hear what she is saying. At the very least, you are joining with her in her concerns rather than getting into an argument with her.

The strategic point of reflections is that you will *get more* of what you *reflect back*. Notice that there is little need for the pastoral caregiver to assert her opinion. What we choose to reflect back is what makes a difference to the conversation, because we emphasize some points while minimizing others. So what we reflect back helps to guide the themes that will continue as the conversation develops. For instance, if someone is complaining about his family being hard on him, he may be using the distancing technique that we discussed in the preceding chapter: drugs are not my problem, my family is my problem. We might want to argue with him by saying, "But you are hurting your family!" Or we might jump down the rabbit hole of the complaint: "Let's find a solution to this marriage problem!" But a change-based reflection might say, "You really wish that things were different with your family." We might then ask an open-ended question to get more information on his relationship to his family or what they think about his use.

Finally, *summaries* are basically longer reflections that help us place signposts on the conversation as we continue, so we know where we have been and where we are going. Summaries help caregivers collect the gist of the conversation over a time period and offer it back to a person in a complete picture. They can pull together disparate pieces of information and help someone see the whole. If we are getting lost in the many threads of the conversation, summaries can give us a snapshot of the ground that we are covering. People begin to feel more secure when they see that we as pastoral caregivers are monitoring the conversation and helping to build a coherent picture, especially when they feel scattered, scared, or chaotic inside.

Summaries are a useful tool in all good pastoral care.The particular trick with a change-oriented summary is to begin with problems but end with values, goals, strengths, and affirmations. It is better that the whole summary emphasizes signs of change. We help reframe problem-saturated narratives into questions about the addicts' hopes and desires for their lives, affirming their struggles but also the capacity that they have for imagining a different life in the future. Finally, summaries provide an opportunity for us to ask questions like "Does that sound about right?" "What else?" or "Am I missing anything?" Through these basic listening skills, we help people explore their thoughts and feelings about their behaviors, think about consequences, and begin to attribute their problems to the addiction.

Navigating a Motivational Interviewing Conversation
Engage Change Language
Avoid Argument
Roll with Resistance
Support Self-Efficacy

There are certainly people who come to us with clarity about their addiction and move quickly into recovery. There are many others who feel desperate for change because the emotional or practical consequences have become too great. Yet, even some who have been desperate for change do not anticipate the challenges of withdrawal or the pain that comes with replacing these well-worn grooves in their behavioral habits. Recovery is indeed a kind of grieving process. The addict is identified with his legion and loses part of himself at its dissolution. MI encourages us to expect this ambivalence, as we seek to strengthen the decisional balance and self-efficacy associated with change. We should not be anxious about the presence of doubt, hesitation, or resistance. We can ask about the pros and cons of use, exploring what is lost as well as what is gained and asking open-ended questions about their ambivalence. People who are on the fence about a behavior will hold both positions in their heads at the same time, a situation that can further incapacitate any decision to make a change.

As we join with the addict regarding her perception of her problem, we can begin to *engage change language*. We can notice and reflect back any change language that we hear. MI uses another handy acronym to spot this language called DARN: desire, ability, reasons, or needs that point to change.[7] As pastoral listeners, we have influence over how much change language builds up in a conversation, because we will get more of what we focus on. When it doesn't seem obvious, we can often discover it within complaints or concerns about stopping use. For instance, if someone says, "I feel bad about my kids, but I just can't seem to stop," we have a choice as to how we will respond. We might reflect back, "You just can't stop," which won't take us much further out of being stuck. Another option is to reflect back a value, such as "You really care about your kids." Our next open-ended question could seek to build up the change side of the decisional balance.[8] What does she hope for herself as a mother, or what would be different in a year if she made the change? Or we could ask whether there was a time when her relationship with her kids seemed more hopeful. If we know that she has stopped or lessened use in the past, we could ask her what helped her then, or how she managed to make that change. Or we might ask about what she would need to feel hopeful about change.

On the other hand, if we ask more about why she can't stop, we will probably get more of what is called "sustain language." Sustain language is the status quo: it is the story that she has been telling herself about her suffering. If we focus on why change has never worked for her, or we follow her down a path of complaints about her life and why she can't change, we are moving the decisional balance in the wrong direction. This doesn't mean that we discount her suffering. We listen, empathize, and give the time needed for her to feel heard. But we are also not simply following wherever the speaker leads. First, we are listening for information to summarize or reframe later. In most self-defeating statements, we hear how people see themselves (or what they have been told about themselves) but we can also find a longing for the opposite to be true. Second, we are trying to find out what matters to her so that we can help her come to a considered decision to change. We are guiding someone through a conversation with our eye toward self-awareness, self-efficacy, and change.

During this process, we can sometimes hit places of resistance, where someone begins to tip back over toward the sustain and temptation sides of the balance. Resistance is usually caused by the listener pushing too hard, not taking ambivalence seriously enough, or not empathizing well enough with the individual's perception of his problem. We've moved too fast, and staying near his legion begins to look very good to the addict. When someone resists by making excuses about his use, we might be tempted to argue with him or to list all the ways that his life would get better if he would make this change. Instead, MI teaches us to *avoid argument.* People who are on the fence about change respond to arguments naturally with counterarguments. By arguing against them, we might actually strengthen their ambivalence or the sustain language that is building in their heads. Furthermore, as we fall into a power struggle with the person, we might also alienate him.

We can often *roll with resistance* by simply changing the subject. Or we could come alongside someone's perspective, thus neutralizing the potential argument. For instance, if someone says, "I don't like that woman at the AA meeting, so I'm not going anymore," we could agree that people can get on our nerves and then ask, "What do you think would help you best in your commitment to recovery?" Or someone says, "I'm going to stop drinking, except for beer." We can ask him what has happened in the past, or help him make a list about the pros and cons of this choice. Or in another case, someone says, "I want to be clean, but I can't tell my boyfriend not to use in front of me." We could reflect back the importance of the relationship and begin to explore the boyfriend's influence on her life. Finally, when people insist that they have control over their behaviors, I've often rolled through a moment of resistance by affirming that only they know if they need to stop.

Supporting self-efficacy is central to recovery because people don't make change without feeling capable or hopeful about its possibility. People easily internalize their problems until they feel that they are fated to always have those problems. They may not realize their strengths, talents, or commitments toward other values in their lives unless we reflect them back and summarize them. We also help them explore what strategies best fit their personality and context, so that they can better succeed in their goals for recovery. *Affirming* any small step forward is also important, including the step of seeking you out for help or advice. We also empower them by respecting their right to choose. In the give-and-take of a supportive conversation, it is important that we place the decision to recover continually and actively back into the hands of those who have to make the real decision to change. I respect that a soul-sickness resists its own dissolution, and I know that this will happen on their schedule and not on mine. None of this needs to diminish my care and admiration for their strength and resilience.

Intrinsic Motivation and Cultural Values

Part of managing our righting reflex throughout the process of change requires developing respect for different cultures, contexts, and worldviews. As pastoral caregivers, we have to be careful about attributing our own values to a person or interpreting another through our value system. This is especially true if we are working with those who are different from us in terms of class, culture, racial identity, or sexual/gender identity. Counselors have less emotional and cognitive empathy for distress stemming from unfamiliar cultural norms.[9] Since this style of addictions care is based on empathy and the exploration of another person's motivational life, it is important for us to be curious about how culture and context might come into play in the decision to change. We can then develop appropriate skills for conversation about the challenges of recovery that resonate with an indivdidual's particular cultural and social positioning, values, and practices.[10]

As pastoral caregivers, we possess a worldview that arises from our own social positioning. In order to be more aware of difference in others, we actually have to first get to know where we come from ourselves. We may forget that our identities are not innate but come from somewhere: they are contextual and socially constructed. So the first step of multicultural humility is to become aware of the privileges, challenges, values, or assumptions that we soak up by being identified with a particular social or cultural group. This ability to step back and observe what we are bringing to pastoral care relationships is crucial to our care. What influences our values, or how we organize life from our cultural positioning? What is most important to us? Are we direct or indirect in our communication style? How do we understand agency or prioritize goals? What are the privileges we hold that might be different from somebody else? What makes life easy for us? How do we understand sickness and health from our cultural point of view?

Being aware of where we come from helps us to understand the criteria by which we assess the other. With our schema-obsessed brain, it is foolish to think that we have not been affected by stereotypes or biases against those who do not look, act, or love as we do. It is human nature to interpret people, and we will do so callously if we are not aware of our own biases and assumptions. At the most basic level, simply being aware of the presence of competing worldviews can encourage us to pause before we interpret other people's lives for them. Before deciding that an addict is resisting change, we might consider that our advice concerning change might not resonate with her values, cultural priorities, or experiences of life. We can assume that our own beliefs and priorities might be different from the addict's, and we might try to imagine what value she is expressing even if it seems foreign to our own.

Multicultural humility in pastoral care also requires knowledge of another context's attitudes toward mental illness, substance use, healing, and help-seeking patterns and practices.[11] We might notice whether there are different ways to describe distress or different cultural idioms through which mental health or substance use are understood. There might be greater lenience or stigma attached to certain substances, or there might be different criteria for what constitutes problematic substance use. Concepts of mental health and cultural or spiritual practices necessary for healing also might look different to different groups of people.[12] It's always good for pastoral caregivers to keep learning from study, conversation, or even immersion in other cultures. But we are never experts on someone else, especially not someone from a different cultural, racial, or social group identity. Individuals acculturate and celebrate their identities differently, so it is up to us to broach the conversation about how their culture or social positioning might be important to how they understand their addiction and recovery. While we might experience anxiety about engaging differences in race, culture, gender, or sexual identity, seeking conversation from a posture of unconditional positive regard for the other can be a way to join with others in their life experiences, meanings, and values as they come to a decision to change.

In terms of multicultural communication, three potential areas of cultural difference may influence conversations on addictions: locus of control, individualism versus collectivism, and communication styles.[13] Locus of control refers to the perceived degree of control someone feels he has over life's circumstances. In some worldviews, there can be a sense of fatalism associated with suffering because it is expected: suffering appears to be the accepted reality of the individual's gender, class, or caste. Strong beliefs about God's will and control over life may also need exploring during these early stages. For instance, some Latino/a worldviews may hold to an external locus of control: they may believe that life is determined by external forces related to fate, spiritual energies such as curses or demonic forces, or God's will.[14] Christians from charismatic healing traditions may also struggle if they are not miraculously healed. Such beliefs could limit motivation for change, but they could also provide some spiritual themes for us to explore. We can ask what bad luck or God's will might mean to the individual, rather than assuming that he is simply avoiding responsibility for his actions by claiming that he is fated to be addicted.

Individualism and collectivism further involve issues of values, identity, and sense of agency. Western culture leans toward individualism, which considers personal liberty and pursuit of individual happiness more important than communal harmony or conformity. For Western pastoral counselors, this might mean assuming that a mature person is one who differentiates from family pressures, speaks openly to loved ones about feelings, asserts her needs apart from others, and seeks personal happiness over self-sacrifice. In collectivist cultures, the needs of the family, the influence of social hierarchies, and decision-making that prioritizes filial or societal norms may affect motivation to change. Depending on acculturation to Western values, Asian American addicts may express collectivist values and experiences at both the family and social level. The addiction might bring shame to the whole family, it may not be discussed openly, and the addict may find little support from family for taking the time and emotional work on long-term recovery.[15] African Americans also may value family needs over their own, or wish to avoid direct hurtful communication with certain family members.[16] Addicts from collectivist cultures may resist conversations about tasks such as setting boundaries with family members, asserting their opinion to an important family member, or prioritizing personal recovery over broader filial and social responsibilities. The addict is not necessarily avoiding change, but he may need help to solve problems concerning how to change within his context and values.

Finally, Peter Bell's book *Chemical Dependency and the African American* reminds us that a person's acculturation to the dominant culture can also make a difference in recovery.[17] He explains acculturation as the balance between the way one meets personal needs, such as relationships, spirituality, or recreation, and survival needs, such as employment, affirmation, or political affiliation. Those who acculturate fully meet both personal and survival needs mostly in the dominant Eurocentric culture. Bicultural African Americans move between cultures to get both needs met, and the emphasis depends on the individual and her life history. What Bell calls "culturally immersed African Americans" get both personal and survival needs met by African American culture, and they avoid white culture. Recovery needs for the individual may differ, depending on how the individual accesses these two kinds of cultures.

Bell suggests a particular relapse challenge for individuals who claim a bicultural identity: if the addict functions comfortably in both cultures and she recovers more in one cultural idiom than the other, she may not be prepared to face contextual triggers when she seeks her needs in the other idiom. This bicultural experience may be true for anyone who has to shift from a nondominant cultural identity into the dominant straight, white, Western mode of culture in order to access recovery. If an individual from a minority group leaves a typical American rehab and is now returning to family for the holiday or returning to an old neighborhood and friends, her resources may not translate to her home idiom. She may not have thought out a high-risk situation in light of cultural pressures or group norms. Empathic listening continues to be crucial for us to get to know the recovering person's world from her perspective, and thus to better address her needs.

FRAMES Brief Intervention

If you are a pastor, you may have the luxury to build a relationship and shepherd an individual struggling with addiction over a much longer period of time. If you are a hospital chaplain or you serve an outreach ministry where your contact with others is fluid, you may get only one or two pastoral conversations with a person. In such instances, how do we broach our concerns while still respecting the fact that people need to come to their own decision to change? One tool that can help us structure our conversation is called the FRAMES model of brief intervention. FRAMES stands for feedback, responsibility, affirmation, menu of options, empathy, and supporting self-efficacy.[18] These principles can be engaged for brief interventions, when we have limited time to explore addicts' substance use, express our concerns, and encourage their self-efficacy toward recovery.

FRAMES involves giving *feedback*—gently and without judgment—about our thoughts or concerns regarding the person's substance use. We could do this simply by summarizing what we've heard about his using and then expressing our concern. Or we might reflect back a pattern that we are noticing. He is drinking every night to deal with anxiety; he is smoking pot in the morning before work; he is taking more and more prescription narcotics for vague physical ailments and may be progressing toward iatrogenic addiction. We then elicit his thoughts about our observations. We keep the *responsibility* for change firmly with the addict. We do not try to convince a person to change, nor do we pressure him into a confession. We avoid getting into arguments because that puts us in the position of taking responsibility for the change. We verbally let him know that it is his decision and his perception that matters.

We can also provide *advice*, or further education, about addiction. We can simply suggest that an addict consider the effects of her substance use on the rest of her life. Going to a therapist or an AA meeting, or talking to someone in church who is in recovery, might also be a way for the individual to explore whether or not she has a problem. Education is also important, because people do not know what is happening to their brains and bodies. Their anxiety or stress might be related to the cycle of withdrawal and craving, and this knowledge could be valuable. If mental-health symptoms like anxiety and depression are worsened rather than improved by her use, she also needs to know that information. Remember that we do not want to hold the ball for long without throwing it back. Any input from our side must be respectful, loving, and succinct, so that we can return our focus back to her.

Affirmations also keep the conversation hopeful and focused on the individual's ability to change. If an addict feels shame and hopelessness, it is powerful for him to hear someone reflect back signs of strength and success. If he is wondering about change or wants to know more, a *menu* of options for recovery activities—rather than an ultimatum to get sober—keeps the choice with the addict. Depending on your area, there are 12-step groups, outpatient programs, counseling centers that specialize in addiction care, therapists, rehab programs, and Christian recovery options. They may also decide to try moderating use, and you can help them evaluate that option. Finally, throughout our conversation, we continue *empathic* MI listening skills and keep the conversation and affirmations moving toward *self-efficacy*. Remember that a soul-sickness takes away our hopes for the future. If we remain positive about individuals and their possibilities of change, if we point to their strengths rather than berate them for their weaknesses, then they will feel that recovery might be a hopeful option for them.

FRAMES Feedback and the "Elicit-Provide-Elicit" Model of Intervention

Realistic feedback offered by a knowledgeable and caring individual can be motivating and empowering.[19] But how do we attend to our pastoral power in this process? It is easy to get caught in the anxiety of a conversation and find ourselves preaching, teaching, or attempting to save the other. Sometimes we feel what counselors call a countertransference to people with addictions, where their communication patterns or issues trigger unconscious thoughts or patterns of behavior related to our own family histories.[20] This can lead to strong compulsions to rescue, save, judge, or reject addicts. Biding our time through the slow work of change can also be frustrating. Taking over the conversation or teaching them what we think they need in order to change might be ways for us to distance from our own reactivity. Or we might find that we have personal difficulties with people who need us too much or, if they are resistant, don't need us enough. Being the authority on someone's life might be a comfortable position for us, a role that we fall into when we are feeling anxious about our relationship with another person.

Carrie Doehring, in her book *The Practice of Pastoral Care,* also draws on Motivational Interviewing listening skills for the pastoral care encounter.[21] She reminds us that when caregivers get caught up in their own empathic distress for another, they are more likely to try to make things right by offering interpretations, giving advice, or proposing spiritual practices to perceived problems.[22] These are our particular pastoral versions of the "righting reflex," and they are attempts to fix, change, or control the other. Doehring is particularly concerned that pastoral caregivers learn to be aware of their own power in the pastoral relationship. When we take over and offer directive care, we have taken over too much power. In other words, our ideas, voices, and actions become the central agents in the relationship with the other. The conversation really turns to focus on our own perspectives and needs, and we stop respecting the agency of the individual.

I have mentioned several times in this book that education on the medical condition is helpful. I've also claimed that pastors need to educate for the task of meaning-making, and can draw from our rich heritage of spiritual tools for recovery. Doehring's concerns about pastoral power remind us to be cautious about how we offer these kinds of feedback. She suggests that caregivers can shift from a receptive role to a guiding role, but only once trust has been established through skillful listening.[23] Chances are that you and I want to offer feedback way too soon. After all, what caring person would not want to prevent a person from harming herself? I tend to interpret quickly and not always correctly. When I do that, I don't pay much attention to how my own social biases or cultural worldview are controlling that interpretation, and I don't notice how my own anxieties or needs are triggered in the conversation. I think that I just want to be helpful, but it is anxiety about the other's distress or my own "righting reflex" that compels my hasty response. I am focused on my uncomfortable emotional state and am not seeing the situation through the eyes of the other. These moments remind me that I must tolerate the other's self-harming now if I am to be of service in the long term.

So how do we contribute to the conversation while monitoring our power? Studies suggest that brief interventions like FRAMES can be highly effective, but they must be conducted with empathy and respect.[24] MI offers a standard for this work through the "elicit-provide-elicit" model.[25] After listening well to the individual's perspective on his problems, we might elicit permission to talk about the topic of substances. We let him know that we would like to broach the subject of his use—if he is willing. If he agrees, we briefly state our concern or offer a short summary of the conversation that presents the signs of a potential problem. Afterwards, we elicit his response. We ask the individual what he thinks about this concern or whether the input was helpful. This returns the ball back to the speaker, so that you remain in a mutual conversation. It also shows that you are willing to be corrected by the other, allowing for some relational repair if your feedback irked him or compromised the alliance between the two of you. The elicit-provide-elicit model thus allows us to offer brief nonjudgmental feedback while still respecting the addict's agency.

Some education about the progression of the disease and its symptoms can also be helpful. In the elicit-provide-elicit model, we ask for permission to share information. We might even first ask what they know about alcohol or drug use or what they would like to know about addiction. We then provide clear, concise information in a nonjudgmental way. We conclude by eliciting their opinion about that information. For instance, in our conversational game of catch, I might throw the ball and ask, "You said that you are depressed and stressed out, and I am wondering if it is related to your drinking. Do you know about how alcohol affects emotions?" The individual may simply tell me that he knows alcohol makes him feel better. I could send the ball back by affirming, "That's true, it does! Can I tell you a little more about that?" If he agrees, then I catch the ball and explain briefly about the cycle of addiction: feeling better when we drink, then feeling worse again in withdrawal, then drinking again to solve the withdrawal. It's about dependence: we need the alcohol to feel normal. I can end by eliciting his thoughts about this information. I throw the ball back by asking, "Does that make sense?" or "Does that fit your experience?" or even "Is that helpful?"

We can do this spiritually as well, if we keep in mind the common signs of a soul-sickness. After we have listened well (and checked in with our own righting reflex), we can use the elicit-provide-elicit model to offer feedback about how the spiritual life becomes more distressed with the progression of one's use. We can let them know that feelings of self-loathing, hopelessness, and isolation are a part of the spiritual oppression of the addiction. If they feel estranged from God or others, we can affirm that this is a common feeling for people who struggle with substance use. It is part of how the cycle of addiction tightens around us, until life feels unreal and we can't connect with others or with God. All of our energy becomes wrapped up in shame and survival. We can describe the divided mind of addiction—how it uses our will but also extends beyond it—then elicit the addict's thoughts about that experience. We can explain that these are all common spiritual struggles in addiction. It is liberating to realize that what seems like unique suffering is actually shared with others, connected to a clear problem, and therefore not the way that life—or the spiritual life—has to be.

To summarize these skills: we first listen well, trying to understand the situation from the person's perspective; we ask open-ended questions, reflect back strategically, and summarize the details of the conversation; we keep a "wondering" attitude and a posture of positive regard; when we want to add our input, we ask permission to share, offer it without judgment, and then ask what they think about it. Of course, if someone doesn't want our feedback, we can always save it for another day. Even if I am expressing concerns or offering education, I often repeat that it is not my decision or my life. Only they can know if they have a problem, and they are the only ones who can decide what to do about it. That's how I keep throwing the ball back into their court.

EXCURSUS: The Loved Ones of a Legion

As the legion protects itself through distancing, deflection, and denial, family and friends are rarely sure what to believe or how best to respond. They often feel guilty for setting firm limits, such as not allowing alcohol in the home, not giving money, not saving addicts from consequences, or even asking a loved one to move out if they continue using. Beverly Conyers, in *Everything Changes,* also explains that going to rehab rarely solves the problem immediately. Addicts are not going into surgery to have a tumor removed. They are detoxing, and the hope is that they begin to learn some basic tools for managing the self and the cravings of addiction, which they must then put into practice. Loved ones have to prepare themselves emotionally for what will be a long journey, not a short solution.

As pastoral caregivers, we can help a family member think about what limits she wishes to set and what her hopes and fears are about those limits. It might be good for loved ones to know that confrontations such as yelling, arguing, guilt-tripping, or monitoring the addict's behavior rarely work. These tactics usually fall into whatever pattern of communication the family member has already developed with the addict. If a night of intoxication always leads to a big fight, a cold shoulder, or attempts to make the other see the light, then it becomes a part of the cycle of the condition. So it is good to collaborate on some concrete strategies for how she will approach setting those limits. The best posture is to be matter of fact, loving, and yet firm when pressured or manipulated. A change in communication strategy, along with a change in the level of emotional reactivity, is helpful when we set new expectations for the addict.

Family members also need to reflect on their own actions, whether they tend to pursue, protect, enable, or feel victimized by the addict. Conyers warns loved ones that their own lives can become chaotic and unmanageable when they allow the addict's struggles to become their own.[26] They cannot make the addict get sober, but they have the power to choose their own actions and responses. Alanon programs suggest that friends and family detach with love, remaining supportive but not taking personal responsibility for solving the addiction or its consequences. This doesn't mean that people can't set boundaries, or even consequences, for actions. Detaching with love means that the loved one decides against letting the addict rule her emotional world. Instead, she starts setting her own priorities for a fulfilling life. She is supportive of the addict's efforts to seek recovery, but she places the responsibility for that recovery directly in the hands of the addict.

Of course, this is easier written than done. It is difficult for family and friends to set limits with addicts. It can feel like giving up on those we love; it might even feel like a threat to one's identity as a loving person. It is hard to do something different in our response, because our relational patterns are also a part of our self-identity. Who am I, after all, if I am not the overprotective father or the self-sacrificing mother or the caretaking sister? How does a good Christian or a good parent survive the guilt of not somehow enacting this change? And what about the harm that the addict does to family members and friends—seemingly taking it in stride?

Since this is also a situation of ambivalence for the loved one, pastoral care can use the same MI listening skills to be respectfully present to the concerns of loved ones, to respond with empathy, to explore options, and to avoid arguments or resistance to change. Conyers suggests that family members need permission to know their own limits as far as controlling or fixing their loved ones is concerned. They need to be able to talk out what they are willing and not willing to do to support the addict, including weighing the implications of giving an ultimatum, such as a choice between rehab or divorce/separation. They need a place for their own anger, resentment, and guilt. They will also need a pastoral caregiver's help to talk honestly about where they find God in this situation, especially if God does not answer their prayers for change.

Interventions are also a possibility, as long as they are well-planned, calm, and each person involved is committed to the process. Interventions are about showing someone the reality of his disease, its progress, and its effects on others through the eyes of people who are meaningful to the addict. The book *Intervention* by the Johnson Institute offers the following principles for organizing an intervention:[27]

1. Meaningful people in the addict's life are involved.
2. They all write down specific data about the events and behaviors that show the legitimacy of their concern.
3. They all tell the addict how they feel about what has been happening in their lives with the addict, without judgment.
4. The addict is offered very specific choices that have been contacted ahead of time, for example, this treatment center or that hospital.

I am frankly cautious about pastoral caregivers taking part in an intervention. While well-planned interventions can be helpful, up to 80 percent of families refuse to go through with a family confrontation.[28] Families are unsure of how best to care for the addict and whether or not it is safe to be honest or to set limits with their loved one. We must be careful in this process, especially if we do not know the family or the addict well. We often know only part of the story, usually from the person who attends our church or ministry. If this is the case, we can support our immediate parishioner in planning and prayer, and as caregivers we can make ourselves available to the addict for support before or after the intervention if he or she needs to talk through the experience.

Pastoral Care and the Self

We all develop an identity through our way of living, regardless of whether those habits are positive or negative. If our habitual thoughts and behaviors make up our sense of self in the world, then who are we without those behaviors? Who is Legion without his many voices? He is healed. Certainly, he is in his right mind; but he is also no longer himself. For the first time, he is facing the silence of being alone in his own head. There are losses to grieve. This is a lot harder for pastoral caregivers than we perhaps suppose. We enter into ministry because we believe that we are called to do good in

God's name. We see such self-harming conditions as behavioral problems to solve rather than ways of being that must first be understood. If we have never suffered addiction, it is harder to understand why someone would protect what is so obviously killing her. It is hard to understand how the irrational excuses, emotional derailments, or sudden cheerful walls of denial are actually expressions of a soul-sickness marked by loss and grief.

When we accompany an addict into considering change, we are challenged in our own spiritual lives. We have to walk by faith, and give the results of our conversations back into God's hands. Because chronic behavioral conditions are indeed chronic, they frustrate our sense of success. They are rarely gratifying to our egos. When people do not change, we may want to play the judge and condemn. Or we may distance ourselves, because our anxiety about their pain or our own fears of failure put a wall between our empathy and addicts' needs. Our own desire to enable or to save, to blame or to reject, may come to the surface.

When we are able to tend to these signs, we can invite Jesus into our own brokenness. We can take time to prayerfully examine our countertransference: what the other is evoking in our history, relational patterns, unconscious desires, or unfinished business. It is unwise either to deny this side of our own righting reflex or to condemn ourselves for it. Instead, we are responsible for bringing what is less than optimal in our reactions and responses back to God and to other wise counselors who can help us meet addicts where they are—in each individual situation—knowing that this is also where they are met by Jesus.

It is interesting to note that, in the Gospel of Mark, Jesus heals each demoniac differently. The first demon in the synagogue he removes with one command. He coaxes the Gerasene's legion out via a magician's duel. He heals the Syrophoenician woman's daughter at a distance through the wit of her mother (Mark 7:24–30). A young son's demon is particularly painful in his resistance to cure, and Jesus tells the disciples that that demon can only come out by use of prayer (Mark 9:14-29). In the end, the disciples are half-blind in the very healing work to which they are called, as they walk with Jesus through each intense need. We also do our best to heal, but we are not the real Physician. We do our best to provide moments of redemption, but we are not the One who redeems. And while we can act as guides through all that is overwhelming in this process, there is only one Good Shepherd who meets us on the shores of our own legions. The care of addicts challenges us to put into practice the belief that God is the one who is sovereign over every child's life.

Chapter Seven

Moving into Change

> The student of right action must come to embrace in an effective way the actions that he has come to believe are right. And this takes time and practice, which is to say that this takes habituation.
>
> —Kent Dunnington, *Addiction and Virtue: Beyond the Models of Disease and Choice*

> [S]uffering produces endurance, and endurance produces character, and character produces hope, and hope does not disappoint us, because God's love has been poured into our hearts through the Holy Spirit that has been given to us.
>
> —Romans 5:3–5

Some 12-step meetings belong to the old guys. They can be former motorcycle gang members with skulls tattooed on their necks or rich retired businessmen who still pop the collars on their polo shirts. But what they have in common is a twinkle in their eye and a "squire of the village" kind of benevolence. They are the guys who always sit in the same place at every meeting. The kind of guys who lean in and elbow you meaningfully before they tell you a story. And they are ready to impart their wisdom to any sweet young forty-six-year-old seminary professor who comes their way. My favorite old-guy story is:

"Did you hear the one about the frogs on the lily pad? You remember that one?"

"No," I lie.

"Okay. So—two frogs are on a lily pad in this stream and one decides to jump off into the water. Now, how many frogs are still on the lily pad?"

I shrug, "One?"

"Nah. Two. Just because one of them decides to jump doesn't mean he did anything about it."

Never was there a truer AA-old-guy story. I don't bother telling my friend that the joke could go even longer. Really, the frog has to stretch his legs for a while and contemplate jumping, nudge up to the edge of the lily pad, crawl back, change his mind and argue with the frog next to him, perhaps rail against whoever put the lily pad in the middle of the pond, slide forward one more time, dip the corner of his frog-flipper in the water, and then maybe jump. Change is a process, not an event. There are different stages that encompass the decisions and the actions involved in changing chronic, habitual behaviors, and each stage benefits from a different kind of care. We plan our care for that person depending on where she or he is on that lily pad of contemplation.

Change Theory (formally called the Transtheoretical Model of Intentional Change) is a framework for imagining the process of changing chronic behaviors. This model has five stages: precontemplation, contemplation, preparation, action, and maintenance.[1] Relapse may be a part of this process at any time, bringing the individual back to an earlier stage. Not every addict moves in an obvious succession through these stages. The stages are more like a broad map or a heuristic to help us better understand the process that can help pastoral caregivers respond more skillfully to the varied tasks of recovery. Just as in grief work, we meet with individuals at certain points in their relationship with addiction. Each stage has a different task of recovery, so the pastoral caregiver adjusts care according to the goals of that stage. There is never just one response to the addict. There is not an ideal timeline or even an assured result; but there are common reflective and action-oriented tasks related to where addicts find themselves in their own commitment to change.

Stages of Change Map[2]

1. The Precontemplation Stage
   The addict does not believe that she has a problem or is not motivated to change

   Task: Increase awareness of need for change. Increase concerns about the current pattern of the behavior. Develop discrepancies between addiction and the addict's desire or perception of her life.
   Goal: Become conscious of the behavior and consider the need for change.

2. The Contemplation Stage
   The addict considers that she might have a problem or want to limit use. She is beginning to seriously imagine changing the behavior within the next six months or so.

Task: Analyze the pros and cons of current behavior patterns and the costs and benefits for change. Explore her ambivalence when it comes to decision-making. Look for values and motivations from the individual's perspective that could lead to a substantive decision to change.
Goal: A considered evaluation that can "tip the decisional balance" toward a substantive decision to change.

3. The Preparation Stage
The addict would like to make changes to the problem. She is actively planning for cessation of behavior and addressing continued doubts and fears regarding the decision to change.

Task: Increase the commitment to change and create a plan. Includes manageable goals and problem-solving concerned with triggers. Continue to explore ambivalence, and increase self-efficacy and hope.
Goal: Create an action plan to be implemented in the next stage.

4. The Action Stage
The addict is ready to initiate plans to help manage difficulties of stopping/reducing use. She takes steps to change the current behavior and begin a new behavior pattern.

Task: Implement strategies for change, revising plan as needed, sustaining commitment in face of difficulty. Try out coping skills regarding new situations. Review strengths, encourage self-efficacy.
Goal: Take successful action for changing current pattern. About six months is minimal for this change to settle in.

5. The Maintenance Stage
The addict wants to sustain her gains. Consolidated into lifestyle, new behaviors have become a new set of habits.

Tasks: Sustain change over time across a wide range of situations. Integrate the behavior into the person's life. Avoid slips and relapses back to the old pattern of behavior.
Goals: Make a long-term, sustained change of the old pattern and establish a new pattern.

Encounters with Change

Imagine that a man comes to you for pastoral care after being laid off from his job. He admits to you that his supervisor discovered him asleep at his desk last week, after a liquid lunch with his office colleagues. He is considering suing his supervisor, because he believes that she targeted him because of his age. He is near retirement, and his much younger co-workers were not even reprimanded. The office has been hell ever since she got promoted. You ask if he is drinking too much. He becomes uncomfortable and seems frustrated with you. After all, it's the holidays. Everyone is going to office parties. He tells you stories about the antics among his colleagues. You remind him that not everyone falls asleep at work after the party. He becomes visibly annoyed and looks away. Then he tells you that he is going through a rough time right now. He talks at length about the stress of being unemployed and the problems in his family life. You listen well, ask a few questions, and make a suggestion or two about his family. But on the alcohol issue, you are not sure how to proceed. After all, his life does seem out of balance and stressful right now.

Consider another example: A woman comes to tell you that she has been taking prescription narcotic medications every day since she hurt her back a year ago. Her family has finally confronted her, and she is ready to begin a new life. She threw away her medications last week. You affirm her commitment and ask if she is in some kind of recovery. She says that she tried an NA meeting at her family's request, but she did not like it because it was a rough crowd of people using dangerous drugs like heroin and cocaine. She didn't fit in there. You suggest the local outpatient counseling center. She tells you it's a great idea. Maybe she will contact them. But she has to admit that she has never felt better and has no desire to use anymore. She almost lost everything. She has learned her lesson and will never touch pain medication again. That is what she really wanted to talk to you about. She is excited and is ready to begin a new life. She thinks God has blessed her with a chance at a new beginning. She wants to join your discipleship group and she wants suggestions for Bible study. You pray with her, and after that she comes to the discipleship group once or twice. Two months later, she relapses.

These two individuals are both struggling with addiction, but they are not at the same stage of change. The alcoholic is in the precontemplation stage: in other words, he is not willing to think about his behaviors. He is still resisting consciousness about his alcohol use, and he needs to come to his own realization that alcohol is his primary problem. He is avoiding his addiction in ways typical for this stage: distancing and deflection. He points to other conditions associated with the behavior (everyone drinks during the holidays) and blames another factor (his age) for the consequence (his job loss). He distances the conversation by moving it toward his general stress. He may be actively hiding the truth, or he may simply be in complete denial, caught in his mind's split between alcohol and his responsibilities to work and family.

The prescription addict is in the midst of the contemplation stage, which means that she is just coming to a decision to change. She admits that her prescription drug use is problematic. She must stop because her family wants her to stop. Unfortunately, she has made the common mistake of believing that if she's thinking about recovery, then she's already as good as recovered. Remember that all aspects of the Gerasene's life are defined by his demon possession. It has taken on a life of its own and fights for its own survival. Long-term change must move from the emotional intensity of the moment and into actual plans for recovery. She needs to move on from contemplation and into the work of the preparation stage by deepening her commitment and planning for this change. So, the addict's place in the process of making a decision affects how we plan our goals for the pastoral care moment and how we engage strategies toward change.

The Precontemplation Stage

Precontemplators remind me of a saying I used to hear in recovery groups: "Normal people adjust their behaviors to meet their goals in life, while alcoholics adjust their goals in life to meet their behaviors." That is an apt description of addicts in this stage. They feel that they have kept their use under control or managed whatever consequences have come their way. When they get in trouble, they identify family, relationships, job, church, or courts as the real problem. They have adjusted their lives to their behavior, and often they will say something like "I'm just having fun" or "I'm not harming anyone" or "I can do what I want on my free time." They suffer the estrangement and the sense of unreality that are characteristic of a soul-sickness. Other precontemplators have attempted to quit and have failed. They are merely trying to avoid the pain of withdrawal or the pain of conscious living. While they may earnestly talk about the problems of their behavior, it has become their only companion, and they cannot imagine any other way of surviving life.

Remember that the Gerasene was so wrapped into the voice of his possession that he did not see his tormented life as a problem, but instead saw Jesus's attempts at healing him as the problem that he needed to resist.

The task of the precontemplation stage is to explore their thoughts and feelings about the behavior, in order to arrive at some realization that substance use is a problem that might need changing. First, we explore why they have come to us. Like the alcoholic man in the example above, an addict often comes to us for help regarding problems that he thinks are disconnected from his substance abuse. He may have been referred by a family member, and so he considers that family member to be the problem. In some cases, he realizes that a major consequence, such as losing his driver's license or injuring himself, has occurred because of his substance use. But he thinks that he can control the consequences in the future, and he has no real intention of changing. Finally, an addict may have many of the legion of stressors we have been discussing throughout this book: childhood and adult losses, trauma, or social suffering, which require extended care. He might not realize that his substance use is making it even harder to address the other emotional and practical difficulties in his life.

Motivational Interviewing suggests that we take some time listening before we focus on any particular topic or goal.[3] The pastoral caregiver enters into a conversation where she shows curiosity and interest in the person's life: what is important to him and what he thinks and feels about his substance use. She reflects back any metaphors or figures of speech that the addict uses to describe his life, in order to create a sense of his internal frame of reference. She learns his spiritual language. This is a part of "joining," or developing an alliance with the individual. We are seeking to strengthen our relationship as a partner in this endeavor and to get a feel for how a person perceives his problems and behaviors. If we don't listen well to the many themes that thread through his conversation, we can focus too soon on one string that interests us without figuring out what most interests him. So we try to keep mental track of all that is being said to us and make sure that we have respectfully noted the person's perspective. Once we have summarized the issues that have brought the addict to us, we can begin to focus our time together.

The addict may first want to address another issue, such as how he feels about losing his job, or how she feels excited about her spiritual growth. We can respect that thread of the conversation and give them some time, empathy, and reflective listening. During this time, we are still paying attention to signs of their ambivalence about their substance use. If they do not bring up substance use themselves, we can broach the issue of their using substances *once we have listened well* to how they frame the problems in their lives. Note that the pastor in the example above asked the man quite precipitously whether he thought he was drinking too much. That was not an open-ended invitation; it was a yes-or-no kind of closed question. Instead, after listening well, we can use the elicit-respond-elicit model to ask if the addict is open to talking about his use of substances. This is our chance to briefly mention that we are concerned about what we have heard and are wondering what he thought about his substance use, or if he is willing to talk more about it.

If the addict is willing to talk about his substances, we can encourage him to explore what a usual day or evening of drinking looks like for him, what he values about the behavior, and what worries him about its effects on his life. Like Kathleen Greider in the example of spiritual care in the preceding chapter, we can begin to utilize his spiritual language about the condition and note what faith issues or "ultimate concerns" are resonant in his substance use. We use OARS throughout this process of exploration. A simple reflection—"So last night's drinking worried you"—will lead to more conversation. Or a double-sided reflection and follow-up question can be helpful: "You felt relieved after you took the pills, and you didn't like how you checked out from your family. Can you tell me more about that?" Double-sided reflections are very useful to mirror back discrepancies between the positives and negatives associated with using that come up in the conversation. By staying firmly in these skills, we begin to draw more and more focus on the ambivalence about using.

By being curious about the addict's experience of using—and reflecting back any ambivalence that we hear—we are trying to develop a sense of discrepancy between how he is living and how he would like to live. We are trying to affirm the benefits that the addict finds in his use while also lifting up a pattern of harm that is often lost in the haze of the addictive cycle. This helps him realize, even in small ways, that the addictive behavior is no longer in line with his values, goals, or desires for his life. If the individual gets frustrated or starts defending his behavior, it means that we are going too fast and need to use MI skills to redirect the conversation. There will be opportunities to offer education or feedback once we have established a respectful relationship, but we must first set our feet very firmly on the side of not being God. The addict is the one who must decide that he has a problem, and thus it is the addict who has to engage this evaluative process.

Motivational Strategies in the Precontemplation Stage

1. Connect with empathy and interest, using MI listening skills.
2. Explore the event or problem that brought the person to you.
3. Get to know the situation in his words, but also explore what others around him think about it.
4. Broach the topic of substance use.
5. Elicit the person's perception of the substance use, both its pros and cons.
6. Notice any doubts, concerns, or ambivalence about addictive behaviors.
7. Notice any values, goals, or a longing for change that might be out of phase with the addictive behavior.
8. Offer facts about substance use, if useful (drug effects, withdrawal/craving cycle).
9. Frame spiritual aspects of the problem through the addict's own spiritual language. Reflect back his "ultimate concerns" and notice what the strengths and struggles of his faith are.
10. Express your concern for the addict, keep responsibility in his court, and keep the door open.[4]

Along with exploring substance use, we can also ask what addicts want for their lives or what is important to them. Do they have goals or commitments that keep them going, day after day? Sometimes it is hard for the addict to imagine that she has different values and goals for her life than the ones that she is currently enacting. She suffers from a divided mind, where the good she wants seems unreal and the cravings seem the most salient part of her life. So another way to develop discrepancy is for the listener to notice and reflect back any small value, goal, or desire for her life that seems in contrast with the current addiction.[5] We are trying to focus on her strengths and also to identify intrinsic motivators for change. As one alcoholic man described it to me once, "Your bottom is when the last thing you lost or the next thing you are going to lose is more important than the drinking." What we notice or reflect back can help evoke those important values.

Our ability to do this work depends on how we use reflections and summaries. For instance, if someone says she does not want to go back to jail, we might reflect back that she values her freedom or that she really wants to be present for her children. If someone says that he just wants his spouse off his back, we could reflect back that his marriage is important to him. For the alcoholic man in our example above, a value would be the importance of his employment or being a provider for his family. He values his dignity; his relationship with his co-workers is important to him; he values his independence and fears being homeless and without a job. We could simply reflect back that this is hard for him: losing a job is very painful. These might all hit on some intrinsic motivators to change, especially if contrasted to his current behavior or situation. As active listeners, we provide a kind of mirror to the person so that he can see what he is saying in a different light.

Extrinsic motivators, such as losing one's job, can also lead one to examine addictive behaviors, but only if the addict can connect this loss to his using and thus decide that it is not what he wants for his life. Consequences such as jail, a threat of divorce, or loss of children commonly lead addicts to contemplate change, but it is equally common for addicts to brush off these major consequences. Outer consequences must touch an intrinsic motivator—valuing family, freedom, work, social position, parenthood—that can lead to a sustained decision to change. We can help addicts identify why this particular consequence touches something important to them. In one recovery meeting, I can hear a dozen reasons for why a person began to think about change. One was a functioning alcoholic who nonetheless felt "spiritually bankrupt." Another didn't care about the consequences for his spiritual life, but he was threatened with divorce. Another lost his family, survived two overdoses, and still kept on using drugs. He finally caught his own reflection in a window, and what got him was the realization that he couldn't even look himself in the eye. Another held an important job but was a binge drinker. She didn't know why she woke up one day after a weeklong binge and simply said, "That is enough." The point is that an addict's coming to consciousness about a problem arises from what is important to that individual, not what is important to us.

If the addict is in the precontemplation stage and refuses to explore his substance use when you broach the topic, it is not helpful to try to argue with him. We can certainly express our concern about his use, but if we choose to get into an argument, the power dynamic will shift into a focus on winning that conflict. The person will actually forget about his substance-use issues and focus his attention on the pastoral caregiver as the problem. Instead, we can continue to listen to how he perceives the problems that have brought him to our door. If the opportunity arises, we can reflect back any ambivalence about his use that we hear in his conversation, and ask some open-ended questions about it. For instance, someone may say that his use is not a problem but then mention, several sentences later, that his family is bothering him about his use. We might ask him to tell us more about that. Another might say that she is "just having fun," but then describe some rather unfunny sources of pain that have arisen from her partying. It might be the time to reflect back those situations or feelings and ask if that has happened at other times. We can be curious about that dissonance in her story without being judgmental. A general stance of "not knowing" or "wondering" is useful here, because we are not trying to trap someone into a confession; we are trying to get to know how she sees her situation. Of course, she may be completely unwilling to address the issue—at least not now—and that is her choice.

We need to monitor our own anxiety in this process. As listeners, we can be tempted to disengage from a conversation when we think that the person is stuck and is not going to change, or we can turn to more direct styles in a last-ditch effort to convince him. Instead, imagine that we are building a bridge the individual can use to return to us at a later date. At some point, as our conversation is drawing to a close, we could use elicit-respond-elicit one more time to note some signs that might be troubling. We can explain how substance use can progress into a chronic stage. We can affirm that only he can really know whether he has a problem. We are available to talk if he ever needs help. Remember that the main task at this stage is to get the conversation going, not to get the person into treatment. That is for another stage. Here we are trying to see his world and his problems through his point of view, so that he keeps on talking to us as he moves through these stages. The pastoral goal at this early stage is to maintain a caring and trusting relationship as the person begins to assess his behaviors.

The Contemplation Stage

To transfer out of the precontemplation stage is to realize that one does indeed have a problem that is getting in the way of a fulfilling life. In the contemplation stage, the addict begins to consider the possibility of change. There is often a sense of ambivalence or fear associated with stopping the behavior. Sometimes addicts will say that they want to change and then will find themselves in the throes of their addiction again, as if they are taken over by the possession inside of them. Others talk about change, but they stall and resist. They may worry about what they will lose personally or socially if they enter into recovery, but they may not feel comfortable sharing that with a pastoral caregiver unless you broach the question about loss or grief. It is hard to talk honestly about the goods someone loses when she stops a socially unacceptable behavior.

Our goal in the contemplation stage is to help tip the decisional balance toward change, so that the gains of stopping substance use outweigh the benefits that the substance seems to provide. We use many of the same strategies that we used for precontemplation—listening to the positives and negatives, building discrepancies, reflecting back values—because we are trying to strengthen the commitment to change while we respect the loss that it brings. We also expand our conversation to include the person's feelings about what it might be like to change the behavior. Our tone is empathic and our outlook hopeful rather than punitive or moralizing. We affirm the strengths that we see in her. We hold the possibility of change lightly and leave the responsibility with the person, because she has to make the decision to change. We approach our conversation this way in order to encourage clients' self-efficacy concerning their ability to make that change. Our ultimate goal is to help tip the decisional balance from the *idea* of change into a *decision* to change.

We might begin simply by asking why the person is seeking change now. This can provide us with information about the consequences that brought her to us and will also furnish some idea about how she perceives these problems. Sometimes personal or practical problems propel an addict into reconsidering her behavior. Others may have just survived a bad experience of drinking or drug using, and they have come to us feeling broken or scared. We can ask open-ended questions to expand the conversation. What happened? Why now? What is different about the consequence or a family reaction?—questions that search for the motivation behind the person's seeking for advice about change at this moment. For the contemplation stage, here are some MI questions that can help people think about change:[6]

1. Why would you want to make this change?
2. What are the pros and cons of continuing the behavior?
3. What are the three best reasons for you to make this change?
4. What do you think you will miss most if you stop?
5. What would be different in your life in a year's time if you made the decision to change?
6. How do you think you should go about it?
7. What do you think is God's part in this? How can the church support you?

We also explore ambivalence about the idea of changing. Often addicts will not tell fellow Christians about the perceived benefits of staying with their behavior. They think that you only want to hear their "good side," the side that wants to change or to embrace socially acceptable values and goals. Ambivalence lessens some of its hold when we can look honestly at what we are afraid to lose as well as what we hope to gain from change. So we dig into ambivalence, considering the pros and cons that surround the decision to change, and the risks/rewards of ceasing or continuing the behavior. We want people to bring both sides to consciousness.

We are the ones that guide this conversation, and our goal is to reflect back and ask more questions about the change side of the equation. As I mentioned in the preceding chapter, change language is about desires, actions, reasons, or needs to change. Change language can also be found in the values or life goals that are out of phase with the behavior. On the other hand, sustain language occurs when people keep talking about all the reasons why they are stuck—or can't change. The former is movement forward, and the latter is staying put. We want to tip the decisional balance toward change by strengthening the movement forward, and we succeed in that when the person sees a good reason for change, finds the behavior dissonant with her life or values, and feels as though there is hope that she has the ability to make this change. As we discussed in the last chapter, reflections and summaries that gather change language are particularly important in this process. Through summaries we can acknowledge the concerns about change that we have heard, but we try to end them with the positive desires or thoughts surrounding change.

As we reflect back her reasons for change or her goals for her life, the addict might push the other direction. She might begin to argue for reasons why change won't work for her. This may mean that we are going too fast or are inserting our own agenda directly into the reflection. We've stopped listening closely. The cost is higher than we have acknowledged, and she is inviting us to count that cost with her. So we can return to the "wondering" stance and ask, "What do you think about that challenge?" or "I don't know. What would you do in that situation?" This helps return the conversation back to the individual, so that the caregiver does not get into a tug of war with the addict about change. Remember the legion: stopping a behavior that has infiltrated mind, body, and spirit feels like a torment. It is good to be positive, but ignoring the real struggle of recovery helps no one. While our strategy is to be affirming and to reflect and summarize toward intrinsic change, we must avoid doing this in a manipulative way. We have to remain real and genuine, open to the pain of the other.

The Preparation Stage

Once a person has made a considered decision to change, he has entered into the preparation stage, which is the transition from decision to action. There are two main tasks in this stage: first, we continue to encourage a strong enough commitment to adequately support the work of change; second, we develop a plan for the addict to manage triggers and to take care of himself in the face of the early challenges of sobriety. Conversations about the pros and cons of use and recovery continue as we seek to strengthen that commitment and to be honest about ambivalence. Addicts must also feel some sense of self-efficacy: in other words, they must feel that they possess sufficient personal and social resources to manage the difficulties that will come with stopping the behavior. They need encouragement and affirmation as they begin to experiment with change. We can also collaborate with them on how to break goals into manageable parts, so that change feels less overwhelming to them.

While the preparation stage is about making plans to change, we must also keep one eye focused on commitment. Strengthening change commitment is important, because we can often think about change and even desire it without really being able to accomplish it. Let me put this in terms of the prescription drug abuser's motivational factors. The woman in one of our examples above had an extrinsic source of motivation when her family confronted her. But she did not realize that her intrinsic motivator was to stop feeling immediate pain. Both her addiction and her family dynamics had become a source of suffering. She responded by throwing away her medication and reuniting with her family and her faith. This action removed the immediate source of pain, and by the time she arrived at the caregiver's office, she was on a spiritual high. She did not want to sully that spiritual high with plans for recovery—or really with any thoughts of her addiction at all. Avoiding discomfort is a good sign that someone is in the midst of a spiritual high and not a graced conversion. Since ending pain was her real motivator, when the spiritual high ended and she was in pain again, she shifted back to the drug use. She did not make it to the second part of deepening her commitment or planning for this behavioral change.

The preparation stage is a time to partner with the individual in problem-solving the challenges of his particular context. Recovery takes time, energy, and sometimes financial resources. A person seeking recovery might need to talk about how to manage daily outpatient treatment with a busy work schedule. Or he might need help in prioritizing a host of problems, such as employment needs, court proceedings, divorce, or childcare challenges. It is also good to get a feel for his social support or relationship with parents, family, or loved ones. These are not always positive influences. Since we are taking away a coping skill that helps regulate stress, it is important to figure out which relationships are supportive and which actually cause more stressful problems. Finally, he needs to begin planning around high-risk situations, dealing with triggers, and managing his emotions and social life without the substance.

Some Areas to Evaluate during the Preparation Stage

1. How is the person feeling about the change?
2. How can I strengthen hope, offer a sense of possibility, point to inner resources?
3. What are the outer resources or social supports?
4. What are other practical or spiritual problems, and how does the addict feel about them?
5. Is the addict able to plan around high-risk situations?
6. What will it feel like to change friends, be home with family, manage stress, or return to an old neighborhood?
7. What are the resources of prayer, worship, and relationship with God and the church community that can strengthen and nourish the addict during change?[7]

When caring for a person on the verge of change, it is good to remember that one does not have to prepare perfectly *before* entering into some kind of treatment. Some people try out an AA meeting or go into detox even when they are not completely sure that they can sustain sobriety. Some also try limiting their use to see if they really have a problem. Treatment programs are of varied quality, and it can take people time to identify what kind of recovery activities best support their goals. It is also good to remember that we cannot want recovery for addicts more than they want it for themselves. But we can be a spiritual mentor and a sounding-board: a wise and knowledgeable companion for this journey. This is the "cool engagement" of accompanying another through the stages of change. We ask them what they think they need to get sober. We offer them local resources, if those may be of use to them. We talk through the challenges that they face: the friends they used with, the workplace challenges related to using, the family dynamics that trigger their use. We continue to educate on addiction. We explore where they see God in this process of change, and what spiritual challenges and opportunities lie ahead. But we also remember that there is no perfect plan. So we keep positive and build a sense that addicts can accomplish their decision for sobriety over time.

The Action Stage

Once the addict sets a date to put her recovery into practice, she has entered the action stage. This stage is the first time addicts attempt to abstain from substance use for a significant period of time. The individual starts treatment of some kind, or she takes steps to change her current addictive behaviors and replace them with new ones. The main tasks of the action stage are to follow through with treatment plans, develop new strategies with which to meet daily challenges, and begin the task of emotion and stress regulation without substances. Pastoral caregivers should not be the addict's primary addiction counselor, unless they are trained and certified for that role. I strongly advise referring the addict to some kind of professional care, even if you have an addiction ministry, because we do not know the extent of the mental or physical health issues that may need to be addressed alongside the addictive behavior. Pastoral caregivers can still provide vital support, a listening ear, and spiritual counsel. In fact, we might be very important to an addict's sense of hope and self-efficacy as she seeks to make connections between recovery and faith.

"Coaching" is probably the best way to describe our role in the action and maintenance stages, as we problem-solve together and share ideas about the challenges of recovery. People in early recovery need help forming structure in their new lives. But there will be times when ambivalence and resistance return, or the two barometers of changing/sustaining and self-efficacy/temptation sway back and forth. During those times, we turn more fully to the MI guiding skills in the preceding chapter: avoiding argument, rolling with resistance, and reflecting back values and strengths toward change. We can also use the OARS listening skills of open-ended questions, affirmation, reflections, and summaries to develop a consistent and safe conversation that focuses on understanding and reflecting back the recovering person's perspectives and needs regarding change.

For the action stage, we can be a calming presence and support to help the person in recovery to keep a "one-day-at-a-time" perspective. The recovering addict experiences many "firsts," and she needs to figure out how to navigate the temptations or stresses of life without her customary behaviors. It is rarely a simple process of sustained gains: some days feel more hopeful, others less hopeful. Addicts in early recovery can pile on their problems or get lost in self-defeating thoughts. Others isolate themselves and do not know how to ask for help. We can help them focus on one thing at a time and pare down goals into manageable parts. We can also model a nonanxious and positive perspective. "Now" statements and questions help to focus the recovering addict: "What would help right now?" "What do you need to do today?" "What is the priority right now?" Strength-based explorations can also be useful: "How have you managed this before?" or "What have you done in similar situations?" We manage our own anxiety about their recovery, and so we help them to stay in the moment with us. Being in the moment, the here and now, and holding it lightly, is precisely the skill that they will need for long-term recovery.

Note that while pastoral caregivers may begin with empathizing and exploring feelings, we often end with affirming strengths, talking about goals, or exploring actions. Doing something shifts our emotional states. In chapter 3, we talked about the importance of mindfulness meditation and our many Christian prayer practices that can help with grounding and regulation. We also explored the importance of activities when we considered Kim's needs for affect regulation. Addicts tend to isolate, so they have to practice learning how to reach out to others, to spend time in community, or to call people when they are feeling down. They are often disconnected from their needs for healthy food and exercise, playful hobbies, or proper rest. Recovery from substance abuse is not constrained by talk therapy. It is replacing old behavioral cues with new behavioral cues, and thus old actions with new actions.

The Pastoral Caregiver's Support during the Action Stage

1. Celebrate his immediate victories and strengths.
2. Help him develop a new story through your witness. At every meeting, summarize how you see the positive steps he is taking now.
3. Offer spiritual and congregational resources for further healing and nourishment.
4. Explore high-risk situations as they arise—holidays, family visits, relational problems, new stressors at work.
5. Help him discover resonant spiritual and cultural tools to help manage negative thoughts and feelings or to survive dynamic high-risk situations.
6. Find ways of explaining the long process of change via Scripture stories or practices in your church that he might find meaningful.
7. Check in on social support and self-care: Who is he calling? What is he doing? How is his prayer life, and what cultural practices or support system are helping him?

Our empathy and encouragement can be vital for an addict's sense of hope and self-efficacy as she embarks on recovery. We can celebrate her successes and be impressed by her strengths. We can also use reflections and summaries to mentalize: to show her that we truly see her as a thinking and feeling self in her own right. We can notice the change that we see in her. For instance, "I really like how you managed that problem at work. I remember last year when the deadlines made you crazy, but this year you really reached out and got help. What do you think has changed for you?" or "I remember months ago that you had a hard time sitting still. Now, you seem to feel more comfortable in your own skin. Is that about right?" Paying respectful attention to people's histories makes an extraordinary difference. Change is so gradual, and sometimes people who are newly recovered are the last ones to notice the benefits of recovery or the strengths in their personality shining through the difficulties.

Along with supporting recovering people in the daily emotional and practical challenges of recovery, we are there as spiritual companions. Addiction is a spiritual bondage, the condition of the soul in distress. We are the ones equipped to explain this aspect of addiction to people in recovery in order to alleviate the sense of shame and self-loathing that might keep them from turning to God for hope and renewal. We can companion with them as they slowly reconnect to a life of spiritual growth, to their love of others, and to their belovedness as children of God. Involvement in worship, prayer, and fellowship activities becomes a vital part of developing a new sober identity. In these environments of intimacy and spiritual surrender, the vigilance associated with recovery can fall away, and the recovering addict can receive the healing and grace offered to all of God's children. But perhaps more importantly, recovering individuals can feel connected to the touchstone of their Christian community, and feel that you as their pastoral caregiver see them as sacred and respected children of God.

Maintaining Recovery

After approximately six months of change, the individual finally finds herself in the maintenance stage. She is well into the work of consolidating new behaviors into her lifestyle and sense of identity, and the task of the maintenance stage is to continue to sustain this change over time and across a wide range of situations. Relapse-prevention in the midst of high-risk situations remains crucial, as the recovering addict develops skills for managing the challenges of daily life. The goal of this stage is to make the practice of sobriety into its own habit, with a new set of behavioral and emotional cues.

In this replacement of old actions with new ones, the swings of decisional balance and self-efficacy/temptation remain signposts at least for the first few years of recovery. For instance, to return to my New Year's Eve resolutions, I might actually sustain an exercise plan for six months. Allegedly, I have now engaged it long enough to qualify for the maintenance stage. But I am not a fully recovered couch-sitter. While I feel better and have changed many behaviors related to my previous sedentary lifestyle, the realities of increased stress, time-management issues, or mere complacency can tip the decisional balance back to my old behaviors. They can lower my sense of self-efficacy and make me feel like it is all too much work to continue. That's when the chocolate comes out. The task of the maintenance stage is to maintain the new behavior by paying attention to the little adjustments and the changes in life that might need extra care or problem-solving as time passes.

Nurturing Self-Efficacy and Strengthening New Habits in the Maintenance Stage

1. Social affiliations that provide a sense of community-belonging and meaning.
2. Activities—sports, volunteering, hobbies, spirituality—that connect to others and/or aid in emotional regulation and self-efficacy.
3. Continued management of any psychological medications or co-morbid mental health conditions.
4. Continued safety planning about new situations, losses, or life stressors.
5. Continued evaluation of the natural ebb and flow of closeness to God, involvement in prayer and worship, connection to the church community.

During the maintenance stage, a recovering addict may enter into another ambivalent season in which the decisional balance requires some attention. He might start wondering whether he was making up his problem. Perhaps he fantasizes about drinking or using like a "normal person" again. He may face an emotionally intense event that returns his cravings to use substances—such as a parent's death, a job loss, or a divorce. Whenever resistance is on the rise, we should refrain from any arguing and instead get him talking. We should ask more open-ended questions and return to paraphrasing and summarizing signs of dissonance between his past using and his present life of recovery. We also should ask about what he would gain or lose in using, or how he managed cravings or difficult life situations in the past. We should always end a conversation with action: What are you going to do tonight? What do you think you need to stay sober? How will you take care of yourself? In the end, the decision is his. We just want to get people out of the echo chamber of their heads and review the potential consequences so that they are able to make a more informed decision.

Relapse Prevention

Continued planning around high-risk situations is a large part of the action and maintenance stages. According to studies in relapse prevention, the addict enters high-risk situations with a baseline of personal resources or challenges.[8] This baseline makes up the cards the addict is dealt at the beginning of her recovery. It can include genetics, depression levels, the chronic nature of substance use, mental-health issues, physical health concerns, and any of the contextual stressors we have been discussing that create the background to change. Note that in relapse prevention, the term "relapse" is distinguished from individual instances of "lapse." One may have a single lapse that sets recovery plans back, while full relapse constitutes a complete return to the addictive pattern of behavior.

Along with this baseline of characteristics, the experience of physical and psychological withdrawal also differs from person to person. For those suffering withdrawal symptoms, best practices suggest combining medication with recovery treatment. It is very difficult to recover when one is caught in the swing of withdrawal. Note that while drugs like heroin or crack have the greatest media attention for being dangerous substances, it is actually more often fatal to detox from alcohol without medical assistance. Those who are highly addicted daily drinkers or who experience delirium, psychosis, or the shakes when they have a break in their drinking schedule (called delirium tremens) should seek medical attention before detoxing from alcohol.

As the addict carries this baseline of characteristics and his withdrawal symptoms into the realities of daily living, he confronts *static* and *dynamic* high-risk situations.[9] *Static* high-risk situations are the ones that almost always lead to a lapse. Many people require some planning in order to deal with dangerous situations like family gatherings, the old neighborhood where they formerly bought their drugs, friends they used with, or work and relationship stressors that predictably lead to substance use. Since many of these static situations involve the emotions associated with using, they can trigger withdrawal and craving, even if these states seem to have disappeared in other environments.

This is why we need to explain to addicts who are newly into recovery that "I don't feel like using anymore" is not a surprising feeling for them to express when sitting in the pastor's office, since it is not the place, one would hope, that they associate with their substance use. Humans have a social brain that responds to its environment, and static high-risk situations can thus trigger withdrawal symptoms as they further bombard the addict with behavioral and social cues to engage in the behavior. The good news is that static high-risk situations are easier to plan around: in 12-step language, the addict watches for "people, places and things" related to her using history. The challenge is that these situations represent a loss. Much of the addict's identity might be connected to familiar faces, activities, and neighborhoods that are also static high-risk situations for substance use.

The second kind of situation, the *dynamic* high-risk situation, arises from the mixing of individual and social variables, and thus it is harder to plan for. We may be walking around in the itch of physical withdrawal or the aching emptiness many addicts feel as they grieve the loss of the addiction. But we are committed to recovery and we think we've got it under control. Then we might run into a problem within a relationship, or might feel shame or anger at work, or we can't stop thinking about our fears for the future. These cognitive and affective challenges pile on top of our baseline of itchiness. Then, that evening, we might find ourselves chatting with a friend we used with, and we relive the glory days. Or it is a bright, sunny day and we imagine sitting on the lawn with a cold drink. These are simple behavioral cues, but the combination becomes difficult to resist. Whether the addict survives, the temptation is related to her sense of self-efficacy and her practical coping skills in the moment. When negative affect is high (self-pity, depression, anger, or shame) or cognitive distortions are swirling in the addict's head (self-defeating thoughts, perfectionism, resentment, or denial), she is at greater risk of making poor decisions or feeling a lowered sense of self-efficacy.

When a recovering person is in a dynamic high-risk situation, his actions depend on his strength and optimism in the moment. In other words, he can feel pretty positive about a change overall, but if he is tired, overwhelmed with stress, shamed, or angry because of something that has happened in his life, he might not be able to engage his coping skills. If he then hits a high-risk situation, a perfect storm could be brewing. This is why continued planning and new nourishing habits of life are just as important as trusting self-efficacy in the moment. Remember, addiction is not a disease of excess; it is a disease that attacks self-regulation. This means that cutting down or stopping is only part of the answer. He now needs to learn how to self-regulate. AA groups often teach their members the acronym HALT: if you feel irritable, check to see if you are *hungry, angry, lonely,* or *tired*, and first address those issues. The person in recovery can also problem-solve ahead of time for moments when he feels overwhelmed or tempted. It is necessary to be very direct about that possibility so that when he is too depleted to face temptation, he can engage in a preplanned behavior, such as calling a friend (or other person who is in recovery) for support, attending a recovery meeting, calling his therapist, or praying.

Finally, faith can be involved in how one engages in high-risk situations. This can be a pastoral issue if the person in recovery is confusing a positive feeling of overall self-efficacy in the moment with a sense that God will deliver her from any trouble in the future. It is our job as pastoral caregivers to help separate good feelings from future realities. We need to remove any false belief that, if someone had "real faith," she could go to the old neighborhood, the old using boyfriend, or the drunken family barbecue and not be tempted. A good quotation to guide your conversation with a recovering person comes from Luke 14:28: "For which of you, intending to build a tower, does not first sit down and estimate the cost, to see whether he has enough to complete it?" Faith and planning are not mutually exclusive. One might also reflect on how Jesus did not throw himself off the corner of the temple and expect angels to save him. God may indeed be supporting us, but that does not mean that we get to eschew our personal responsibility. When emotional or cognitive negativity is high or temptation is great, God is the one telling us to avoid that dangerous situation, to call a supportive friend, or to enter into any other action that can restore our balance.

Supporting Spiritual Growth

Recovery is not a return from a mistake; it is a movement forward into discipleship. It is a way of life that matures over time as those who are recovering seek God's will for their sober lives. Whether we draw from John Bunyan's *Pilgrim's Progress,*[10] Saint Paul's missionary adventures, Richard Foster's *Celebration of Discipline,*[11] or the mystic's slow progress to union with God, we have an incredibly varied history of thought that teaches Christian discipleship as a long process rather than a quick fix. In the same way as the Gerasene embarks on the path of following Jesus, he is sent back home so that he can work on the slow restoration of his body and soul, as well as his reintegration into his community. For all Christian discipleship, we first meet and surrender to the love of God in Christ. Then we must learn how to live in the light of that love. That process has its consolations and blessings, but it also has its spiritual deserts and dark nights. We need to live in the moment as we go through these experiences one day at a time. After years, we look back and see that our faithfulness during both kinds of experiences draws us closer to spiritual maturity and to our relationship with God.

So, rather than imagining recovery as something compartmentalized from our spiritual lives, we can see recovery as a particular spiritual path. It is a way of doing discipleship. As pastoral caregivers, we help connect the themes people find in recovery to the themes of the church year, to worship, and to Scripture study. We explore signs of God's love and direction in the lives of those recovering. We help integrate actions of faith and worship with the person's emotional and practical goals of recovery. We learn her spiritual language and offer her rich theological resources. We provide her with a safe, dependable environment in which to examine her moral past and enter into acts of confession and forgiveness. Throughout the spiritual and emotional work of recovery, we help her integrate the new life that arises from this death.

As a part of the discipleship process, pastoral caregivers also need to be able to address the moral sin that is involved in addictions and the shame and guilt over the "I'll never do *that*" lists that addicts break as the soul-sickness progresses. Some of this work involves each faith tradition's practices of naming and releasing guilt and shame—in other words, engaging in rituals of penance or repentance and proclaiming the promise of absolution or forgiveness. First, we listen well and engage in the assurance of God's love and forgiveness. We can wonder what it is like for the recovering person to talk about this situation. We can be curious about how this action was helpful at the time, or what it might have protected or achieved for him. We can explore whether or not this action reflects a common behavior pattern or emotional theme in his life or across his relationships.[12] We can ask what God wanted for the person at the time, and what God wants now for his future. Beyond offering the assurance of God's grace, we become curious about what God is teaching through these difficult emotional and spiritual losses.

Finally, while reconciliation with others can be part of our Christian discipleship, it is important to check the motivation behind seeking forgiveness. Staying in Holy Saturday may be more important than quickly seeking to resurrect a relationship that we have harmed. If the goal is to relieve the recovering addict's guilt, to change the person's feelings about her, or to get something from the person, then she is not ready to make an apology. A real apology does not insist on being received, and it is not an arena for our excuses. It does not erase the other's point of view or magically achieve relationship. In other words, it should not be a strategy to control others. Furthermore, if the apology—or making any contact with the offended party—will traumatize them or cause them more harm than good, the individual should not make the apology. Part of the penance is to sacrifice the satisfaction that the recovering addict is seeking from the apology. Some other symbolic acts or some acts of service might take the place of directly contacting the offended individual.

EXCURSUS: Mental-Health Conditions

Focusing on skills that build on self-reflection, intrinsic motivation, and collaboration toward change can be much more challenging if the addict also suffers from a mental-health condition. It is estimated that 8.1 million adults have a substance-use disorder that is co-occurring with a mental, behavioral, or emotional disorder.[13] The high prevalence of co-occurring disorders may reflect attempts at self-medication, either because these conditions share similar neural pathways in the brain or because they are engaged to manage the high stress that comes with mental-health challenges.[14]

For instance, antisocial personality disorder is highly correlated with substance-use disorder. These individuals may seek to control and manipulate, may feel little actual remorse for their actions, and may be unable to reflect on their part in any dispute.[15] Those who suffer borderline personality disorder may have traits such as impulsivity, along with intense interpersonal cycles of need and rage that are further exacerbated by substance-use disorders.[16] Those struggling with bipolar conditions may abuse substances in depressive or manic phases of their disorder. Schizophrenia also has a high rate of co-occurring substance use.[17] Co-occurring disorders can lead to higher potential for negative outcomes for an addict, including higher rates of relapse, hospitalization, violence, victimization, and incarceration compared to individuals with a mental-health disorder alone.[18] So the journey to recovery may be longer and more fraught with relapses or personal crises. It is possible that individuals may need to focus on harm reduction measures rather than abstinence, or may need to manage cyclical involvement in addictive behaviors related to the shifts in their mental-health condition. There is not a "one size fits all" way to imagine the long work of recovery.

This is a topic fraught with misunderstanding, so let me be clear: pastoral caregivers do not diagnose others. Addicted people (and just about anyone on a church committee) can be emotionally challenging, and drug effects can mimic mental-health problems like mania or paranoia. The early stages of recovery also can cause swings in moods or even temporary feelings of psychosis as one suffers withdrawal from heavy substance use. Sometimes caregivers may label some people as "borderline" or "narcissistic" to rationalize why they don't want to work with them. But other times, pastoral caregivers can overengage, believing that they must give and give for someone else, must explore and respond to every emotional need, and are responsible for the other's well-being. These well-meaning responses can reinforce problematic emotional states and relational patterns. Plus, of course, they can exhaust caregivers and congregations. In these cases, we are actually putting our need to be needed above the individual's need for gentle but firm boundaries. We are here to love unconditionally, but part of that love is to offer stable and caring limits that help people with personality difficulties feel that we are secure and consistent, even if they fight against that stability.

MI skills are used by professional mental-health providers to help motivate lifestyle changes, like consistent compliance to medication and treatment. Skills like avoiding argument or rolling with resistance can help us to keep a conversation on track without getting pulled into the emotional or relational undertow. But if we are not trained in the management of serious mental-health conditions, simply asking open-ended questions or reflecting back discrepancies may not be structured enough for people who struggle with intense emotional and relational patterns. They may not be able to step back from emotional states and self-reflect. Instead, they may need more gently directive and problem-solving kinds of care. We can also set basic standards for how the individual treats others in the community and how to correct inappropriate behavior—especially if it is aggressive or hurtful to others.[19] We can suggest recovery resources, like dual-diagnosis inpatient or outpatient programs, dialectical behavioral therapists (DBT), or "double trouble" peer recovery support groups.

People with mental-health conditions can also challenge our empathy, because we can easily forget that they are suffering. We can get offended when someone rages against us for perceived slights, tries to control us, or seems to be lying to us.[20] Pastoral theologian Carol Schwietzer offers some important points for individuals with borderline personality disorder that can be useful for any mental-health condition that is chronically or emotionally dysregulated.[21] Set limits to your time and to the help offered by pastor or congregation. Shepherd your pastoral counseling with the intention of emotionally containing those recovering, rather than opening them up to the vagaries of emotional exploration. In other words, keep to specifics, keep explanations simple, and ask concrete clarifying questions about what the individual needs. Be a little irreverent and playful to both connect with the client and to break the intensity of the engagement. Offer mental-health treatment options. Keep grounded by having another wise caregiver help you process your own experience of the individual. We can offer these limits while still respecting the human dignity of the individual and honoring her resilience and survival.

Opening to Change

In chapter 1, I explained that addictions are about multiplicity: the many organize into one. Throughout this work I have pulled on many of the threads that entangle a vulnerable person into an addiction. I have discussed the progression of the disease on the mind and the soul. I have drawn from the assumption of our fundamental relationality: the fact that we need each other to become whole, and that we must find other ways to cope when our environments lack empathy and attunement. I have threaded Mark's story of the Gerasene and his self-protective legion throughout these chapters, and I have talked about avoiding simple solutions. I have tried to tarry with the death of Jesus to consider what new life looks like for conditions that were once sources of survival. I have talked about recovery as a kind of grieving—in the words of the legion, a "torment"—as we seek to untangle our identity from the possession. It is a process marked by ambivalence, because it represents a loss—even as the legion seeks to kill us.

Within the weave of these dynamics, an addict comes to you for care. Or he ends up in your office in the precontemplation stage, talking about addiction when he thinks he is complaining about other problems in his life. What now? First, take time. Understand the problem from his perspective. Ask open-ended questions. Affirm his values, and learn his spiritual language. Summarize what you are hearing. After listening well, broach the question of substance use if he has not already brought it up. Ask more open-ended questions and reflect back the values and motivations that are important to him—or any desire to change—and ask more about them. Use double-sided reflections to mirror back discrepancies in a nonjudgmental way. Keep the ball in his court. Use elicit-respond-elicit to share what you notice in his story or to give some information about substance use. Focus fuzzy, inchoate affect by naming emotions. Summarize the conversation periodically in a way that honors ambivalence while ending in signs of strength and change.

Don't bother arguing with or fighting resistance. When he pushes back with an excuse, roll with it rather than confronting it head-on. It is a sign that you are out of sync with the person, or pushing too quickly or too hard. Avoid argument by either affirming some aspect of his point of view, changing the topic, or asking more questions. Keep a cool engagement. If he is open to talk about his substance use as a problem, look for the spiritual language: the themes of ultimate concern that frame his use for him. Ask him how he is doing in his relationship with God and others. If you find that he is in the precontemplation stage and says that he has his use under control, then affirm that he is the only one who can know what is going on with him. Explore his point of view to get to know him better. Use elicit-respond-elicit to ask if you can leave him with some information on addiction. If he responds in the affirmative, let him know that substance use can be progressive. If he begins to feel like he can't control how much he uses, finds himself in blackouts, or life starts feeling really horrible, you are there for him if he wants to explore this more. The door is always open.

If he is concerned about his substance use, then he is in the contemplation stage. Continue to get to know his problem from his perspective, and then perhaps consider the pros and cons of change. Develop discrepancies between behaviors and values by reflecting them back with a "wondering" kind of curiosity. Keep using your OARS to build on change language. Ask about how life might be different in the future if he makes the change. If he is curious about recovery options, offer a menu of possibilities and talk about them together.

If someone comes to you in the action stage, it is probably because he wants his pastor to know that he has started recovery. Your support is important to him. Ask what brought him to this decision, if he is willing to talk about it. Ask about his plans. Ask what is changing in his life now as he enters recovery. Affirm his strengths and build self-efficacy. Explore his spiritual language concerning his experience of addiction and recovery. Ask what you or the church can do to support him. If useful, provide a safe space for reflection on relationship challenges or feelings of guilt related to friends, family, or God.

That's a lot of advice drawn from Change Theory and Motivational Interviewing. And it sounds too simple. I find these conversations very difficult. They require that the pastoral caregiver hold the kind of double-consciousness required to listen well while also building change language and self-efficacy. Like playing a musical instrument, these skills take a lot of practice before they become more intuitive. But the skills do help us to monitor our own reactions and respond with a mind to support change. Rather than trying to convince or argue with the addict (or recovering person), we become aware of our righting reflex and keep the conversation going with affirmation and respect. Rather than getting lost in deflections based on blame or rationalizations, we point to values and intentions that we find embedded in the discussion. We gently explore the discrepancy between what she wants for her life and what is happening to her in her substance abuse. We do a lot of reframing toward strengths and signs of change.

In all of these ways, we can accompany an addict through the stages of change. But we will miss the point entirely if we think that these skills help us gain control over another person's journey toward the good that God wants for her life. None of these skills is guaranteed to work, if by "work" we mean a smooth journey into sobriety. So let me attempt to return us to what is really important. I've mentioned that we need a holy curiosity—a respect and interest in others because they are beloved children of God. I have also mentioned that people are sacred, and they are sacred especially at the depths of their suffering. I have mentioned that addictions tell stories of suffering: opaque histories, traumatic memories, or the losses throughout the expanding circles of the social body. They tell stories of attempts to manage life with few emotional resources, attempts to grow up too fast or numb out too quickly, which, in our immaturity, can go horribly wrong. This suffering is now addressed to us as pastoral caregivers, and we have a choice about what story we are able to hear and to hold regardless of whether or not the person changes.

We might see the addiction of addicts as a story of failure, of irrational self-harm, or of prideful rebellion. But consider what it could be if we were to see it through the many voices of the legion? It could be a symbolic cry—a witness to trauma or a protest of oppression—or a story stored in the violation of the body, numbed by substances. Or it could be an attachment grief, an escape from an internalized relational emptiness that felt like a death. Or it might have grown from a life transition into high school or into college that combined with a genetic susceptibility. A situation of social loneliness that, in youth's immaturity, seemed easily met by substances. It could have been substance use neatly compartmentalized behind an otherwise successful life. A functional addiction fueled by fears of vulnerability and intimacy. Or, at the opposite extreme, it could be a mess: a self-loathing that got bundled up in bad jobs and bad relationships, victimizing people when drunk or high, ending later in jails and on probation, a life that seemed from the beginning to be nothing but a slow death by drowning. There is no one way to become an addict. But in every story we hear the profundity of our human fragility. We hear the grief and loss that compelled the Word to become flesh.

This is why a book about definitions can be so dangerous. Perhaps some of these answers are right, at least technically. We could say, "You have a problem with alcohol; your brain is changing; your drug use will continue to progress until you damage your body or kill yourself." Those answers are correct, and the required change seems so obvious. But we cannot capture the whole of what it means for that person to suffer or to assert himself symbolically through his behaviors. We don't know what it costs to protect himself from a sense of loss that feels worse than death. Because maybe these things are true about alcohol and drug use, or any other chronic, habitual condition; but maybe there are other equally correct answers. Maybe we could say, "You are also broken and traumatized; you feel anxious and alone. Maybe you want to numb out from the exhaustion of functioning in a racist society. Or you are enraged about the homophobia that has given you the message that you are worthless and irredeemable. Or you wish that you could no longer feel so hyped up, so out of control, so empty, or so afraid of others. So full of shame or regret. Maybe, after everything, you are a survivor."

The more strategic advice we as pastoral caregivers get, the more we risk turning to an instrumental view of care. We think to ourselves, "How can I help?" But another way of saying this is: "How can I control the outcome?" It is so easy to move from helping to controlling because we want what is best for the other. We feel helpless when we are up against the legion's tactics of self-preservation—the distancing, deflection, and denial used to protect behavior from change. But we have no control over someone else's sobriety. We have no control over someone else's complicated, relapsable, chronic behavioral condition. But we do have control over whether or not we will allow what breaks God's heart to break our own.

What is perhaps most uncomfortable about addiction is that it does not just communicate other people's suffering. It teaches us about ourselves. The characteristic ambivalence, resistance, and avoidance of addicts are more than roadblocks on our way to progress; they ferret out our own brokenness. They push on our egos and our own need for success. They turn up the volume on the judgmental tapes that we don't want to admit play in the background in our heads. We might think that the other person is full of self-pity or is lying to us. The other doesn't seem to take our good advice, or may not even really want to recover. The other doesn't respect our authority, or she may evoke too much emotion in us. We begin to want recovery for the addict more than she wants it for herself. So what we learn is that we are deeply affected, trapped in some way with the person and her legion. We have been moved into an engagement: we have been touched and pulled down into our own wounded flesh.

Where do we go from here—both of us—wrapped in the net of the legion as it plays its self-protective game? I have my OARS, but I cannot singlehandedly row us both to the shore. Could it be that we both have to be here in the middle of this storm, feeling a little helpless? Recovery remains a mystery bound to our personal and social resources, our relational histories, and the progression of the disease upon us. So pastoral *mastery* in the end must be replaced by *faithfulness*. Before our good plans for another person's life, we stand in the holiness of our calling, the sacredness of being invited into the kind of suffering that breaks the heart of God. And what if it could break our own hearts? Would we be a little closer to the paradise we had lost, the call to love the other as ourselves? Loving the addicts may or may not change *them*. But it could indeed change *us*.

Notes

Foreword

1. Susan Sontag, *Illness as Metaphor and AIDS and Its Metaphors* (London: Penguin Classics, 1991), 60.

Acknowledgments

1. Jewish Fairy Godmother.

Introduction

1. American Psychiatric Association, *Diagnostic and Statistical Manual of Mental Health Disorders: DSM 5* (Arlington, VA: American Psychiatric Publishing, 2013), 481–90.

2. Rebecca S. Chopp, *The Praxis of Suffering: An Interpretation of Liberation and Political Theologies* (Eugene, OR: Wipf and Stock, 2007), 4.

3. Elaine Graham, *Transforming Practice: Pastoral Theology in an Age of Uncertainty* (Eugene, OR: Wipf and Stock, 2002), 139.

4. This phrase was coined by one of the founders of the chaplaincy movement, Anton Boisen, and further developed by Charles Gerkin, *Living Human Document: Re-Visioning Pastoral Counseling in a Hermeneutical Mode,* 2nd ed. (Nashville: Abingdon, 1984), 40.

5. Bonnie J. Miller-McLemore, *Christian Theology in Practice: Discovering a Discipline* (Grand Rapids: Eerdmans, 2012), 46–69.

6. See Archie Smith Jr., *Navigating the Deep River: Spirituality in African American Families* (Cleveland: United Church Press, 1997); Edward Wimberly, *African American Pastoral Care and Counseling: The Politics of Oppression and Empowerment* (Cleveland: Pilgrim, 2006); and Lee Butler, *Liberating Our Dignity, Saving Our Souls* (St. Louis: Chalice, 2006).

7. Ryan LaMothe, *Care of Souls, Care of Polis: Toward a Political Pastoral Theology* (Eugene, OR: Cascade Books, 2017), 2–5.

8. Graham, *Transforming Practice,* 211.

9. Carlo DiClimente, "Natural Change and the Troublesome Use of Substances: A Life-Course Perspective," in William Miller and Kathleen Carroll, eds., *Rethinking Substance Abuse: What the Science Shows, and What We Should Do about It* (New York: Guilford Press, 2010), 81–96.

10. Groups not connected to the AA/NA program, including unofficial coalitions of women in recovery, and in a local treatment center, where I serve as a volunteer chaplain.

Chapter 1

1. For an account of relational perspectives in pastoral counseling, see Barbara J. McClure, *Moving Beyond Individualism in Pastoral Care and Counseling: Reflections on Theory, Theology, and Practice* (Eugene, OR: Cascade Books, 2009).

2. Christopher H. Cook, *Alcohol, Addiction and Christian Ethics* (Cambridge, UK: Cambridge University Press, 2008), 42–43.

3. Augustine, *The Confessions: Saint Augustine of Hippo*, trans. Maria Boulding, ed. David Vincent Meconi (San Francisco: Ignatius Press, 2012), VI.ii.2; 131. For Augustine's account of his mother's progress into wine drinking, see *Confessions* IX.viii.18; 245–46.

4. Thomas Aquinas, "Of Drunkenness," in *Summa Theologica* II–II, Q. 150, trans. Fathers of the English Dominican Province (New York: Christian Classics, 1981), 1793–96.

5. Cook, *Alcohol, Addiction and Christian Ethics*, 67.

6. Martin Luther, "Princes Who Are an Example to Their Subjects," No. 3514 in *Table Talk*, ed. and trans. Theodore Tappert, *Luther's Works*, vol. 54, (Minneapolis: Fortress, 1967), 218.

7. Martin Luther, "Drunkenness as a Common Vice of Germans," No. 4917 in *Table Talk*, 371.

8. *Geneva Catechism, or Instruction on the Christian Religion: Prepared by the Pastors of Geneva for the Use of the Swiss and French Protestant Churches*, 1814 new trans. ed. (London: Sherwood, Neely, and Jones, 1815), 191.

9. Augustine, *Confessions* I.i.1, 3.

10. John Calvin, *Catechism of Geneva, Being a Form of Instruction for Children*, 1.1, Center for Reformed Theology and Apologetics, accessed May 24, 2018, http://www.reformed.org/documents/calvin/geneva_catachism/geneva_catachism.html.

11. *Westminster Shorter Catechi*sm, Westminster Assembly 1643–1652, Center for Reformed Theology and Apologetics, accessed May 24, 2018, http://www.reformed.org/documents/wsc/index.html?_top=http://www.reformed.org/documents/WSC_frames.html.

12. Mark H. Moore and Dean R. Gerstein, *Alcohol and Public Policy: Beyond the Shadow of Prohibition*, National Research Council (US) Panel on Alternative Policies Affecting the Prevention of Alcohol Abuse and Alcoholism (Washington, DC: National Academies Press, 1981), https://www.ncbi.nlm.nih.gov/books/NBK216414/.

13.Lyman Beecher, *Six Sermons On The Nature, Occasions, Signs, Evils, and Remedy of Intemperance*, tenth edition (New York: American Tract Society, 1833), 52.

14. Beecher, *Six Sermons*, 57.

15. Jason Lantzer, *"Prohibition Is Here to Stay": The Reverend Edward S. Shumaker and the Dry Crusade in America* (Notre Dame, IN: University of Notre Dame Press, 2009), 98–104.

16. Joseph Locke, *Making the Bible Belt: Texas Prohibitionists and the Politicization of Southern Religion* (Oxford: Oxford University Press, 2017), 136.

17. Marvin D. Seppala and Mark E. Rose, *Prescription Painkillers: History, Pharmacology, and Treatment* (Center City, MN: Hazelden, 2011), 24.

18. David T. Courtwright, *Dark Paradise: A History of Opiate Addiction in America*, en-

larged ed. (Cambridge, MA: Harvard University Press, 2001), 76. Opium dens were gathering places for buying and smoking opium.

19. Edward Marshall, "Uncle Sam Is the Worst Drug Fiend in the World," *New York Times*, March 12, 1911, 1–9. http://www.druglibrary.net/schaffer/History/e1910/worstfiend.htm.

20. Courtwright, *Dark Paradise*, 104.

21. Johan Hari, *Chasing the Scream: The First and Last Days of the War on Drugs* (New York: Bloomsbury USA, 2015), 18. Harry Anslinger was appointed by Herbert Hoover to be the first director of the Federal Bureau of Narcotics, and served from 1930 until 1962.

22. Dan Baum, "Legalize It All," *Harper's Magazine*, April 2016, https://harpers.org/archive/2016/04/legalize-it-all/.

23. Michelle Alexander, *The New Jim Crow: Mass Incarceration in the Age of Colorblindness* (New York: The New Press, 2012), 95-133.

24. Bruce Western, *Punishment and Inequality in America* (New York: Russell Sage Foundation, 2006), 44.

25. Marie Gottschalk, *Caught: The Prison State and the Lockdown of American Politics* (Princeton, NJ: Princeton University Press, 2014), 4.

26. William L. White, *Slaying the Dragon: The History of Addiction Treatment and Recovery in America*, 2nd ed. (Bloomington, IL: Chestnut Health Systems, 2014), 3.

27. White, *Slaying the Dragon*, 63.

28. Sarah W. Tracy, "Medicalizing Alcoholism One Hundred Years Ago," *Harvard Review of Psychiatry* 15, no. 2 (April 3, 2007): 86–91, doi:10.1080/10673220701307562.

29. Charles Terry and Mildred Pellens, *The Opium Problem* (Camden, NJ: Haddon Craftsmen, 1928), 517–628.

30. Anonymous, *The Big Book of Alcoholics Anonymous*, 4th ed. (New York: Alcoholics Anonymous World Services, Inc., 2001), xxvi.

31. Humberto Fernandez and Theresa Libby, *Heroin: Its History, Pharmacology, and Treatment*, 2nd ed. (Minneapolis: Hazelden, 2011), 28.

32. Substance Abuse and Mental Health Services Administration Center for Substance Abuse Treatment, "Detoxification and Substance Abuse Treatment, Treatment Improvement Protocol (TIP) Series, No. 45," HHS Publication No. (SMA) 15-4131 (Rockville, MD: Center for Substance Abuse Treatment, 2006), xv–xix.

33. Jared Leone, "Read: Full Transcript of Trump's Rally Speech in Florida," *Palm Beach Post*, February 18, 2017, http://www.palmbeachpost.com/news/national/read-full-transcript-trump-rally-speech-florida/DeDCpoNEKLQmWcIKndWBoM/.

34. Marc Lewis, *The Biology of Desire: Why Addiction Is Not a Disease* (New York: Public Affairs, 2015), 1–26.

35. Coral E. Gartner, Adrian Carter, and Brad Partridge, "What Are the Public Policy Implications of a Neurobiological View of Addiction?" *Addiction* 107, no. 7 (July 2012): 1199–1200, http://doi.org/10.1111/j.1360-0443.2012.03812.x.

36. Howard J. Clinebell, *Understanding and Counseling Persons with Alcohol, Drug, and Behavioral Addictions*, revised and enlarged ed. (Nashville: Abingdon, 1998), 287–91.

37. National Institute on Drug Abuse, "Opioid Overdose Crisis," National Institute on Drug Abuse, February 2018, https://www.drugabuse.gov/drugs-abuse/opioids/opioid-overdose-crisis#nine.

38. Centers for Disease Control and Prevention, "Prescription Painkiller Overdoses in

the US," *CDC Vital Signs,* November 2011, https://www.cdc.gov/VitalSigns/PainkillerOverdoses/index.html.

39. George Unick et al., "The Relationship between US Heroin Market Dynamics and Heroin-Related Overdose, 1992-2008," *Addiction* 109, no. 11 (November 2014): 1889–98, doi:10.1111/add.12664.

40. Colleen Walsh, "Rising Threat: Death by Fentanyl," *Harvard Gazette,* June 2017, http://news.harvard.edu/gazette/story/2017/06/mass-general-hospital-addiction-specialist-explains-fentanyl-threat/.

41. Marvin D. Seppala and Mark E. Rose. *Prescription Painkillers: History, Pharmacology, and Treatment* (Center City, MN: Hazelden, 2011), 11.

42. US Department of Justice Drug Enforcement Administration, "2015 National Drug Threat Assessment Summary," DEA Strategic Intelligence Section, October 2015, https://www.dea.gov/docs/2015%20NDTA%20Report.pdf.

43. See, e.g., Sam Quinones, *Dreamland: The True Tale of America's Opiate Epidemic* (New York: Bloomsbury Press, 2015).

44. See, e.g., Andre Cohen, "How White Users Made Heroin a Public Health Problem," *Atlantic,* August 12, 2015, https://www.theatlantic.com/politics/archive/2015/08/crack-heroin-and-race/401015/.

45. Katharine Seelye, "In Heroin Crisis, White Families Seek Gentler War on Drugs," *New York Times,* October 30, 2015, https://www.nytimes.com/2015/10/31/us/heroin-war-on-drugs-parents.html.

46. Naomi I. Eisenberger, "The Neural Basis of Social Pain: Findings and Implications," in Geoff MacDonald and Lauri A. Jensen-Campbell, eds., *Social Pain: Neuropsychological and Health Implications of Loss and Exclusion* (Washington, DC: The American Psychological Association, 2011), 53–78.

47. Naomi I. Eisenberger, "The Pain of Social Disconnection: Examining the Shared Neural Underpinnings of Physical and Social Pain," *Nature Reviews Neuroscience* 13, no. 6 (June 2012): 421–34, doi:10.1038/nrn3231.

48. William R. Miller, Alyssa Forcehimes, and Allen Zweben, *Treating Addiction: A Guide for Professionals* (New York: Guilford Press, 2011), 23-28.

49. Markus Heilig, *The Thirteenth Step: Addiction in the Age of Brain Science* (New York: Columbia University Press, 2015), 147.

50. Warren Bickel and Marc Potenza, "The Forest and the Trees: Addiction as a Complex Self-Organizing System," in William Miller and Kathleen Carroll, eds., *Rethinking Substance Abuse: What the Science Schows and What We Should Do about It,* (New York: Guilford, 2010), 15.

51. National Institute on Alcohol Abuse and Alcoholism, "Alcohol Use Disorder: A Comparison Between DSM–IV and DSM–V," NIH Publication No. 13–7999 (November 2013): 1–2, https://pubs.niaaa.nih.gov/publications/dsmfactsheet/dsmfact.pdf.

52. Mild withdrawal from alcohol would be like a hangover: feeling shaky or nauseous, feeling withdrawn or irritable, and having difficulty focusing or processing new information. Withdrawal syndrome from prolonged and heavy alcohol use, traditionally called delirium tremens, is much more dangerous: Stage One includes tremors, rapid heartbeat, heavy sweating, loss of appetite, and insomnia: Stage Two includes auditory, visual, and tactile hallucinations; Stage Three includes delusions, disorientation, and delirium; Stage Four includes seizures. Detoxification from chronic alcohol abuse is best attempted under medical supervision. See

Carl Hart and Charles Ksir, *Drugs, Society, and Human Behavior*, 14th ed. (New York: McGraw-Hill Education, 2010), 223.

53. Cornelius Plantinga Jr., *Not the Way It's Supposed to Be: A Breviary of Sin* (Grand Rapids: Eerdmans, 1995), 148.

54. Terry D. Cooper, *Sin, Pride and Self-Acceptance: The Problem of Identity in Theology and Psychology* (Westmont, IL: IVP Academic, 2009), 65.

55. Gerald G. May, *Addiction and Grace: Love and Spirituality in the Healing of Addictions* (San Francisco: HarperOne, 2007).

56. James B. Nelson, *Thirst: God and the Alcoholic Experience* (Louisville: Westminster John Knox, 2004).

57. Nelson, *Thirst*, 28.

Chapter 2

1. Drunkenness is, like many issues in the Bible, primarily constructed around discourses related to men. Drunkenness has a definite social valence related to male roles and responsibilities as warriors, patriarchs of the household, and leaders in the community. It is also nuanced around the masculine value of self-control. But Titus does include women in that Epistle's advice against drunkenness.

2. Not everyone has a textbook development from hedonic recreational use to the compulsive stage of addiction. For some people, the fall into binge using or addiction seems immediate and compulsive, while for others, it might be considered "subclinical" (not scoring on the DSM-V symptom list but still using heavily) for most of their lives. One's trajectory can depend on genetic makeup and temperament, as well as the personal and social stressors that we will be addressing in the next two chapters. But ultimately an addiction is the progression into a binge-withdrawal-craving loop, seeking out more substances to solve the problem the substances cause.

3. Dan L. Longo et al., "Neurobiologic Advances from the Brain Disease Model of Addiction," *The New England Journal of Medicine* 374, no. 4 (January 28, 2016): 363–71, http://search.proquest.com/docview/1761134089/abstract/406E75E6935A4B09PQ/1.

4. George F. Koob and M. Le Moal, "Plasticity of Reward Neurocircuitry and the 'Dark Side' of Drug Addiction," *Nature Neuroscience* 8, no. 11 (2005): 1442–44, http://doi.org/10.1038/nn1105-1442.

5. George F. Koob, "The Neurobiology of Addiction: A Neuroadaptational View Relevant for Diagnosis," *Addiction* 101 (September 2, 2006): 23–30, doi:10.1111/j.1360-0443.2006.01586.x.

6. Koob and Le Moal, "Plasticity of Reward Neurocircuitry," 1443.

7. I am using cocaine in my second example to vary my substances between the liquid and dry, legal and illegal variety; but let me emphasize that both alcohol and cocaine are drugs. It is possible to be a recreational user of cocaine, just as one can use alcohol recreationally. By using both examples, I wish to emphasize that alcohol use is not as different from drug use as we might imagine. Both can become an addiction.

8. Omar Manejwala, *Craving: Why We Can't Seem to Get Enough* (Center City, MN: Hazelden, 2013), 49.

9. Michael Kuhar, *The Addicted Brain: Why We Abuse Drugs, Alcohol, and Nicotine* (Upper Saddle River, NJ: FT Press, 2015), 43.

10. Kuhar, *The Addicted Brain,* 146.

11. Longo et al., "Neurobiologic Advances," 363–71.

12. This is one of the many sayings passed on in AA/NA meetings.

13. This evolutionarily older portion is often called the "primitive" side of our brain, but I am trying to avoid the way that the term "primitive" has historically connoted the inferior or the under-developed. There is nothing inferior about this part of the brain. By using the term "instinctual," I am emphasizing that this part of the brain functions largely outside of conscious awareness. I understand that it is a stretch of the term, as the old neighborhood of our brain holds both our instinctual drives (such as sex, attachment, aggression) and also conditioned responses that are learned over time, such as addiction or trauma reactions. Yet, as a descriptor, "instinctual" better captures the split-second, automatic, nonconscious aspect of the old brain's functioning.

14. Warren Bickel and Marc Potenza, "The Forest and the Trees: Addiction as a Complex Self-Organizing System," in William Miller and Kathleen Carroll, eds., *Rethinking Substance Abuse: What the Science Shows and What We Should Do about It,* (New York: Guilfor,2010), 10.

15. The orbital medial prefrontal cortex is the first neighborhood next to the instinctual brain, and it is a mediating figure between the limbic system and the cerebral cortex. For a simple review of the cortex, see Louis Cozolino, *The Neuroscience of Human Relationships: Attachment and the Developing Social Brain* (New York: Norton, 2006), 54–56.

16. George Fein and Valerie A. Cardenas, "Neuroplasticity in Human Alcoholism," *Alcohol Research: Current Reviews* 37, no. 1 (2015): 125–41.

17. Charles Dackis and Charles O'Brien, "Neurobiology of Addiction: Treatment and Public Policy Ramifications," *Nature Neuroscience* 8, no. 11 (2005): 1431–36, http://doi.org/10.1038/nn1105-1431.

18. Atika Khurana et al., "Working Memory Ability Predicts Trajectories of Early Alcohol Use in Adolescents: The Mediational Role of Impulsivity," *Addiction* 108, no. 3 (2013): 506–15, http://doi.org/10.1111/add.12001.

19. Seo Dongju and Rajita Sinha, "Neuroplasticity and Predictors of Alcohol Recovery," *Alcohol Research: Current Reviews* 37, no. 1 (2015): 143-52.

20. Abigail M. Polter and Julie A. Kauer, "Stress and VTA Synapses: Implications for Addiction and Depression," *European Journal of Neuroscience* 39, no. 7 (April 2014): 1179–88. https://doi.org/10.1111/ejn.12490.

21. Markus Heilig, *The Thirteenth Step: Addiction in the Age of Brain Science* (New York: Columbia University Press, 2015), 68.

22. Longo et al., "Neurobiologic Advances," 363–71.

23. Manejwala, *Craving,* 52.

24. US Department of Health and Human Services (HHS), Office of the Surgeon General, "Neurobiology" in *Facing Addiction in America: The Surgeon General's Report on Alcohol, Drugs, and Health* (Washington, DC: HHS, November 2016), 2.

25. Manejwala, *Craving,* 63–65.

26. Marian L. Logrip, George F. Koob, and Eric P. Zorrilla, "Role of Corticotropin-Releasing Factor in Drug Addiction," *CNS Drugs* 25, no. 4 (April 2011): 271–87, doi: 10.2165/11587790-000000000-00000.

27. Koob, "The Neurobiology of Addiction," 24.

28. Heilig, *The Thirteenth Step,* 127.

29. Kenneth Paul Rosenberg, Patrick Carnes, and Suzanne O'Connor, "Evaluation and

Treatment of Sex Addiction," *Journal of Sex and Marital Therapy* 40, no. 2 (April 3, 2014): 77–91, https://doi.org/10.1080/0092623X.2012.701268.

30. Donald Hilton, Stefanie Carnes, and Todd Love, "Neurobiology of Behavioral Addictions: Sexual Addiction," in Alan Swann, F. Gerard Moeller, and Marijn Lijffijt, eds., *Neurobiology of Addiction* (Oxford: Oxford University Press, 2016), 179.

31. Bonnie Phillips, Raju Hajela, and Donald L. Hilton Jr., "Sex Addiction as a Disease: Evidence for Assessment, Diagnosis, and Response to Critics," *Sexual Addiction and Compulsivity* 22, no. 2 (April 2015): 167–92, https://doi.org/10.1080/10720162.2015.1036184.

32. Gary Wilson, *Your Brain on Porn: Internet Pornography and the Emerging Science of Addiction* (Margate, Kent, UK: Commonwealth, 2014), 58–59.

33. Hilton, Carnes, and Love, "Neurobiology of Behavioral Addictions: Sexual Addiction," 183.

34. Robert Weiss, *Sex Addiction 101: A Basic Guide to Healing from Sex, Porn, and Love Addiction* (Deerfield Beach, FL: Health Communications), 10.

35. Doug Weiss, *Sex Addiction: 6 Types and Treatment*, Kindle Ed. (Anaheim, CA: Discovery Press, 2017), Loc 359.

36. Stefanie Carnes, "Sex Addiction: Neuroscience Etiology and Treatment," lecture, NAADAC Annual Conference, Denver, CO, September 25, 2017.

37. Alex Kwee, Amy Dominguez, and Donald Ferrell, "Sexual Addiction and Christian College Men: Conceptual, Assessment, and Research Challenges," *Journal of Psychiatry and Christianity* 26, no. 1 (2007): 3–13.

Chapter 3

1. Edward J. Khantzian, "The Self-Medication Hypothesis and Attachment Theory: Pathways for Understanding and Ameliorating Addictive Suffering," in Richard Gill, ed., *Addictions from an Attachment Perspective: Do Broken Bonds and Early Trauma Lead to Addictive Behaviours?* (London: Karnac Books, 2014), 34.

2. 12-step meetings are often mistaken for group-therapy meetings. While talking about childhood difficulties is honored, the culture usually limits sharing to how these issues affect one's sobriety so that others can learn how to stay sober in the midst of similar challenges. The speaker shared his story with the group in order to identify where he had come from, and then to highlight how sobriety enabled him "show up" to the challenges of life in the present. Recovering addicts in AA/NA who struggle with trauma histories are encouraged to find therapeutic support or trauma-informed outpatient addiction programs as an adjunct to the work of 12-step recovery.

3. Edward J. Khantzian, "Addiction as a Self-Regulation Disorder and the Role of Self-Medication," *Addiction* 108, no. 4 (April 2013): 668–69, doi:10.1111/add.12004. Khantzian's full theory is that addicts intuitively self-medicate psychiatric disorders or traumas with specific kinds of drugs that correspond to their condition, which has not been substantiated in later studies. But the larger framework is that addictions arise from efforts to manage distressing affective states and traumatic sequels, and many studies do explore this connection.

4. Khantzian, "The Self-Medication Hypothesis," 52.

5. Beatrice Beebe and Frank M. Lachmann, *The Origins of Attachment: Infant Research and Adult Treatment* (New York: Routledge, 2013), 44–52.

6. Allan N. Schore, *Affect Dysregulation and Disorders of the Self* (New York: Norton, 2003), 14.

7. John Bowlby, *A Secure Base: Parent-Child Attachment and Healthy Human Development*, reprint ed. (New York: Basic Books, 1988), 11.

8. Peter Fonagy et al., *Affect Regulation, Mentalization, and the Development of Self* (New York: Other Press, 2005), 54–59.

9. Low dopamine function, possibly developed through childhood neglect, is thought to lead to impulsive, compulsive, and addictive behaviors. See Kenneth Blum et al., "Reward Deficiency Syndrome: A Biogenetic Model for the Diagnosis and Treatment of Impulsive, Addictive, and Compulsive Behaviors," *Journal of Psychoactive Drugs* 32, Suppl. (2000): 1–112.

10. Fonagy et al., *Affect Regulation,* 130.

11. David Howe, *Attachment across the Lifecourse: A Brief Introduction* (New York: Palgrave Macmillan, 2011), 25.

12. Mary Sykes Wylie and Lynn Turner, "The Attuned Therapist: Does Attachment Theory Really Matter?" *Psychotherapy Networker* 35, no. 2 (March/April 2011), https://www2.psychotherapynetworker.org/magazine/recentissues/1261-the-attunded-therapist. I am indebted to my doctoral student Sarah Chae for this reference.

13. Howe, *Attachment across the Lifecourse,* 124.

14. Daniel Siegel, *The Developing Mind: How Relationships and the Brain Interact to Shape Who We Are*, 2nd ed. (New York: Guilford, 2015), 103.

15. Schore, *Affect Dysregulation and Disorders of the Self*, 29.

16. Beebe and Lachmann, *The Origins of Attachment*, 113.

17. Siegel, *The Developing Mind*, 101.

18. Siegel, *The Developing Mind*, 123.

19. Schore, *Affect Dysregulation and Disorders of the Self*, 38.

20. Howe, *Attachment across the Lifecourse*, 107.

21. Siegel, *The Developing Mind*, 134.

22. Philip J. Flores, *Addiction as an Attachment Disorder* (Lanham, MD: Jason Aronson, 2004), 140.

23. Beebe and Lachmann, *The Origins of Attachment*, 135.

24. Siegel, *The Developing Mind*, 111.

25. Flores, *Addiction as an Attachment Disorder*, 59.

26. Alex Zautra, John Stuart Hall, and Kate Murray, "Resilience: A New Definition of Health for People and Communities," in John Reich, Alex Zautra, John Hall, eds., *Handbook of Adult Resilience* (New York: Guilford Press, 2010), 3–34.

27. Ryan Mills et al., "Alcohol and Tobacco Use among Maltreated and Non-Maltreated Adolescents in a Birth Cohort," *Addiction* 109, no. 4 (April 2014): 672–80, doi:10.1111/add.12447.

28. Carolyn E. Sartor et al., "Childhood Sexual Abuse and Early Substance Use in Adolescent Girls: The Role of Familial Influences," *Addiction* 108, no. 5 (May 2013): 993–1000, doi:10.1111/add.12115.

29. Shane Darke and Michelle Torok, "The Association of Childhood Physical Abuse with the Onset and Extent of Drug Use among Regular Injecting Drug Users," *Addiction* 109, no. 4 (April 2014): 610–16, doi:10.1111/add.12428.

30. Shane Darke, "Pathways to Heroin Dependence: Time to Re-Appraise Self-Medication," *Addiction* 108, no. 4 (April 2013): 659–67, doi:10.1111/j.1360-0443.2012.04001.x.

31. Darke, "Pathways to Heroin Dependence," 660.

32. Chris Taplin et al., "Family History of Alcohol and Drug Abuse, Childhood Trauma, and Age of First Drug Injection," *Substance Use & Misuse* 49, no. 10 (August 2014): 1311–16, doi:10.3109/10826084.2014.901383.

33. Jon G. Allen, *Traumatic Relationships and Serious Mental Disorders* (New York: John Wiley and Sons, 2001), 18.

34. Jon G. Allen, *Coping with Trauma: Hope Through Understanding*, 2nd ed. (American Psychiatric Publishing, Inc., 2005), 207.

35. Matthew Friedman, *Post-Traumatic and Acute Stress Disorders: The Latest Assessment and Treatment Strategies* (Kansas City, MO: Compact Clinicals, 2006), 4–6.

36. Babette Rothschild, *The Body Remembers: The Psychophysiology of Trauma and Trauma Treatment* (New York: Norton, 2000), 65–73.

37. Bessel A. van der Kolk, "The Complexity of Adaptation to Trauma: Self-Regulation, Stimulus Discrimination, and Characterological Development," in Bessel A. van der Kolk, A. C. McFarlane, and L. Weisaeth, eds., *Traumatic Stress: The Effects of Overwhelming Experience on Mind, Body, and Society* (New York: Guilford, 1996), 182–213.

38. Schore, *Affect Dysregulation and Disorders of the Self*, 85.

39. L. Pani, A. Porcella, and G. L. Gessa, "The Role of Stress in the Pathophysiology of the Dopaminergic System," *Molecular Psychiatry* 5, no. 1 (January 2000): 14, doi:10.1038/sj.mp.4000589

40. Sophie Duranceau, Mathew G. Fetzner, and R. Nicholas Carleton, "Low Distress Tolerance and Hyperarousal Posttraumatic Stress Disorder Symptoms: A Pathway to Alcohol Use?" *Cognitive Therapy and Research* 38, no. 3 (June 2014): 280–90, doi: 10.1007/s10608-013-9591-7.

41. Dusty Miller, "Addictions and Trauma Recovery: An Integrated Approach," *Psychiatric Quarterly* 73, no. 2 (2002): 157.

42. Marina A. Bornovalova et al., "Extending Models of Deliberate Self-Harm and Suicide Attempts to Substance Users: Exploring the Roles of Childhood Abuse, Posttraumatic Stress, and Difficulties Controlling Impulsive Behavior When Distressed," *Psychological Trauma: Theory, Research, Practice, and Policy* 3, no. 4 (December 2011): 349–59, doi:10.1037/a0021579.

43. Bornovalova et al., "Extending Models of Deliberate Self-Harm," 349–59.

44. Allen, *Traumatic Relationships*, 106.

45. Gabor Maté, *In the Realm of Hungry Ghosts: Close Encounters with Addiction* (Berkeley, CA: North Atlantic Books, 2010), 36.

46. Lynn Greenwood, "Taking the Toys Away: Removing the Need for Self-harming Behavior," in Richard Gill, ed., *Addictions from an Attachment Perspective, Do Broken Bonds and Early Trauma Lead to Addictive Behaviors?* (London: Karnac Books, 2014), 69–93.

47. Flores, *Addiction as an Attachment Disorder*, 85.

48. National Eating Disorders Association, "Co-occurring Disorders and Special Issues," www.NationalEatingDisorders.org, accessed December 10, 2017, https://www.nationaleatingdisorders.org/learn/general-information/co-occurring-disorders-and-special-issues.

49. Academy of Eating Disorders, "Eating Disorders: A Guide to Medical Care," 3rd edition, AED Report 2016, https://higherlogicdownload.s3.amazonaws.com/AEDWEB/05656ea0-59c9-4dd4-b832-07a3fea58f4c/UploadedImages/Learn/AED-Medical-Care-Guidelines_English_02_28_17_NEW.pdf.

50. National Eating Disorders Association, "Trauma and Eating Disorders," www.Na

tionalEatingDisorders.org, accessed December 11, 2017, https://www.nationaleatingdisorders.org/sites/default/files/ResourceHandouts/TraumaandEatingDisorders.pdf.

51. Gregory L. Jantz and Ann Mcmurray, *Hope, Help, and Healing for Eating Disorders: A New Approach to Treating Anorexia, Bulimia, and Overeating* (Colorado Springs, CO: WaterBrook, 2010), 171–80.

52. To better understand the varied antecedents and dynamics of this mental health condition, see Harriet Brown, *Brave Girl Eating: A Family's Struggle with Anorexia* (New York: HarperCollins Publishers, 2011); Jenni Schaeffer, *Life Without Ed: How One Woman Declared Independence from Her Eating Disorder and How You Can Too*, anniversary ed. (McGraw-Hill Education, 2003); Becky Thompson, *A Hunger So Wide, So Deep: A Multi-Racial View of Women's Eating Problems* (Minneapolis: University of Minnesota Press, 1996).

53. Carolyn Costin, *The Eating Disorders Sourcebook: A Comprehensive Guide to the Causes, Treatments, and Prevention of Eating Disorders*, 3rd ed. (New York: McGraw-Hill, 2007), 75–79.

54. Carolyn Costin and Gwen Schubert Grabb, *8 Keys to Recovery from an Eating Disorder: Effective Strategies from Therapeutic Practice and Personal Experience* (New York: Norton, 2012), 95.

55. P. Scott Richards, *Spiritual Approaches in the Treatment of Women with Eating Disorders* (Washington, DC: American Psychological Association, 2007), 53–57.

56. See the many advice columns on early sobriety in Anonymous, *Living Sober* (New York: AA World Services, 2002).

57. Bessel van der Kolk, *The Body Keeps the Score: Brain, Mind, and Body in the Healing of Trauma* (New York: Viking Adult, 2014), 115.

58. Claudia Black, "Addiction and Trauma: The Complexity of Treating the Young Adult," keynote lecture, NAADAC Annual Conference, Denver, CO, September 23, 2017.

59. To start your education on the signs and symptoms of mood and personality disorders, see the National Alliance on Mental Illness website, "Mental Health Conditions," at https://www.nami.org/ and The National Institute of Mental Health website, "Mental Health Information," at https://www.nimh.nih.gov/health/topics/index.shtml. They offer accessible information on mood and personality conditions such as anxiety, depression, and bipolar disorders, eating disorders, borderline personality, ADHD, posttraumatic stress disorder, and also severe mental health challenges like psychosis and schizophrenia.

60. Shelly Rambo and Catherine Keller, *Spirit and Trauma: A Theology of Remaining* (Louisville: Westminster John Knox, 2011), 26.

61. Rambo and Keller, *Spirit and Trauma*, 76.

62. Rambo and Keller, *Spirit and Trauma*, 79.

Chapter 4

1. Nancy Boyd-Franklin, *Black Families in Therapy: Understanding the African American Experience*, 2nd ed. (New York: Guilford, 2006), 149.

2. Philip J. Flores, *Addiction as an Attachment Disorder* (Lanham, MD: Jason Aronson, 2004), 54.

3. Marijn Lijffijt, "Stress and Addiction," in Alan Swann, F. Gerard Moeller, and Marijn Lijffijt, eds., *Neurobiology of Addiction* (Oxford: Oxford University Press, 2016), 153.

4. Anthony D. Ong, Thomas Fuller-Rowell, and Anthony L. Burrow, "Racial Discrimina-

tion and the Stress Process," *Journal of Personality and Social Psychology* 96, no. 6 (June 2009): 1259–71, doi:10.1037/a0015335.

5. Alex L. Pieterse et al., "Perceived Racism and Mental Health among Black American Adults: A Meta-Analytic Review," *Journal of Counseling Psychology* 59, no. 1 (January 2012): 1–9, doi:10.1037/a0026208.

6. Robert T. Carter, "Race-Based Traumatic Stress," *Psychiatric Times* 23, no. 14 (December 2006): 37, http://www.psychiatrictimes.com/cultural-psychiatry/race-based-traumatic-stress/page/0/1.

7. Meifen Wei, Kenneth T. Wang, Puncky Paul Heppner, and Yi Du, "Ethnic and Mainstream Social Connectedness, Perceived Racial Discrimination, and Posttraumatic Stress Symptoms," *Journal of Counseling Psychology* 59, no. 3 (July 2012): 486–93, doi:10.1037/a0028000.

8. J. Scott Brown, Sarah O. Meadows, and Glen H. Elder Jr., "Race-Ethnic Inequality and Psychological Distress: Depressive Symptoms from Adolescence to Young Adulthood," *Developmental Psychology* 43, no. 6 (November 2007): 1295–1311, doi:10.1037/0012-1649.43.6.1295.

9. For a general review of the diverse connections between racism and substance use for African American and Hispanic youth, see: Yonette F. Thomas and LeShawndra N. Price, eds., *Drug Use Trajectories among Minority Youth* (New York: Springer, 2016).

10. Frederick X. Gibbons et al., "Prospecting Prejudice: An Examination of the Long-Term Effects of Perceived Racial Discrimination on the Health Behavior and Health Status of African Americans," in Thomas and Price, eds., *Drug Use Trajectories*, 199–232.

11. Kathy Sanders-Phillips et al., "Perceived Racial Discrimination, Drug Use, and Psychological Distress in African American Youth: A Pathway to Child Health Disparities," *Journal of Social Issues* 70, no. 2 (June 1, 2014): 279–97, https://doi.org/10.1111/josi.12060.

12. Dan Hauge, "The Trauma of Racism and the Distorted White Imagination," in Stephanie Areland and Shelly Rambo, eds., *Post Traumatic Public Theology* (Basingstoke, UK: Palgrave Macmillan, 2016), 89–114.

13. Gibbons et al., "Prospecting Prejudice," 213.

14. Ilan H. Meyer, "Prejudice, Social Stress, and Mental Health in Lesbian, Gay, and Bisexual Populations: Conceptual Issues and Research Evidence," *Psychological Bulletin* 129, no. 5 (September 2003): 674–97, doi:10.1037/0033-2909.129.5.674.

15. S. E. James et al., "Executive Summary of the Report of the 2015 US Transgender Survey" (Washington, DC: National Center for Transgender Equality, 2016), https://transequality.org/sites/default/files/docs/usts/USTS-Executive-Summary-Dec17.pdf.

16. Grace Medley et al., "Sexual Orientation and Estimates of Adult Substance Use and Mental Health: Results from the 2015 National Survey on Drug Use and Health," October 2016, https://www.samhsa.gov/data/sites/default/files/NSDUH-SexualOrientation-2015/NSDUH-SexualOrientation-2015/NSDUH-SexualOrientation-2015.htm#topofpage.

17. Ethan H. Mereish, Conall O'Cleirigh, and Judith B. Bradford, "Interrelationships between LGBT-based Victimization, Suicide, and Substance Use Problems in a Diverse Sample of Sexual and Gender Minorities," *Psychology, Health and Medicine* 19, no. 1 (January 2, 2014): 1–13, doi:10.1080/13548506.2013.780129.

18. Caitlin Ryan et al., "Family Rejection as a Predictor of Negative Health Outcomes in White and Latino Lesbian, Gay and Bisexual Young Adults," *Pediatrics* 123, no. 1 (2009): 346. Quoted in Cody Sanders, *A Brief Guide to Ministry with LGBTQIA Youth* (Louisville: Westminster John Knox, 2017), 104.

19. Elizabeth A. Schilling, Robert H. Aseltine Jr, and Susan Gore, "Adverse Childhood Experiences and Mental Health in Young Adults: A Longitudinal Survey," *BMC Public Health* 7, no. 1 (January 2007): 30–40, doi:10.1186/1471-2458-7-30.

20. John A. Rich and Courtney M. Grey, "Pathways to Recurrent Trauma Among Young Black Men: Traumatic Stress, Substance Use, and the 'Code of the Street,'" *American Journal of Public Health* 95, no. 5 (May 2005): 816–24, doi:10.2105/AJPH.2004.044560.

21. Kerstin Pahl, Judith S. Brook, and Jung Yeon Lee, "Joint Trajectories of Victimization and Marijuana Use and Their Health Consequences among Urban African American and Puerto Rican Young Men," *Journal of Behavioral Medicine* 36, no. 3 (June 2013): 305–14, doi:10.1007/s10865-012-9425-1.

22. Sari L. Reisner et al., "Sexual Orientation Disparities in Substance Misuse: The Role of Childhood Abuse and Intimate Partner Violence Among Patients in Care at an Urban Community Health Center," *Substance Use and Misuse* 48, no. 3 (February 12, 2013): 274–89, doi:10.3109/10826084.2012.755702.

23. Michael Ungar, ed., *Handbook for Working with Children and Youth: Pathways to Resilience across Cultures and Contexts* (Thousand Oaks, CA: Sage Publications, 2005), 6–7.

24. Frederick X. Gibbons et al., "Exploring the Link between Racial Discrimination and Substance Use: What Mediates? What Buffers?" *Journal of Personality and Social Psychology* 99, no. 5 (November 2010): 785–801, doi:10.1037/a0019880.

25. John M. Wallace et al., "Race/Ethnicity, Religiosity and Differences and Similarities in American Adolescents' Substance Use," in Thomas and Price, eds., *Drug Use Trajectories*, 105–21.

26. Robert T. Carter et al., "Race-Based Traumatic Stress, Racial Identity Statuses, and Psychological Functioning: An Exploratory Investigation," *Professional Psychology: Research and Practice* 48, no. 1 (February 2017): 30–37, doi:10.1037/pro0000116.

27. Thomas E. Fuller-Rowell et al., "Racial Discrimination and Substance Use: Longitudinal Associations and Identity Moderators," *Journal of Behavioral Medicine* 35, no. 6 (December 2012): 581–90, doi:10.1007/s10865-011-9388-7.

28. Tiffany Yip, Gilbert C. Gee, and David T. Takeuchi, "Racial Discrimination and Psychological Distress: The Impact of Ethnic Identity and Age among Immigrant and United States-Born Asian Adults," *Developmental Psychology* 44, no. 3 (May 2008): 787–800, doi:10.1037/0012-1649.44.3.787.

29. Gibbons et al., "Prospecting Prejudice," 200–202.

30. Substance Abuse and Mental Health Services Administration, Center for Behavioral Health Statistics and Quality, "Treatment Episode Data Set (TEDS): 2005-2015, National Admissions to Substance Abuse Treatment Services," BHSIS Series S-91, HHS Publication No. (SMA) 17-5037 (Rockville, MD: Substance Abuse and Mental Health Services Administration, 2017), https://www.samhsa.gov/data/sites/default/files/2015%20TEDS%20National%20Admissions.pdf.

31. Lloyd D. Johnston et al., "Demographic Subgroup Trends among Adolescents in the Use of Various Licit and Illicit Drugs, 1975–2016," Monitoring the Future Occasional Paper No. 88 (Ann Arbor: Institute for Social Research, The University of Michigan, 2017), http://www.monitoringthefuture.org/pubs/occpapers/mtf-occ88.pdf.

32. Josefina Alvarez et al., "Substance Abuse Prevalence and Treatment among Latinos and Latinas," *Journal of Ethnicity in Substance Abuse* 6, no. 2 (2007): 115–41.

33. Jorge Delva et al., "Agenda for Longitudinal Research and Substance Use and Abuse

with Hispanics in the U.S. and with Latin American Populations," in Thomas and Price, eds., *Drug Use Trajectories*, 63–83.

34. Louis Alvarez and Pedro Ruiz, "Substance Abuse in the Mexican American Population," in Shulamith Lala Ashenberg Straussner, ed., *Ethnocultural Factors in Substance Abuse Treatment* (New York: Guilford, 2001), 122.

35. See Ruth McNair et al., "A Model for Lesbian, Bisexual and Queer-Related Influences on Alcohol Consumption and Implications for Policy and Practice," *Culture, Health and Sexuality* 18, no. 4 (April 2016): 405–21, https://doi.org/10.1080/13691058.2015.1089602; see also Karen Trocki and Laurie Drabble, "Bar Patronage and Motivational Predictors of Drinking in the San Francisco Bay Area: Gender and Sexual Identity Differences," *Journal of Psychoactive Drugs* (November 2, 2008): 345–56.

36. Substance Abuse and Mental Health Services Administration, Center for Substance Abuse Treatment, "A Provider's Introduction to Substance Abuse Treatment for Lesbian, Gay, Bisexual, and Transgender Individuals," HHS Publication No. (SMA) 12–4104 (Rockville, MD: Substance Abuse and Mental Health Services Administration, 2012), http://store.samhsa.gov/shin/content//SMA12-4104/SMA12-4104.pdf.

37. Connie R. Matthews, Peggy Lorah, and Jaime Fenton, "Treatment Experiences of Gays and Lesbians in Recovery from Addiction: A Qualitative Inquiry," *Journal of Mental Health Counseling* 28, no. 2 (April 2006): 111–32.

38. Urban Ministries of Durham, accessed March 21, 2017, http://playspent.org/. I would also encourage you to consider: http://www.gamesforchange.org/games/.

39. Jasmine Tucker and Caitlin Lowel, "National Snapshot: Poverty Among Women and Families, 2015," Data on Poverty and Income, National Women's Law Center, September 14, 2016, https://nwlc.org/resources/national-snapshot-poverty-among-women-families-2015/.

40. Leonard I. Pearlin et al., "Stress, Health, and the Life Course: Some Conceptual Perspectives," *Journal of Health and Social Behavior* 46, no. 2 (June 2005): 205–19, doi: 192.231.177.99.

41. Pearlin et al, "Stress, Health, and the Life Course," 206.

42. Racial discrimination is connected to distinct patterns of cortisol release, which suggests a dysregulated stress system. See Maximus Berger and Zoltán Sarnyai, "'More than Skin Deep': Stress Neurobiology and Mental Health Consequences of Racial Discrimination," *Stress: The International Journal on the Biology of Stress* 18, no. 1 (January 2015): 1–10, doi:10.3109/10253890.2014.989204.

43. Bernadette D. Proctor, Kayla R. Fontenot, and Melissa A. Kollar, "Income and Poverty in the United States: 2015. United Census Bureau," accessed July 31, 2017, https://www.census.gov/content/dam/Census/library/publications/2016/demo/p60-256.pdf.

44. For a primer on global market capitalism, see William Robinson, "Understanding Global Capitalism," Discussion Paper CSGP D2/08 (Peterborough, ON: Trent University, January 25, 2008), http://www.soc.ucsb.edu/faculty/robinson/Assets/pdf/understandingglobalcapitalism.pdf.

45. US Department of Education, National Center for Education Statistics, "Employment and Unemployment Rates by Educational Attainment," The Condition of Education, NCES 2017-144, last updated April 2016, https://nces.ed.gov/fastfacts/display.asp?id=561.

46. Anthony Cilluffo, "5 Facts About Student Loans," Pew Research Center, August 24, 2017, http://www.pewresearch.org/fact-tank/2017/08/24/5-facts-about-student-loans/.

47. Catherine E. Ross and John Mirowsky, "Social Structure and Psychological Func-

tioning Distress, Perceived Control, and Trust," in John DeLamater, ed., *Handbook of Social Psychology,* 3rd ed. (New York : Kluwer Academic/Plenum Publishers, 2003), 411–47.

48. See Sam Quinones, *Dreamland: The True Tale of America's Opiate Epidemic* (New York: Bloomsbury, 2015); see also Nick Reding, *Methland: The Death and Life of an American Small Town*, reprint ed. (New York: Bloomsbury, 2010).

49. Peggy A. Thoits, "Stress and Health: Major Findings and Policy Implications," *Journal of Health and Social Behavior* 51, no. 1, suppl. (March 2010): S41–53, doi:http://dx.doi.org/10.1177/0022146510383499.

50. Rudolf Moos, "Social Contexts and Substance Abuse," in William Miller and Kathleen Carroll, eds., *Rethinking Substance Abuse: What the Science Shows, And What We Should Do about It* (New York: Guilford, 2010), 195.

51. Kimberly A. Tenorio and Celia C. Lo, "Social Location, Social Integration, and the Co-Occurrence of Substance Abuse and Psychological Distress," *American Journal of Drug and Alcohol Abuse* 37, no. 4 (July 2011): 218–23, https://doi.org/10.3109/00952990.2011.568079.

52. Robin Room, "Stigma, Social Inequality and Alcohol and Drug Use," *Drug and Alcohol Review* 24, no. 2 (March 2005): 143–55, doi:10.1080/09595230500102434.

53. Ryan LaMothe, "Neoliberal Capitalism and the Corruption of Society: A Pastoral Political Analysis," *Pastoral Psychology* 65, no. 1 (February 2016): 5–21, https://doi.org/10.1007/s11089-013-0577-x.

54. LaMothe, "Neoliberal Capitalism," 20.

55. Bruce Alexander, *The Globalization of Addiction: A Study in Poverty of the Spirit* (New York: Oxford University Press, 2010), 57–84.

56. Alexander, *The Globalization of Addiction*, 60.

57. Gene M. Heyman, "Addiction and Choice: Theory and New Data," *Frontiers in Psychiatry* 4 (May 6, 2013), doi:10.3389/fpsyt.2013.00031.

58. Michelle Alexander, *The New Jim Crow: Mass Incarceration in the Age of Colorblindness* (New York: The New Press, 2012), 95–33.

59. Pew Research Center, "Chapter 3: Demographic and Economic Data, by Race," in *King's Dream Remains an Elusive Goal: Many Americans See Racial Disparities,* Report from Social and Demographic Trends Project, August 22, 2013, http://www.pewsocialtrends.org/2013/08/22/chapter-3-demographic-economic-data-by-race/#incarceration.

60. Christopher Ingraham, "Charting the Shocking Rise of Racial Disparity in Our Criminal Justice System," *Washington Post*, July 15, 2014, https://www.washingtonpost.com/news/wonk/wp/2014/07/15/charting-the-shocking-rise-of-racial-disparity-in-our-criminal-justice-system/?utm_term=.441055bbb87a.

61. Marie Gottschalk, *Caught: The Prison State and the Lockdown of American Politics* (Princeton, NJ: Princeton University Press, 2014), 259.

62. Marie VanNostrand, *New Jersey Jail Population Analysis: Identifying Solutions to Safely and Responsibly Reduce the Jail Population,* Luminosity and the Drug Policy Alliance, March 2013, https://www.drugpolicy.org/sites/default/files/New_Jersey_Jail_Population_Analysis_March_2013.pdf.

63. Bruce Western, *Punishment and Inequality in America* (New York: Russell Sage Foundation, 2006), 76.

64. Ages twenty to twenty-four, 26% incarceration versus 19% employment. Rates were comparable for African American men in their late twenties with no high school diploma. See George Gao, "Chart of the Week: The Black-White Gap in Incarceration Rates,"

Pew Research Center, July 18, 2014, http://www.pewresearch.org/fact-tank/2014/07/18/chart-of-the-week-the-black-white-gap-in-incarceration-rates/.

65. Gottschalk, *Caught*, 129.

66. Gottschalk *Caught*, 1.

67. Gottschalk, *Caught*, 135.

68. Gottschalk, *Caught*, 6.

69. ACLU-NJ, "Report Reveals Deep Racial Disparities in NJ Marijuana Arrests," June 15, 2017, https://www.aclu-nj.org/news/2017/06/15/aclu-nj-report-reveals-deep-racial-disparities-nj-marijuana.

70. Harry G. Levine, Jon B. Gettman, and Loren Siegel, "Arresting Blacks for Marijuana in California," *The Drug Policy Alliance*, October 2010, https://www.drugpolicy.org/sites/default/files/ArrestingBlacks.pdf.

71. Alexander, *The New Jim Crow*, 96.

72. For more information on prison reform and advocacy against the war on drugs, see the Drug Policy Alliance: http://www.drugpolicy.org/about-us/about-drug-policy-alliance. The NAADAC, the Association of Addiction Professionals, can send advocacy alerts directly to your inbox, at https://www.naadac.org/. For health care, see the American Public Health Association: https://www.apha.org/policies-and-advocacy/advocacy-for-public-health.

73. The Marshall Project, "Death in Police Custody: A Curated Collection of Links," accessed November 22, 2017, https://www.themarshallproject.org/records/543-death-in-police-custody.

74. See Lee H. Butler, *Liberating Our Dignity, Saving Our Souls: A New Theory of African American Identity Formation* (St. Louis: Chalice, 2006); Kelly Brown Douglas, *Stand Your Ground: Black Bodies and the Justice of God* (Maryknoll, NY: Orbis, 2015); and James H. Cone, *The Cross and the Lynching Tree* (Maryknoll, NY: Orbis Books, 2013).

75. Keith Bedford, "Read a transcript of Trump's remarks in N.H.," *Boston Globe*, March 19, 2018, https://www.bostonglobe.com/news/politics/2018/03/19/read-transcript-trump-remarks/6Iie27RlDkc1VgtIZvUBfL/story.html

76. Philip Browning Helsel, *Pastoral Power Beyond Psychology's Marginalization: Resisting the Discourses of the Psy-Complex* (New York: Palgrave Macmillan, 2015), 77.

77. Helsel, *Pastoral Power*, 41.

78. Gary Enos, "Programs Face Hurdles in Knowledge and Client Safety in LGBTQ Care," *Alcoholism and Drug Abuse Weekly* 28, no. 18 (May 2, 2016): 1–7, https://doi.org/10.1002/adaw.30558.

79. Deniece Reid, "Addiction, African Americans, and a Christian Recovery Journey," in Jo-ann Krestan, ed., *Bridges to Recovery: Addiction, Family Therapy, and Multicultural Treatment* (New York: Free Press, 2000), 145–72.

80. Substance Abuse and Mental Health Services Administration, "Enhancing Motivation for Change in Substance Abuse Treatment, Treatment Improvement Protocol (TIP) Series, No. 45," HHS Publication No. (SMA) 13-4212 (Rockville, MD: Substance Abuse and Mental Health Services Administration, 2013), 3, https://store.samhsa.gov/shin/content/SMA13-4212/SMA13-4212.pdf.

81. See Mark Lewis Taylor, *The Executed God: The Way of the Cross in Lockdown America*, 2nd ed. (Minneapolis: Fortress, 2015). Taylor describes lockdown America as the combination of police violence and surveillance practices, mass incarceration, and the death penalty. It is part of a broader network of socioeconomic and political oppression.

Chapter 5

1. Joel Marcus, *Mark 1–8: A New Translation with Introduction and Commentary* (New York: Anchor Bible, 2002), 336.

2. Marcus, *Mark 1–8*, 350.

3. Douglas W. Geyer, *Fear, Anomaly, and Uncertainty in the Gospel of Mark* (Lanham, MD: Scarecrow Press, 2001), 128.

4. Dr. Clifton Black, personal communication with the author; see also Black's delightful commentary *Mark,* Abingdon New Testament Commentary Series (Nashville: Abingdon, 2011).

5. Marcus, *Mark 1–8,* 344.

6. Camille Focant, *The Gospel According to Mark: A Commentary*, trans. L. R. Keylock (Eugene, OR: Wipf and Stock, 2012), 204.

7. Hans Leander, *Discourses of Empire: The Gospel of Mark from a Postcolonial Perspective* (Atlanta: Society of Biblical Literature, 2015), 206.

8. Geyer, *Fear, Anomaly,* 136.

9. Leander, *Discourses of Empire,* 203.

10. Paul Hollenbach, "Jesus, Demoniacs, and Public Authorities: A Socio-Historical Study," *Journal of the American Academy of Religion* 49, no. 4 (1981): 567–88, http://www.jstor.org/stable/1462450.

11. Frantz Fanon, *The Wretched of the Earth*, trans. R. Philcox, reprint ed. (New York: Grove, 2005), 182.

12. Ched Myers, *Binding the Strong Man: A Political Reading of Mark's Story of Jesus*, 20th anniversary ed. (Maryknoll, NY: Orbis, 2008), 191.

13. Robert T. Carter et al., "Initial Development of the Race-Based Traumatic Stress Symptom Scale: Assessing the Emotional Impact of Racism," *Psychological Trauma: Theory, Research, Practice, and Policy* 5, no. 1 (January 2013): 1–9, https://doi.org/10.1037/a0025911.

14. R. Alan Culpepper, *Mark,* Vol. 20 of Smyth and Helwys Bible Commentary (Macon, GA: Smyth and Helwys, 2007), 165.

15. Richard Sugg, *The Secret History of the Soul: Physiology, Magic and Spirit Forces from Homer to St Paul* (Newcastle upon Tyne: Cambridge Scholars Publishing, 2013), 224.

16. Michelle Alexander, *The New Jim Crow: Mass Incarceration in the Age of Colorblindness* (New York: The New Press), 96.

17. Mark Lewis Taylor, *The Executed God: The Way of the Cross in Lockdown America*, 2nd ed. (Minneapolis: Fortress, 2015), 262.

18. Carlo C. DiClemente, *Addiction and Change: How Addictions Develop and Addicted People Recover* (New York: Guilford, 2006), 115–20.

19. DiClemente, *Addiction and Change*, 54.

20. If individuals are in a 12-step process, they may require your spiritual guidance at about the fourth step, which is a moral inventory of the resentments, harms to others, financial and sexual conduct that is burdening their minds and spirits. It mirrors ideas of confession and forgiveness in the Christian church. If they are not in this kind of program but are seeking your ideas on forgiveness, I would suggest time, prayer, and a gentle examination of motives and expected results. Some questions for exploration include: What are your motives for asking forgiveness? or What would be different if they accepted your apology? or, finally, What will you do if you are not forgiven at this time?

21. Lars Hartman, *Mark for the Nations: A Text- and Reader-Oriented Commentary* (Eugene, OR: Pickwick Publications, 2015), 219.

22. Christine Yuodelis-Flores and Richard K. Ries, "Addiction and Suicide: A Review," *American Journal on Addictions* 24, no. 2 (March 2015): 98–104, doi:10.1111/ajad.12185.

23. World Health Organization, "Preventing Suicide: A Global Imperative" (Geneva, Switzerland: World Health Organization Press, 2014), http://apps.who.int/iris/bitstream/10665/131056/1/9789241564779_eng.pdf.

24. Gabriela Borges et al., "A Meta-Analysis of Acute Use of Alcohol and the Risk of Suicide Attempt," *Psychological Medicine* 47, no. 5 (April 2017): 949–57, doi:10.1017/S0033291716002841.

25. The reader might perceive some of Paul Tillich's themes, such as the tragedy of our finitude and its limitations, estrangement, and a turning inward. While I appreciate this perspective on the human condition, I am locating estrangement from self, others, and God—and the addict's subsequent turning inward—as a symptom of the addiction's emergence rather than part of a universal existential dilemma. I also want to emphasize that this is a perceived estrangement—an estrangement at the level of accident, not essence. It is my conviction that God never leaves us.

26. Mark Baker and Joel Green, *Rediscovering the Scandal of the Cross: Atonement in New Testament and Contemporary Contexts*, 2nd ed. (Downers Grove, IL: InterVarsity, 2011), 23.

27. Carrie Doehring, *The Practice of Pastoral Care* (Louisville: Westminster John Knox, 2015), 147.

28. Kenneth I. Pargament, *The Psychology of Religion and Coping: Theory, Research, Practice* (New York: Guilford, 1997), 99.

29. Kenneth I. Pargament, *Spiritually Integrated Psychotherapy: Understanding and Addressing the Sacred* (New York: Guilford, 2011), 73.

30. Pargament, *Spiritually Integrated Psychotherapy*, 100.

31. Pargament, *Spiritually Integrated Psychotherapy*, 137.

32. For a good resource on this diversity, see Brad Jersak and Michael Hardin, eds., *Stricken by God? Nonviolent Atonement and the Victory of Christ* (Grand Rapids: Eerdmans, 2007).

33. For a primer on the practice of theological reflection, I would suggest Howard W. Stone and James O. Duke, *How to Think Theologically* (Minneapolis: Fortress, 2013).

34. Kathleen J. Greider, "Pastoral Theological Reflection on Sin and Evil vs. Pathology: The Case of the 'Disconnected/Unplugged Man,'" *Journal of Spirituality in Mental Health* 10, no. 3 (August 1, 2008): 227–40, doi:10.1080/19349630802067615.

Chapter 6

1. Arnold M. Washton and Joan E. Zweben, *Treating Alcohol and Drug Problems in Psychotherapy Practice: Doing What Works* (New York: Guilford, 2006), 81.

2. Carl R. Rogers, "The Necessary and Sufficient Conditions of Therapeutic Personality Change," *Psychotherapy: Theory, Research, Practice, Training* 44, no. 3 (2007): 240–48, doi:10.1037/0033-3204.44.3.240.

3. William R. Miller and Stephen Rollnick, *Motivational Interviewing: Helping People Change*, 3rd ed. (New York: Guilford, 2012), 6.

4. Miller and Rollnick, *Motivational Interviewing: Helping People Change*, 88.

5. Melinda Hohman, *Motivational Interviewing in Social Work Practice* (New York: Guilford, 2015), 24.

6. Miller and Rollnick, *Motivational Interviewing: Helping People Change*, 5.

7. Miller and Rollnick, *Motivational Interviewing: Helping People Change*, 161.

8. Hohman, *Motivational Interviewing in Social Work Practice*, 86–89.

9. Joseph Ponterotto, ed., *Handbook of Multicultural Counseling*, 3rd ed. (Thousand Oaks, CA: SAGE Publications, Inc., 2009), 134.

10. Jennifer Erickson and Barry Schreier et al., eds., *Handbook of Multicultural Counseling Competencies* (Hoboken, NJ: Wiley, 2010), 6-7.

11. Substance Abuse and Mental Health Services Administration, "Improving Cultural Competence, Treatment Improvement Protocol (TIP) Series No. 59," HHS Publication No. (SMA) 14-4849 (Rockville, MD: Substance Abuse and Mental Health Services Administration, 2014), http://store.samhsa.gov/shin/content/SMA14-4849/SMA14-4849.pdf.

12. Lydia F. Johnson, *Drinking from the Same Well: Cross-Cultural Concerns in Pastoral Care and Counseling* (Eugene, OR: Wipf and Stock, 2011), 120–37.

13. Nathaniel Ivers et al., "Brief Alcohol Counseling Interventions in a Trauma Setting with Latina/o Clients," in Stephen Southern and Katherine Hilton, eds., *Annual Review of Addictions and Offender Counseling: Best Practices* (Eugene, OR: Wipf and Stock, 2013), 111.

14. Nathaniel Ivers et al., eds., "Brief Alcohol Counseling Interventions in a Trauma Setting with Latina/o Clients," 112.

15. Peter Chang, "Treating Asian/Pacific American Addicts and Their Families," in Jo-ann Krestan, ed., *Bridges to Recovery: Addiction, Family Therapy, and Multicultural Treatment* (New York: Free Press, 2000), 192–218.

16. Nancy Boyd-Franklin, *Black Families in Therapy: Understanding the African American Experience*, 2nd ed. (New York: Guilford, 2006), 126.

17. Peter Bell, *Chemical Dependency and the African American: Counseling and Prevention Strategies*, 2nd ed. (Center City, MN: Hazelden, 2002), 49–62.

18. William Miller, "Motivational Factors in Addictive Behaviors," in William Miller and Kathleen Carroll, *Rethinking Substance Abuse*, 146.

19. Washton and Zweben, *Treating Alcohol and Drug Problems*, 82.

20. For a more thorough treatment of the transference-countertransference dynamic and the Christian faith, see Pamela Cooper-White, *Shared Wisdom: Use of the Self in Pastoral Care and Counseling* (Minneapolis: Fortress, 2004).

21. Carrie Doehring, *The Practice of Pastoral Care* (Louisville: Westminster John Knox, 2015), 56–57.

22. Doehring, *The Practice of Pastoral Care*, 67.

23. Doehring, *The Practice of Pastoral Care*, 57.

24. William Miller and Stephen Rollnick, *Motivational Interviewing: Preparing People to Change Addictive Behavior* (New York: Guilford, 1991), 35.

25. Miller and Rollnick, *Motivational Interviewing: Helping People Change*, 139.

26. Beverly Conyers, *Everything Changes: Help for Families of Newly Recovering Addicts* (Center City, MN: Hazelden, 2009), 104.

27. Vernon E. Johnson, *Intervention: How to Help Someone Who Doesn't Want Help* (Center City, MN: Hazelden, 2009), 66–87.

28. Miller, "Motivational Factors in Addictive Behaviors," 139.

Chapter 7

1. Carlo C. DiClemente, *Addiction and Change: How Addictions Develop and Addicted People Recover* (New York: Guilford, 2006), 26–30.

2. The Change Theory Map is drawn from two main sources. See Carlo C. DiClemente, *Addiction and Change*, 27; see also Substance Abuse and Mental Health Services Administration, Center for Substance Abuse Treatment, "Substance Abuse Treatment for Persons with Co-Occurring Disorders: Treatment Improvement Protocol (TIP) Series, No. 42," HHS Publication No. (SMA) 13-3992 (Rockville, MD: Substance Abuse and Mental Health Services Administration, 2013), http://store.samhsa.gov/shin/content//SMA13-3992/SMA13-3992.pdf.

3. William R. Miller and Stephen Rollnick, *Motivational Interviewing: Helping People Change*, 3rd ed. (New York: Guilford, 2012), 33.

4. Arnold M. Washton and Joan E. Zweben, *Treating Alcohol and Drug Problems in Psychotherapy Practice: Doing What Works* (New York: Guilford, 2006), 171.

5. Miller and Rollnick, *Motivational Interviewing*, 54.

6. Adapted from Miller and Rollnick, *Motivational Interviewing*, 11.

7. Adapted from DiClemente, *Addiction and Change*, 165.

8. Katie A. Witkiewitz and G. Alan Marlatt, eds., *Therapist's Guide to Evidence-Based Relapse Prevention* (Boston: Elsevier Academic Press, 2007), 49.

9. Katie A. Witkiewitz and G. Alan Marlatt, "High Risk Situations: Relapse as a Dynamic Process," in Witkiewitz and Marlatt, *Therapist's Guide to Evidence-Based Relapse Prevention*, 19–33.

10. John Bunyan, *The Pilgrim's Progress*, ed. Cynthia Wall (New York: Norton, 2008).

11. Richard J. Foster, *Celebration of Discipline: The Path to Spiritual Growth*, 3rd ed. (New York: HarperCollins, 2009).

12. I am gleaning this self-reflection on guilt or sin from the 12-step "moral inventory." The key to the moral inventory is that, for every resentment, fear, or guilty action the person lists, she should also explore the emotions or actions tied to the issue: what part did she play in the resentment/guilt/fear, and what was threatened in the self. The individual also examines the whole list for common patterns across her life. For the foundational discourse on this step, see "How It Works" and "Into Action" in *The Big Book of Alcoholics Anonymous*, 4th ed., 58–87.

13. Center for Behavioral Health Statistics and Quality, *Key Substance Use and Mental Health Indicators in the United States: Results from the 2015 National Survey on Drug Use and Health*, HHS Publication No. SMA 16-4984, NSDUH Series H-51 (2016), https://www.samhsa.gov/data/sites/default/files/NSDUH-FFR1-2015/NSDUH-FFR1-2015/NSDUH-FFR1-2015.pdf.

14. Kathleen T. Brady and Sinha Rajita, "Co-Occurring Mental and Substance Use Disorders: The Neurobiological Effects of Chronic Stress," *The American Journal of Psychiatry* 162, no. 8 (2005): 1483–93, doi:10.1176/appi.ajp.162.8.1483.

15. Mark Sanders, *Slipping Through the Cracks: Intervention Strategies for Clients with Multiple Addictions and Disorders* (Deerfield Beach, FL: Health Communications, Inc., 2011), 40.

16. Lauren R. Few et al., "Genetic Variation in Personality Traits Explains Genetic Overlap between Borderline Personality Features and Substance Use Disorders," *Addiction* 109, no. 12 (December 2014): 2118–27, https://doi.org/10.1111/add.12690.

17. Alan I. Green et al., "Schizophrenia and Co-Occurring Substance Use Disorder," *The American Journal of Psychiatry* 164, no. 3 (March 2007): 402–8, doi:10.1176/ajp.2007.164.3.402.

18. S. L. Proctor and N. G. Hoffmann, "Identifying Patterns of Co-occurring Substance

Use Disorders and Mental Illness in a Jail Population," *Addiction Research and Theory* 20, no. 6 (2012): 492–503, http://doi.org/10.3109/16066359.2012.667853.

19. Substance Abuse and Mental Health Services Administration, Center for Substance Abuse Treatment, "Quick Guide for Clinicians: Based on TIP 42: Substance Abuse Treatment for Persons With Co-Occurring Disorders," HHS Publication No. (SMA) 15-4034 (1st printing, 2005; Rockville, MD: Substance Abuse and Mental Health Services Administration, 2015).

20. One study suggests that psychiatric professionals also find it hardest to maintain empathy for patients with co-occuring disorders, especially due to repeated negative experiences when trying to help the most severe in this population. This is problematic due to the high rate of substance-use disorders that co-occur with psychiatric disorders. Jonathan Avery et al., "Changes in Psychiatry Residents' Attitudes towards Individuals with Substance Use Disorders over the Course of Residency Training," *American Journal on Addictions* 26, no. 1 (January 2017): 75–79, https://doi.org/10.1111/ajad.12406.

21. Carol L. Schnabl Schweitzer, "Resilience Revisited: What Ministers Need to Know about Borderline Personality Disorder," *Pastoral Psychology* 64, no. 5 (October 1, 2015): 727–49, https://doi.org/10.1007/s11089-014-0626-0.

Bibliography

Academy of Eating Disorders, "Eating Disorders: A Guide to Medical Care." 3rd edition. AED Report 2016. https://higherlogicdownload.s3.amazonaws.com/AEDWEB/0565ea0-59c9-4dd4-b832-07a3fea58f4c/UploadedImages/Learn/AED-Medical-Care-Guidelines_English_02_28_17_NEW.pdf.

ACLU-NJ. "Report Reveals Deep Racial Disparities in NJ Marijuana Arrests." June 15, 2017. https://www.aclu-nj.org/news/2017/06/15/aclu-nj-report-reveals-deep-racial-disparities-nj-marijuana.

Alexander, Bruce. *The Globalization of Addiction: A Study in Poverty of the Spirit*. New York: Oxford University Press, 2010.

Alexander, Michelle. *The New Jim Crow: Mass Incarceration in the Age of Colorblindness*. New York: The New Press, 2012.

Allen, Jon G. *Coping with Trauma: Hope Through Understnading*, 2nd ed. (American Psychiatric Publishing, Inc., 2005).

———. *Traumatic Relationships and Serious Mental Disorders*. New York: Wiley, 2001.

Alvarez, Josefina, Leonard A. Jason, Bradley D. Olson, Joseph R. Ferrari, and Margaret I. Davis. "Substance Abuse Prevalence and Treatment among Latinos and Latinas." *Journal of Ethnicity in Substance Abuse* 6, no. 2 (2007): 115–41.

Alvarez, Louis, and Pedro Ruiz. "Substance Abuse in the Mexican American Population." In *Ethnocultural Factors in Substance Abuse Treatment*, edited by Shulamith Lala Ashenberg Straussner, 111–36. New York: Guilford, 2001.

American Psychiatric Association. *Diagnostic and Statistical Manual of Mental Health Disorders: DSM 5*. Arlington, VA: American Psychiatric Publishing, 2013.

Anonymous. *The Big Book of Alcoholics Anonymous*. 4th ed. New York: Alcoholics Anonymous World Services, Inc., 2001.

———. *Living Sober*. New York: Alcoholics Anonymous World Services, Inc., 2002.

———. *Twelve Steps and Twelve Traditions*. New York: AA World Services, 2002.

Aquinas, Thomas. "Of Drunkenness." In *Summa Theologica* II–II, Q. 150. Translated by the Fathers of the English Dominican Province. New York: Christian Classics, 1981.

Augustine. *The Confessions: Saint Augustine of Hippo*. Translated by Maria Boulding. Edited by David Vincent Meconi. San Francisco: Ignatius Press, 2012.

Avery, Jonathan, Bernadine H. Han, Guojiao Wu, Elizabeth Mauer, Julie B. Penzner, Erin Zerbo, Joseph Avery, and Stephen Ross. "Changes in Psychiatry Residents' Attitudes towards Individuals with Substance Use Disorders over the Course of Residency Training." *American Journal on Addictions* 26, no. 1 (January 2017): 75–79. https://doi.org/10.1111/ajad.12406.

Baker, Mark, and Joel Green. *Rediscovering the Scandal of the Cross: Atonement in New Testament and Contemporary Contexts.* 2nd ed. Downers Grove, IL: InterVarsity Press, 2011.

Baum, Dan. "Legalize It All." *Harper's Magazine*, April 2016. https://harpers.org/archive/2016/04/legalize-it-all/.

Bedford, Keith. "Read a transcript of Trump's remarks in N.H." *Boston Globe*, March 19, 2018. https://www.bostonglobe.com/news/politics/2018/03/19/read-transcript-trump-remarks/6Iie27RlDkc1VgtIZvUBfL/story.html

Beebe, Beatrice, and Frank M. Lachmann. *The Origins of Attachment: Infant Research and Adult Treatment*. New York: Routledge, 2013.

Beecher, Lyman. *Six Sermons On The Nature, Occasions, Signs, Evils, and Remedy of Intemperance.* 10th ed. New York: American Tract Society, 1833.

Bell, Peter. *Chemical Dependency and the African American: Counseling and Prevention Strategies.* 2nd ed. Center City, MN: Hazelden Publishing, 2002.

Berger, Maximus, and Zoltán Sarnyai. "'More than Skin Deep': Stress Neurobiology and Mental Health Consequences of Racial Discrimination." *Stress: The International Journal on the Biology of Stress* 18, no. 1 (January 2015): 1–10. doi:10.3109/10253890.2014.989204.

Bickel, Warren, and Marc Potenza. "The Forest and the Trees: Addiction as a Complex Self-Organizing System." In Miller and Carroll, *Rethinking Substance Abuse*, 8–24. New York: Guilford, 2006.

Black, Claudia. "Addiction and Trauma: The Complexity of Treating the Young Adult." Keynote Lecture, NAADAC Annual Conference, Denver, CO, September 23, 2017.

Black, Clifton. *Mark.* Abingdon New Testament Commentaries Series. Nashville: Abingdon, 2011.

Blum, Kenneth, Eric R. Braverman, Jay M. Holder, Joel F. Lubar, Vincent J. Monastra, David Miller, Judith O. Lubar, Thomas J. Chen, and David E. Comings. "Reward Deficiency Syndrome: A Biogenetic Model for the Diagnosis and Treatment of Impulsive, Addictive, and Compulsive Behaviors." *Journal of Psychoactive Drugs* 32, Suppl. (2000): 49.

Borges, Gabriela, Courtney L. Bagge, Cheryl J. Cherpitel, Kenneth R. Conner, Ricardo Orozco, and Ingeborg Rossow. "A Meta-Analysis of Acute Use of Alcohol and the Risk of Suicide Attempt." *Psychological Medicine* 47, no. 5 (April 2017): 949–57. doi:http://yeshebi.ptsem.edu:2103/10.1017/S0033291716002841.

Bornovalova, Marina A., Matthew T. Tull, Kim L. Gratz, Roy Levy, and Carl W. Lejuez. "Extending Models of Deliberate Self-Harm and Suicide Attempts to Substance Users: Exploring the Roles of Childhood Abuse, Posttraumatic Stress, and Difficulties Controlling Impulsive Behavior When Distressed." *Psychological Trauma: Theory, Research, Practice, and Policy* 3, no. 4 (December 2011): 349–59. doi:10.1037/a0021579.

Bowlby, John A. *Secure Base: Parent-Child Attachment and Healthy Human Development.* Reprint edition. New York: Basic Books, 1988.

Boyd-Franklin, Nancy. *Black Families in Therapy: Understanding the African American Experience*. 2nd ed. New York: Guilford, 2006.

Brady, Kathleen T., and Rajita Sinha. "Co-Occurring Mental and Substance Use Disorders: The Neurobiological Effects of Chronic Stress." *The American Journal of Psychiatry* 162, no. 8 (2005): 1483–93. doi:10.1176/appi.ajp.162.8.1483.

Brown, Harriet. *Brave Girl Eating: A Family's Struggle with Anorexia*. New York: HarperCollins, 2011.

Brown, J. Scott, Sarah O. Meadows, and Glen H. Elder Jr. "Race-Ethnic Inequality and Psychological Distress: Depressive Symptoms from Adolescence to Young Adulthood." *Developmental Psychology* 43, no. 6 (November 2007): 1295–1311. doi:10.1037/0012-1649.43.6.1295.

Bunyan, John. *The Pilgrim's Progress*. Edited by Cynthia Wall. New York: Norton, 2008.

Butler, Lee H. *Liberating Our Dignity, Saving Our Souls: A New Theory of African American Identity Formation*. St Louis: Chalice, 2006.

Calvin, John. *Catechism of Geneva, Being a Form of Instruction for Children*, 1.1. Center for Reformed Theology and Apologetics. http://www.reformed.org/documents/calvin/geneva_catachism/geneva_catachism.html.

Carnes, Stefanie. "Sex Addiction: Neuroscience Etiology and Treatment." Lecture, NAADAC Annual Conference, Denver, CO, September 25, 2017.

Carter, Robert T. "Race-Based Traumatic Stress." *Psychiatric Times* 23, no. 14 (December 2006): 37. http://www.psychiatrictimes.com/cultural-psychiatry/race-based-traumatic-stress/page/0/1.

Carter, Robert T., Veronica E. Johnson, Katheryn Roberson, Silvia L. Mazzula, Katherine Kirkinis, and Sinead Sant-Barket. "Race-Based Traumatic Stress, Racial Identity Statuses, and Psychological Functioning: An Exploratory Investigation." *Professional Psychology: Research and Practice* 48, no. 1 (February 2017): 30–37. doi:10.1037/pro0000116.

Center for Behavioral Health Statistics and Quality. "Key Substance Use and Mental Health Indicators in the United States: Results from the 2015 National Survey on Drug Use and Health." HHS Publication No. SMA 16-4984. NSDUH Series H-5.1 Rockville, MD: Substance Abuse and Mental Health Services Administration, 2016. http://www.samhsa.gov/data/.

Centers for Disease Control. "Prescription Painkiller Overdoses in the US." *CDC Vital Signs*. November 2011. https://www.cdc.gov/VitalSigns/PainkillerOverdoses/index.html.

Chang, Peter. "Treating Asian/Pacific American Addicts and Their Families." In Krestan, *Bridges to Recovery*, 192–218.

Chopp, Rebecca S. *The Praxis of Suffering: An Interpretation of Liberation and Political Theologies*. Eugene, OR.: Wipf & Stock, 2007.

Cilluffo, Anthony. "5 Facts About Student Loans." Pew Research Center. August 24, 2017. http://www.pewresearch.org/fact-tank/2017/08/24/5-facts-about-student-loans/.

Clinebell, Howard J. *Understanding and Counseling Persons with Alcohol, Drug, and Behavioral Addictions*. Revised and enlarged edition. Nashville: Abingdon, 1998.

Cohen, Andre. "How White Users Made Heroin a Public Health Problem." *The Atlan-*

tic, August 12, 2015. https://www.theatlantic.com/politics/archive/2015/08/crack-heroin-and-race/401015/.

Cone, James H. *The Cross and the Lynching Tree*. Reprint edition. Maryknoll, NY: Orbis Books, 2013.

Connors, Gerard J., Carlo C. DiClemente, Mary Marden Velasquez, and Dennis M. Donovan. *Substance Abuse Treatment and the Stages of Change: Selecting and Planning Interventions*. 2nd edition. New York: Guilford, 2015.

Conyers, Beverly. *Everything Changes: Help for Families of Newly Recovering Addicts*. Center City, MN: Hazelden, 2009.

Cook, Christopher H. *Alcohol, Addiction and Christian Ethics*. Cambridge: Cambridge University Press, 2008.

Cooper, Terry D. *Sin, Pride, and Self-Acceptance: The Problem of Identity in Theology and Psychology*. Westmont, IL: IVP Academic, 2009.

Cooper-White, Pamela. *Shared Wisdom: Use of the Self in Pastoral Care and Counseling*. Minneapolis: Fortress, 2004.

Costin, Carolyn. *The Eating Disorders Sourcebook: A Comprehensive Guide to the Causes, Treatments, and Prevention of Eating Disorders*. 3rd ed. New York: McGraw-Hill, 2007.

Costin, Carolyn, and Gwen Schubert Grabb. *8 Keys to Recovery from an Eating Disorder: Effective Strategies from Therapeutic Practice and Personal Experience*. New York: Norton, 2012.

Courtwright, David T. *Dark Paradise: A History of Opiate Addiction in America*. Enlarged edition. Cambridge, MA: Harvard University Press, 2001.

Cozolino, Louis. *The Neuroscience of Human Relationships: Attachment and the Developing Social Brain*. New York: Norton, 2006.

Culpepper, R. Alan. *Mark*. Vol. 20 of *Smyth & Helwys Bible Commentary*. Macon, GA: Smyth and Helwys, 2007.

Dackis, Charles, and Charles O'Brien. "Neurobiology of Addiction: Treatment and Public Policy Ramifications." *Nature Neuroscience* 8, no. 11 (2005): 1431–36. http://doi.org/10.1038/nn1105-1431.

Darke, Shane. "Pathways to Heroin Dependence: Time to Re-Appraise Self-Medication." *Addiction* 108, no. 4 (April 2013): 659–67. doi:10.1111/j.1360-0443.2012.04001.x.

Darke, Shane, and Michelle Torok. "The Association of Childhood Physical Abuse with the Onset and Extent of Drug Use among Regular Injecting Drug Users." *Addiction* 109, no. 4 (April 2014): 610–16. doi:10.1111/add.12428.

Delva, Jorge, Andrew Grogan-Kaylor, Fernando H. Andrade, Marya Hynes, Ninive Sanchez, and Cristina B. Bares. "Agenda for Longitudinal Research and Substance Use and Abuse with Hispanics in the U.S. and with Latin American Populations." In Thomas and Price, *Drug Use Trajectories among Minority Youth*, 63–83.

DiClemente, Carlo C. *Addiction and Change: How Addictions Develop and Addicted People Recover*. New York: Guilford, 2006.

———. "Natural Change and the Troublesome Use of Substances: A Life-Course Perspective." In Miller and Carroll, *Rethinking Substance Abuse*, 81–96.

Doehring, Carrie. *The Practice of Pastoral Care*. Revised and expanded edition. Louisville: Westminster John Knox, 2015.

Dongju, Seo, and Rajita Sinha. "Neuroplasticity and Predictors of Alcohol Recovery." *Alcohol Research: Current Reviews* 37, no. 1 (2015): 143–52.

Douglas, Kelly Brown. *Stand Your Ground: Black Bodies and the Justice of God*. Maryknoll, NY: Orbis Books, 2015.

Drug Enforcement Administration. "2015 National Drug Threat Assessment Summary." October 2015. https://www.dea.gov/docs/2015%20NDTA%20Report.pdf.

Dunnington, Kent. *Addiction and Virtue: Beyond the Models of Disease and Choice*. Downers Grove, IL: IVP Academic, 2011.

Duranceau, Sophie, Mathew G. Fetzner, and R. Nicholas Carleton. "Low Distress Tolerance and Hyperarousal Posttraumatic Stress Disorder Symptoms: A Pathway to Alcohol Use?" *Cognitive Therapy and Research* 38, no. 3 (June 2014): 280–90. doi: 10.1007/s10608-013-9591-7.

Eisenberger, Naomi I. "The Neural Basis of Social Pain: Findings and Implications." In *Social Pain: Neuropsychological and Health Implications of Loss and Exclusion*, edited by Geoff MacDonald and Lauri A. Jensen-Campbell, 53–78. Washington, DC: The American Psychological Association, 2011.

———. "The Pain of Social Disconnection: Examining the Shared Neural Underpinnings of Physical and Social Pain." *Nature Reviews Neuroscience* 13, no. 6 (June 2012): 421–34. doi:10.1038/nrn3231.

Erickson, Jennifer, Barry Schreier, et al., eds. *Handbook of Multicultural Counseling Competencies*. Hoboken, NJ: Wiley & Sons, 2010.

Eyrich-Garg, Karin M., John S. Cacciola, Deni Carise, Kevin G. Lynch, and A. Thomas McLellan. "Individual Characteristics of the Literally Homeless, Marginally Housed, and Impoverished in a US Substance Abuse Treatment-Seeking Sample." *Social Psychiatry & Psychiatric Epidemiology* 43, no. 10 (October 2008): 831–42. https://doi.org/10.1007/s00127-008-0371-8.

Fanon, Frantz. *The Wretched of the Earth*. Reprint edition. Translated by R. Philcox. New York: Grove, 2005.

Fein, George, and Valerie A. Cardenas. "Neuroplasticity in Human Alcoholism." *Alcohol Research: Current Reviews* 37, no. 1 (2015): 125–41.

Fernandez, Humberto, and Theresa Libby. *Heroin: Its History, Pharmacology, and Treatment*. 2nd edition. Minneapolis: Hazelden, 2011.

Few, Lauren R., Julia D. Grant, Timothy J. Trull, Dixie J. Statham, Nicholas G. Martin, Michael T. Lynskey, and Arpana Agrawal. "Genetic Variation in Personality Traits Explains Genetic Overlap between Borderline Personality Features and Substance Use Disorders." *Addiction* 109, no. 12 (December 2014): 2118–27. https://doi.org/10.1111/add.12690.

Flores, Philip J. *Addiction as an Attachment Disorder*. Lanham, MD: Jason Aronson, Inc., 2004.

Focant, Camille. *The Gospel according to Mark: A Commentary*. Translated by L. R. Keylock. Eugene, OR: Wipf and Stock, 2012.

Fonagy, Peter, Gyorgy Gergely, Elliot Jurist, and Mary Target. *Affect Regulation, Mentalization, and the Development of Self.* New York: Other Press, 2005.

Foster, Richard J. *Celebration of Discipline: The Path to Spiritual Growth.* 3rd ed. New York: HarperCollins, 2009.

Friedman, Matthew. *Post-Traumatic and Acute Stress Disorders: The Latest Assessment and Treatment Strategies.* Kansas City: Compact Clinicals, 2006.

Fuller-Rowell, Thomas E., Courtney D. Cogburn, Amanda B. Brodish, Stephen C. Peck, Oksana Malanchuk, and Jacquelynne S. Eccles. "Racial Discrimination and Substance Use: Longitudinal Associations and Identity Moderators." *Journal of Behavioral Medicine* 35, no. 6 (December 2012): 581–90. doi:http://yeshebi.ptsem.edu:2103/10.1007/s10865-011-9388-7.

Gao, George. "Chart of the Week: The Black-White Gap in Incarceration Rates." Pew Research Center. July 18, 2014. http://www.pewresearch.org/fact-tank/2014/07/18/chart-of-the-week-the-black-white-gap-in-incarceration-rates/.

Gartner, Coral E., Adrian Carter, and Brad Partridge. "What Are the Public Policy Implications of a Neurobiological View of Addiction?" *Addiction* 107, no. 7 (July 2012): 1199–1200. http://doi.org/10.1111/j.1360-0443.2012.03812.x.

Gerkin, Charles V. *Living Human Document: Re-Visioning Pastoral Counseling in a Hermeneutical Mode.* 2nd ed. Nashville: Abingdon, 1984.

Geyer, Douglas W. *Fear, Anomaly, and Uncertainty in the Gospel of Mark.* Lanham, MD: Scarecrow Press, 2001.

Geneva Catechism, or Instruction on the Christian Religion: Prepared by the Pastors of Geneva for the Use of the Swiss and French Protestant Churches. 1814 trans. ed. (London: Sherwood, Neely, and Jones, 1815).

Gibbons, Frederick X., Michelle L. Stock, Ross E. O'Hara, and Meg Gerrard. "Prospecting Prejudice: An Examination of the Long-Term Effects of Perceived Racial Discrimination on the Health Behavior and Health Status of African Americans." In Thomas and Price, *Drug Use Trajectories among Minority Youth*, 199–232.

Gibbons, Frederick X., Paul E. Etcheverry, Michelle L. Stock, Meg Gerrard, Chih-Yuan Weng, Marc Kiviniemi, and Ross E. O'Hara. "Exploring the Link between Racial Discrimination and Substance Use: What Mediates? What Buffers?" *Journal of Personality and Social Psychology* 99, no. 5 (November 2010): 785–801. doi:10.1037/a0019880.

Gill, Richard, ed. *Addictions from an Attachment Perspective: Do Broken Bonds and Early Trauma Lead to Addictive Behaviours?* London: Karnac Books, 2014.

Gottschalk, Marie. *Caught: The Prison State and the Lockdown of American Politics.* Princeton, NJ: Princeton University Press, 2014.

Graham, Elaine. *Transforming Practice: Pastoral Theology in an Age of Uncertainty.* Eugene, OR: Wipf and Stock, 2002.

Green, Alan I., Robert E. Drake, Mary F. Brunette, and Douglas L. Noordsy. "Schizophrenia and Co-Occurring Substance Use Disorder." *The American Journal of Psychiatry* 164, no. 3 (March 2007): 402–8.

Greenwood, Lynn. "Taking the Toys Away: Removing the Need for Self-harming Behavior." In Richard Gill, ed., *Addictions from an Attachment Perspective*, 69–93.

Greider, Kathleen J. "Pastoral Theological Reflection on Sin and Evil vs. Pathology: The

Case of the 'Disconnected/Unplugged Man.'" *Journal of Spirituality in Mental Health* 10, no. 3 (August 1, 2008): 227–40. doi:10.1080/19349630802067615.

Hart, Carl, and Charles Ksir. *Drugs, Society, and Human Behavior*. 14th ed. New York: McGraw-Hill Education, 2010.

Hartman, Lars. *Mark for the Nations: A Text- and Reader-Oriented Commentary*. Eugene, OR: Pickwick, 2015.

Hauge, Dan. "The Trauma of Racism and the Distorted White Imagination." In *Post Traumatic Public Theology*, edited by Stephanie Areland and Shelly Rambo. Basingstoke, UK: Palgrave Macmillan, 2016.

Hari, Johan. *Chasing the Scream: The First and Last Days of the War on Drugs*. New York: Bloomsbury USA, 2015.

Heilig, Markus. *The Thirteenth Step: Addiction in the Age of Brain Science*. New York: Columbia University Press, 2015.

Helsel, Philip Browning. *Pastoral Power beyond Psychology's Marginalization: Resisting the Discourses of the Psy-Complex*. New York: Palgrave Macmillan, 2015.

Heyman, Gene M. "Addiction and Choice: Theory and New Data." *Frontiers in Psychiatry* 4 (May 6, 2013). doi:10.3389/fpsyt.2013.00031. https://www.ncbi.nlm.nih.gov/pmc/articles/PMC3644798/.

Herman, S. E., J. L. James, S. Rankin, M. Keisling, L. Mottet, and M. Anafi. "Executive Summary of the Report of the 2015 U.S. Transgender Survey." Washington, DC: National Center for Transgender Equality, 2016. https://transequality.org/sites/default/files/docs/usts/USTS-Executive-Summary-Dec17.pdf.

Hilton, Donald, Stefanie Carnes, and Todd Love. "Neurobiology of Behavioral Addictions: Sexual Addiction." In Swann, Moeller, and Lijffijt, *Neurobiology of Addiction*, 176–90.

Hohman, Melinda. *Motivational Interviewing in Social Work Practice*. New York: Guilford, 2015.

Hollenbach, Paul. "Jesus, Demoniacs, and Public Authorities: A Socio-Historical Study." *Journal of the American Academy of Religion* 49, no. 4 (1981): 567–88. http://www.jstor.org/stable/1462450.

Howe, David. *Attachment across the Lifecourse: A Brief Introduction*. New York: Palgrave Macmillan, 2011.

Hughes, Tonda L. "Lesbians' Drinking Patterns: Beyond the Data." *Substance Use and Misuse* 38, no. 11–13 (July 2003): 1739–58. http://search.ebscohost.com/login.aspx?direct=true&db=aph&AN=11028975&site=ehost-live.

Ingraham, Christopher. "Charting the Shocking Rise of Racial Disparity in Our Criminal Justice System." *The Washington Post*, July 15, 2014. https://www.washingtonpost.com/news/wonk/wp/2014/07/15/charting-the-shocking-rise-of-racial-disparity-in-our-criminal-justice-system/?utm_term=.441055bbb87a.

Ivers, Nathaniel, Laura J. Veach, Regina R. Moro, Jennifer L. Rogers, and Mary Claire O'Brien. "Brief Alcohol Counseling Interventions in a Trauma Setting with Latina/o Clients." In Southern and Hilton, *Annual Review of Addictions and Offender Counseling*.

Jantz, Gregory L., and Ann Mcmurray. *Hope, Help, and Healing for Eating Disorders: A*

New Approach to Treating Anorexia, Bulimia, and Overeating. Colorado Springs, CO: WaterBrook, 2010.

Jersak, Brad, and Michael Hardin, eds. *Stricken by God? Nonviolent Atonement and the Victory of Christ*. Grand Rapids: Eerdmans, 2007.

Johnson, Lydia F. *Drinking from the Same Well: Cross-Cultural Concerns in Pastoral Care and Counseling*. Eugene, OR: Wipf and Stock, 2011.

Johnson, Vernon E. *Intervention: How to Help Someone Who Doesn't Want Help*. Center City, MN: Hazelden, 2009.

Johnston, Lloyd D., Patrick M. O'Malley, Richard A. Miech, Jerald G. Bachman, and John E. Schulenberg. "Demographic Subgroup Trends among Adolescents in the Use of Various Licit and Illicit Drugs, 1975–2016." Monitoring the Future Occasional Paper No. 88. Ann Arbor: Institute for Social Research, The University of Michigan, 2017. http://www.monitoringthefuture.org/pubs/occpapers/mtf-occ88.pdf.

Khantzian, Edward J. "Addiction as a Self-Regulation Disorder and the Role of Self-Medication." *Addiction* 108, no. 4 (April 2013): 668–69. doi:10.1111/add.12004.

———. "The Self-Medication Hypothesis and Attachment Theory: Pathways for Understanding and Ameliorating Addictive Suffering." In Gill, *Addictions from an Attachment Perspective*.

Khurana, Atika, Dan Romer, Laura M. Betancourt, Nancy L. Brodsky, Joan M. Giannetta, and Hallam Hurt. "Working Memory Ability Predicts Trajectories of Early Alcohol Use in Adolescents: The Mediational Role of Impulsivity." *Addiction* 108, no. 3 (2013): 506–15. http://doi.org/10.1111/add.12001.

Koob, George F. "The Neurobiology of Addiction: A Neuroadaptational View Relevant for Diagnosis." *Addiction 101* (September 2, 2006): 23–30. doi:10.1111/j.1360-0443.2006.01586.x.

Koob, George F., and M. Le Moal. "Plasticity of Reward Neurocircuitry and the 'Dark Side' of Drug Addiction." *Nature Neuroscience* 8, no. 11 (2005): 1442–44. http://doi.org/10.1038/nn1105-1442.

Krestan, Jo-ann, ed. *Bridges to Recovery: Addiction, Family Therapy, and Multicultural Treatment*. New York: Free Press, 2000.

Kuhar, Michael. *The Addicted Brain: Why We Abuse Drugs, Alcohol, and Nicotine*. Upper Saddle River, NJ: FT Press, 2015.

Kwee, Alex, Amy Dominguez, and Donald Ferrell. "Sexual Addiction and Christian College Men: Conceptual, Assessment, and Research Challenges." *Journal of Psychiatry and Christianity* 26, no. 1 (2007): 3–13.

LaMothe, Ryan. *Care of Souls, Care of Polis: Toward a Political Pastoral Theology*. Eugene, OR: Cascade, 2017.

———. "Neoliberal Capitalism and the Corruption of Society: A Pastoral Political Analysis." *Pastoral Psychology* 65, no. 1 (February 2016): 5–21. https://doi.org/10.1007/s11089-013-0577-x.

Lantzer, Jason. *"Prohibition Is Here to Stay": The Reverend Edward S. Shumaker and the Dry Crusade in America*. Notre Dame: The University of Notre Dame Press, 2009.

Leander, Hans. *Discourses of Empire: The Gospel of Mark from a Postcolonial Perspective*. Atlanta: Society of Biblical Literature, 2015.

Leone, Jared. "Read: Full Transcript of Trump's Rally Speech in Florida." *Palm Beach Post*, February 18, 2017. http://www.palmbeachpost.com/news/national/read-full-transcript-trump-rally-speech-florida/DeDCpoNEKLQmWcIKndWBoM/.

Levine, Harry G., Jon B. Gettman, and Loren Siegel. "Arresting Blacks for Marijuana in California." *The Drug Policy Alliance*, October 2010. https://www.drugpolicy.org/sites/default/files/ArrestingBlacks.pdf

Lewis, Marc. *The Biology of Desire: Why Addiction Is Not a Disease*. New York: Public Affairs, 2015.

Lijffijt, Marijn. "Stress and Addiction." In Swann, Moeller, and Lijffijt, *Neurobiology of Addiction*, 153–75.

Locke, Joseph. *Making the Bible Belt: Texas Prohibitionists and the Politicization of Southern Religion*. Oxford: Oxford University Press, 2017.

Logrip, Marian L., George F. Koob, and Eric P. Zorrilla. "Role of Corticotropin-Releasing Factor in Drug Addiction." *CNS Drugs* 25, no. 4 (2011): 271–87. doi: 10.2165/11587790-000000000-00000.

Longo, D. L., N. D. Volkow, G. F. Koob, and A.T. McLellan. "Neurobiologic Advances from the Brain Disease Model of Addiction." *The New England Journal of Medicine* 374, no. 4 (January 28, 2016): 363–71.

Luther, Martin. *Table Talk*. In vol. 54 of *Luther's Works*. Edited and translated by Theodore Tappert. Minneapolis: Fortress, 1967.

Manejwala, Omar. *Craving: Why We Can't Seem to Get Enough*. Center City, MN: Hazelden, 2013.

Marcus, Joel. *Mark 1–8: A New Translation with Introduction and Commentary*. New York: Anchor, 2002.

Marshall Project, The. "Death in Police Custody: A Curated Collection of Links." Accessed November 22, 2017. https://www.themarshallproject.org/records/543-death-in-police-custody.

Maté, Gabor. *In the Realm of Hungry Ghosts: Close Encounters with Addiction*. Berkeley: North Atlantic Books, 2010.

Matthews, Connie R., Peggy Lorah, and Jaime Fenton. "Treatment Experiences of Gays and Lesbians in Recovery from Addiction: A Qualitative Inquiry." *Journal of Mental Health Counseling* 28, no. 2 (April 2006): 111–32.

May, Gerald G. *Addiction and Grace: Love and Spirituality in the Healing of Addictions*. Reissue ed. San Francisco: HarperOne, 2007.

McClure, Barbara J. *Moving beyond Individualism in Pastoral Care and Counseling: Reflections on Theory, Theology, and Practice*. Eugene, OR: Cascade, 2009.

McNair, Ruth, Amy Pennay, Tonda Hughes, Rhonda Brown, William Leonard, and Dan I. Lubman. "A Model for Lesbian, Bisexual, and Queer-Related Influences on Alcohol Consumption and Implications for Policy and Practice." *Culture, Health & Sexuality* 18, no. 4 (April 2016): 405–21. https://doi.org/10.1080/13691058.2015.1089602.

Medley, Grace, Rachel N. Lipari, Jonaki Bose, Devon S. Cribb, Larry A. Kroutil, and Gretchen McHenry. "Sexual Orientation and Estimates of Adult Substance Use and Mental Health: Results from the 2015 National Survey on Drug Use and Health."

NSDUH Data Review. Substance Abuse and Mental Health Services Administration, October 2016. https://www.samhsa.gov/data/sites/default/files/NSDUH-SexualOrientation-2015/NSDUH-SexualOrientation-2015/NSDUH-SexualOrientation-2015.htm#topofpage.

Mereish, Ethan H., Conall O'Cleirigh, and Judith B. Bradford. "Interrelationships between LGBT-Based Victimization, Suicide, and Substance Use Problems in a Diverse Sample of Sexual and Gender Minorities." *Psychology, Health & Medicine* 19, no. 1 (January 2, 2014): 1-13. doi:10.1080/13548506.2013.780129.

Meyer, Ilan H. "Prejudice, Social Stress, and Mental Health in Lesbian, Gay, and Bisexual Populations: Conceptual Issues and Research Evidence." *Psychological Bulletin* 129, no. 5 (September 2003): 674-697. doi:10.1037/0033-2909.129.5.674.

Miller, Dusty. "Addictions and Trauma Recovery: An Integrated Approach." *Psychiatric Quarterly* 73, no. 2 (June 2002): 157.

Miller, William. "Motivational Factors in Addictive Behaviors." In Miller and Carroll, *Rethinking Substance Abuse*, 134–52.

Miller, William, and Kathleen Carroll, eds. *Rethinking Substance Abuse: What the Science Shows, and What We Should Do about It.* New York: Guilford, 2010.

Miller, William, Alyssa Forcehimes, and Allen Zweben. *Treating Addiction: A Guide for Professionals.* New York: Guilford, 2011.

Miller, William, and Stephen Rollnick. *Motivational Interviewing: Helping People Change.* 3rd ed. New York: Guilford, 2012.

Miller, William, and Stephen Rollnick. *Motivational Interviewing: Preparing People to Change Addictive Behavior.* New York: Guilford, 1991.

Miller-McLemore, Bonnie J. *Christian Theology in Practice: Discovering a Discipline.* Grand Rapids: Eerdmans, 2012.

Mills, Ryan, Rosa Alati, Lane Strathearn, and Jake M. Najman. "Alcohol and Tobacco Use among Maltreated and Non-Maltreated Adolescents in a Birth Cohort." *Addiction* 109, no. 4 (April 2014): 672–80. doi:10.1111/add.12447.

Moore, Mark H., and Dean R. Gerstein. *Alcohol and Public Policy: Beyond the Shadow of Prohibition.* National Research Council (US) Panel on Alternative Policies Affecting the Prevention of Alcohol Abuse and Alcoholism. Washington, DC: National Academies Press, 1981. https://www.ncbi.nlm.nih.gov/books/NBK216414/.

Moos, Rudolf. "Social Contexts and Substance Abuse." In Miller and Carroll, *Rethinking Substance Abuse*, 182–200.

Myers, Ched. *Binding the Strong Man: A Political Reading of Mark's Story of Jesus.* 20th anniversary ed. Maryknoll, NY: Orbis Books, 2008.

National Eating Disorders Association. "Co-occurring Disorders and Special Issues." www.NationalEatingDisorders.org. Accessed December 10, 2017. https://www.nationaleatingdisorders.org/learn/general-information/co-occurring-disorders-and-special-issues.

National Eating Disorders Association. "Trauma and Eating Disorders." Accessed December 11, 2017. https://www.nationaleatingdisorders.org/sites/default/files/ResourceHandouts/TraumaandEatingDisorders.pdf.

National Institute on Alcohol Abuse and Alcoholism. "Alcohol Use Disorder: A Comparison Between DSM–IV and DSM–5." NIH Publication No. 13–7999. November 2013.

National Institute on Drug Abuse. "Opioid Overdose Crisis." National Institute on Drug Abuse, February 2018. https://www.drugabuse.gov/drugs-abuse/opioids/opioid-overdose-crisis#nine.

Nelson, James B. *THIRST: God and the Alcoholic Experience*. Louisville: Westminster John Knox, 2004.

Ong, Anthony D., Thomas Fuller-Rowell, and Anthony L. Burrow. "Racial Discrimination and the Stress Process." *Journal of Personality and Social Psychology* 96, no. 6 (June 2009): 1259–71. doi:10.1037/a0015335.

Pahl, Kerstin, Judith S. Brook, and Jung Yeon Lee. "Joint Trajectories of Victimization and Marijuana Use and Their Health Consequences among Urban African American and Puerto Rican Young Men." *Journal of Behavioral Medicine* 36, no. 3 (June 2013): 305–14. http://yeshebi.ptsem.edu:2103/10.1007/s10865-012-9425-1.

Pani, L., A. Porcella, and G. L. Gessa. "The Role of Stress in the Pathophysiology of the Dopaminergic System." *Molecular Psychiatry* 5, no. 1 (January 2000): 14. doi:10.1038/sj.mp.4000589.

Pargament, Kenneth I. *Spiritually Integrated Psychotherapy: Understanding and Addressing the Sacred*. New York: Guilford, 2011.

———. *The Psychology of Religion and Coping: Theory, Research, Practice*. New York: Guilford, 1997.

Pearlin, Leonard I., Scott Schieman, Elena M. Fazio, and Stephen C. Meersman. "Stress, Health, and the Life Course: Some Conceptual Perspectives." *Journal of Health and Social Behavior* 46, no. 2 (June 2005): 205–19. http://yeshebi.ptsem.edu:2103/10.1177/002214650504600206.

Pew Research Center. "Chapter 3: Demographic and Economic Data, by Race." In *King's Dream Remains an Elusive Goal: Many Americans See Racial Disparities*. Published August 22, 2013. http://www.pewsocialtrends.org/2013/08/22/chapter-3-demographic-economic-data-by-race/#incarceration.

Phillips, Bonnie, Raju Hajela, and Donald L. Hilton Jr. "Sex Addiction as a Disease: Evidence for Assessment, Diagnosis, and Response to Critics." *Sexual Addiction & Compulsivity* 22, no. 2 (April 2015): 167–92. https://doi.org/10.1080/10720162.2015.1036184.

Pieterse, Alex L., Nathan R. Todd, Helen A. Neville, and Robert T. Carter. "Perceived Racism and Mental Health among Black American Adults: A Meta-Analytic Review." *Journal of Counseling Psychology* 59, no. 1 (January 2012): 1–9. doi:10.1037/a0026208.

Plantinga, Cornelius, Jr. *Not the Way It's Supposed to Be: A Breviary of Sin*. Grand Rapids: Eerdmans, 1995.

Polter, Abigail M., and Julie A. Kauer. "Stress and VTA Synapses: Implications for Addiction and Depression." *European Journal of Neuroscience* 39, no. 7 (April 2014): 1179–88. https://doi.org/10.1111/ejn.12490.

Ponterotto, Joseph, Manuel Casas, Lisa A. Suzuki, Charlene M. Alexander, and Margo A. Jackson, eds. *Handbook of Multicultural Counseling*. 3rd ed. Thousand Oaks, CA: Sage Publications, Inc., 2009.

Proctor, Bernadette D., Kayla R. Fontenot, and Melissa A. Kollar. "Income and Poverty in the United States: 2015. United Census Bureau." Accessed July 31, 2017. https://www.census.gov/content/dam/Census/library/publications/2016/demo/p60-256.pdf.

Proctor, S. L., and N. G. Hoffmann. "Identifying Patterns of Co-occurring Substance Use Disorders and Mental Illness in a Jail Population." *Addiction Research & Theory* 20, no. 6 (2012): 492–503. http://doi.org/10.3109/16066359.2012.667853.

Quinones, Sam. *Dreamland: The True Tale of America's Opiate Epidemic*. New York: Bloomsbury, 2015.

Rambo, Shelly, and Catherine Keller. *Spirit and Trauma: A Theology of Remaining*. Louisville: Westminster John Knox, 2011.

Rauchenbusch, Walter. *A Theology for the Social Gospel*. Reprint ed. Nashville: Abingdon, 1978.

Reding, Nick. *Methland: The Death and Life of an American Small Town*. Reprint ed. New York: Bloomsbury, 2010.

Reid, Deniece. "Addiction, African Americans, and a Christian Recovery Journey." In Krestan, *Bridges to Recovery*, 145–72.

Reisner, Sari L., Kathryn L. Falb, Aimee Van Wagenen, Chris Grasso, and Judith Bradford. "Sexual Orientation Disparities in Substance Misuse: The Role of Childhood Abuse and Intimate Partner Violence among Patients in Care at an Urban Community Health Center." *Substance Use & Misuse* 48, no. 3 (February 12, 2013): 274–89. doi:10.3109/10826084.2012.755702.

Rich, John A., and Courtney M. Grey. "Pathways to Recurrent Trauma among Young Black Men: Traumatic Stress, Substance Use, and the 'Code of the Street.'" *American Journal of Public Health* 95, no. 5 (May 2005): 816–24. http://yeshebi.ptsem.edu:2073/docview/215085473/abstract/EC44ECBC3BD84019PQ/1.

Richards, P. Scott. *Spiritual Approaches in the Treatment of Women with Eating Disorders*. Washington, DC: American Psychological Association, 2007.

Robinson, William. "Understanding Global Capitalism." Discussion Paper CSGP D2/08. Peterborough, Ontario, Canada: Trent University, January 25, 2008. http://www.soc.ucsb.edu/faculty/robinson/Assets/pdf/understandingglobalcapitalism.pdf.

Rogers, Carl R. "The Necessary and Sufficient Conditions of Therapeutic Personality Change." *Psychotherapy: Theory, Research, Practice, Training* 44, no. 3 (2007): 240–48. doi:10.1037/0033-3204.44.3.240.

Room, Robin. "Stigma, Social Inequality, and Alcohol and Drug Use." *Drug & Alcohol Review* 24, no. 2 (March 2005): 143–55. doi: 10.1080/09595230500102434.

Rosenberg, Kenneth Paul, Patrick Carnes, and Suzanne O'Connor. "Evaluation and Treatment of Sex Addiction." *Journal of Sex & Marital Therapy* 40, no. 2 (April 3, 2014): 77–91. https://doi.org/10.1080/0092623X.2012.701268.

Ross, Catherine E., and John Mirowsky. "Social Structure and Psychological Functioning Distress, Perceived Control, and Trust." In John DeLamater, ed., *Handbook of Social Psychology*, 411–47. New York : Kluwer Academic/Plenum Publishers, 2003.

Rothschild, Babette. *The Body Remembers: The Psychophysiology of Trauma and Trauma Treatment*. New York: Norton, 2000.

Ryan, Catlin, David Huebner, Rafael M. Diaz, and Jorge Sanchez. "Family Rejection as a Predictor of Negative Health Outcomes in White and Latino Lesbian, Gay, and Bisexual Young Adults." *Pediatrics* 123, no. 1 (2009): 346.

Sanders, Cody. *A Brief Guide to Ministry with LGBTQIA Youth*. Louisville: Westminster John Knox, 2017.

Sanders, Mark. *Slipping through the Cracks: Intervention Strategies for Clients with Multiple Addictions and Disorders*. Deerfield Beach, FL: Health Communications, Inc., 2011.

Sanders-Phillips, Kathy, Wendy Kliewer, Taqi Tirmazi, Von Nebbitt, Takisha Carter, and Heather Key. "Perceived Racial Discrimination, Drug Use, and Psychological Distress in African American Youth: A Pathway to Child Health Disparities." *Journal of Social Issues* 70, no. 2 (June 1, 2014): 279–97. https://doi.org/10.1111/josi.12060.

Sartor, Carolyn E., Mary Waldron, Alexis E. Duncan, Julia D. Grant, Vivia V. Mccutcheon, Elliot C. Nelson, Pamela A. F. Madden, Kathleen K. Bucholz, and Andrew C. Heath. "Childhood Sexual Abuse and Early Substance Use in Adolescent Girls: The Role of Familial Influences." *Addiction* 108, no. 5 (May 2013): 993–1000. doi:10.1111/add.12115.

Schaeffer, Jenni. *Life without Ed: How One Woman Declared Independence from Her Eating Disorder and How You Can Too*. Anniversary ed. McGraw-Hill Education, 2003.

Schilling, Elizabeth A., Robert H. Aseltine Jr., and Susan Gore. "Adverse Childhood Experiences and Mental Health in Young Adults: A Longitudinal Survey." *BMC Public Health* 7, no. 1 (January 2007): 30–40. doi:10.1186/1471-2458-7-30.

Schore, Allan N. *Affect Dysregulation and Disorders of the Self*. New York: Norton, 2003.

Schweitzer, Carol L. Schnabl. "Resilience Revisited: What Ministers Need to Know about Borderline Personality Disorder." *Pastoral Psychology* 64, no. 5 (October 1, 2015): 727–49. https://doi.org/10.1007/s11089-014-0626-0.

Seelye, Katharine. "In Heroin Crisis, White Families Seek Gentler War on Drugs." October 30, 2015. https://www.nytimes.com/2015/10/31/us/heroin-war-on-drugs-parents.html.

Seppala, Marvin D., and Mark E. Rose. *Prescription Painkillers: History, Pharmacology, and Treatment*. Center City, MN: Hazelden, 2011.

Siegel, Daniel. *The Developing Mind: How Relationships and the Brain Interact to Shape Who We Are*. 2nd ed. New York: Guilford, 2015.

Southern, Stephen, and Katherine Hilton, eds. *Annual Review of Addictions and Offender Counseling: Best Practices*. Eugene, OR: Wipf & Stock, 2013.

Stone, Howard W., and James O. Duke. *How to Think Theologically*. Minneapolis: Fortress, 2013.

Substance Abuse and Mental Health Services Administration, Center for Behavioral Health Statistics and Quality. "Detoxification and Substance Abuse Treatment, Treatment Improvement Protocol (TIP) Series, No. 45." HHS Publication No. (SMA) 15-4131. Rockville, MD: Center for Substance Abuse Treatment, 2006.

———. "Enhancing Motivation for Change in Substance Abuse Treatment, Treatment Improvement Protocol (TIP) Series No. 35." HHS Publication No. (SMA) 13-4212. Rockville, MD: Substance Abuse and Mental Health Services Administration, 2013. https://store.samhsa.gov/shin/content/SMA13-4212/SMA13-4212.pdf.

———. "Improving Cultural Competence, Treatment Improvement Protocol (TIP) Series No. 59." HHS Publication No. (SMA) 14-4849. Rockville, MD: Substance Abuse and Mental Health Services Administration, 2014. http://store.samhsa.gov/shin/content/SMA14-4849/SMA14-4849.pdf.

———. "A Provider's Introduction to Substance Abuse Treatment for Lesbian, Gay, Bisexual, and Transgender Individuals." HHS Publication No. (SMA) 12–4104. Rockville, MD: Substance Abuse and Mental Health Services Administration, 2012. http://store.samhsa.gov/shin/content//SMA12-4104/SMA12-4104.pdf.

———. "Quick Guide for Clinicians: Based on TIP 42: Substance Abuse Treatment for Persons with Co-Occurring Disorders." HHS Publication No. (SMA) 15-4034. First printing 2005. Rockville, MD: Substance Abuse and Mental Health Services Administration, 2015.

———. "Substance Abuse Treatment for Persons with Co-Occurring Disorders: Treatment Improvement Protocol (TIP) Series, No. 42." HHS Publication No. (SMA) 13-3992. Rockville, MD: Substance Abuse and Mental Health Services Administration, 2013. http://store.samhsa.gov/shin/content//SMA13-3992/SMA13-3992.pdf.

———. "Treatment Episode Data Set (TEDS): 2005–2015. National Admissions to Substance Abuse Treatment Services. BHSIS Series S-91." HHS Publication No. (SMA) 17-5037. Rockville, MD: Substance Abuse and Mental Health Services Administration, 2017. https://www.samhsa.gov/data/sites/default/files/2015%20TEDS%20National%20Admissions.pdf.

Sugg, Richard. *The Secret History of the Soul: Physiology, Magic, and Spirit Forces from Homer to St Paul.* Newcastle upon Tyne, UK: Cambridge Scholars, 2013.

Swann, Alan F., Gerard Moeller, and Marijn Lijffijt, eds. *Neurobiology of Addiction.* New York: Oxford University Press, 2016.

Taplin, Chris, Sahoo Saddichha, Kathy Li, and Michael R. Krausz. "Family History of Alcohol and Drug Abuse, Childhood Trauma, and Age of First Drug Injection." *Substance Use & Misuse* 49, no. 10 (August 2014): 1311–16. doi:10.3109/10826084.2014.901383.

Taylor, Mark Lewis. *The Executed God: The Way of the Cross in Lockdown America.* 2nd ed. Minneapolis: Fortress, 2015.

Terry, Charles, and Mildred Pellens. *The Opium Problem.* Camden, NJ: Haddon Craftsmen, 1928.

Thoits, Peggy A. "Stress and Health: Major Findings and Policy Implications." *Journal of Health and Social Behavior* 51, no. 1, suppl. (March 2010): S41–S53. doi:http://dx.doi.org/10.1177/0022146510383499.

Thomas, Yonette F., and LeShawndra N. Price, eds. *Drug Use Trajectories among Minority Youth.* New York: Springer, 2016.

Thompson, Becky. *A Hunger So Wide, So Deep: A Multi-Racial View of Women's Eating Problems.* Minneapolis: University of Minnesota Press, 1996.

Tracy, Sarah W. "Medicalizing Alcoholism One Hundred Years Ago." *Harvard Review of Psychiatry* 15, no. 2 (April 3, 2007): 86–91. doi:10.1080/10673220701307562.

Trocki, Karen, and Laurie Drabble. "Bar Patronage and Motivational Predictors of Drinking in the San Francisco Bay Area: Gender and Sexual Identity Differences." *Journal of Psychoactive Drugs* (November 2, 2008): 345–56.

Tucker, Jasmine, and Caitlin Lowel. "National Snapshot: Poverty among Women and

Families, 2015." Data on Poverty and Income. National Women's Law Center, September 14, 2016. https://nwlc.org/resources/national-snapshot-poverty-among-women-families-2015/.

Ungar, Michael, ed. *Handbook for Working with Children and Youth: Pathways to Resilience across Cultures and Contexts.* Thousand Oaks, CA: Sage Publications, 2005.

Unick, George, Daniel Rosenblum, Sarah Mars, and Daniel Ciccarone. "The Relationship between US Heroin Market Dynamics and Heroin-Related Overdose, 1992–2008." *Addiction* 109, no. 11 (November 2014): 1889–98. doi:10.1111/add.12664.

US Department of Education, National Center for Education Statistics. "Employment and Unemployment Rates by Educational Attainment." The Condition of Education. NCES 2017-144. Last Updated April 2016. https://nces.ed.gov/fastfacts/display.asp?id=561.

US Department of Health and Human Services (HHS), Office of the Surgeon General. *Facing Addiction in America: The Surgeon General's Report on Alcohol, Drugs, and Health.* Washington, DC: HHS, November 2016.

Van der Kolk, Bessel A. *The Body Keeps the Score: Brain, Mind, and Body in the Healing of Trauma.* New York: Viking, 2014.

———. "The Complexity of Adaptation to Trauma: Self-Regulation, Stimulus Discrimination, and Characterological Development." In *Traumatic Stress: The Effects of Overwhelming Experience on Mind, Body, and Society*, edited by Bessel A. van der Kolk, A. C. McFarlane, and L. Weisaeth, 182–213. New York: Guilford, 1996.

VanNostrand, Marie. *New Jersey Jail Population Analysis: Identifying Solutions to Safely and Responsibly Reduce the Jail Population.* Luminosity and the Drug Policy Alliance, March 2013. New_Jersey_Jail_Population_Analysis_March_2013.Pdf.

Wallace Jr., John M., Patrick M. O'Malley Jr., Jerald G. Bachman, John E. Schulenberg, and Lloyd D. Johnston. "Race/Ethnicity, Religiosity and Differences and Similarities in American Adolescents' Substance Use." In Thomas and Price, *Drug Use Trajectories among Minority Youth,* 105–21.

Walsh, Colleen. "Rising Threat: Death by Fentanyl." *Harvard Gazette*, June 2017. http://news.harvard.edu/gazette/story/2017/06/mass-general-hospital-addiction-specialist-explains-fentanyl-threat/.

Washton, Arnold M., and Joan E. Zweben. *Treating Alcohol and Drug Problems in Psychotherapy Practice: Doing What Works.* New York: Guilford, 2006.

Wei, Meifen, Kenneth T. Wang, Puncky Paul Heppner, and Yi Du. "Ethnic and Mainstream Social Connectedness, Perceived Racial Discrimination, and Posttraumatic Stress Symptoms." *Journal of Counseling Psychology* 59, no. 3 (July 2012): 486–93. doi:10.1037/a0028000.

Weiss, Doug. *Sex Addiction: 6 Types and Treatment.* Kindle Edition. Anaheim: Discovery Press, 2017.

Weiss, Robert. *Sex Addiction 101: A Basic Guide to Healing from Sex, Porn, and Love Addiction.* Deerfield Beach, FL: Health Communications, Inc., n.d.

Western, Bruce. *Punishment and Inequality in America.* New York: Russell Sage Foundation, 2006.

Westminster Shorter Catechism. Westminster Assembly 1643–1652. The Center for Reformed Theology and Apologetics. Accessed May 24, 2018. http://www.reformed.org/documents/wsc/index.html?_top=http://www.reformed.org/documents/WSC_frames.html.

White, William L. *Slaying the Dragon: The History of Addiction Treatment and Recovery in America*. 2nd ed. Bloomington, IL: Chestnut Health Systems, 2014.

Wilson, Gary. *Your Brain on Porn: Internet Pornography and the Emerging Science of Addiction*. Margate, Kent, UK: Commonwealth, 2014.

Wimberly, Edward. *African American Pastoral Care and Counseling: The Politics of Oppression and Empowerment*. Cleveland: Pilgrim, 2006.

Witkiewitz, Katie A., and G. Alan Marlatt. "High Risk Situations: Relapse as a Dynamic Process." In *Therapist's Guide to Evidence-Based Relapse Prevention,* edited by Katie A. Witkiewitz and G. Alan Marlatt, 19–33. Boston: Elsevier Academic, 2007.

World Health Organization. "Preventing Suicide: A Global Imperative." Geneva, Switzerland: World Health Organization, 2014.

Wylie, Mary Sykes, and Lynn Turner. "The Attuned Therapist: Does Attachment Theory Really Matter?" *Psychotherapy Networker* 35, no. 2 (March/April 2011). https://www2.psychotherapynetworker.org/magazine/recentissues/1261-the-attunded-therapist.

Yip, Tiffany, Gilbert C. Gee, and David T. Takeuchi. "Racial Discrimination and Psychological Distress: The Impact of Ethnic Identity and Age among Immigrant and United States-Born Asian Adults." *Developmental Psychology* 44, no. 3 (May 2008): 787–800. doi:10.1037/0012-1649.44.3.787.

Yuodelis-Flores, Christine, and Richard K. Ries. "Addiction and Suicide: A Review." *American Journal on Addictions* 24, no. 2 (March 2015): 98–104. doi:10.1111/ajad.12185.

Zautra, Alex, John Stuart Hall, and Kate Murray. "Resilience: A New Definition of Health for People and Communities." In *Handbook of Adult Resilience,* edited by John Reich, Alex Zautra, and John Hall, 3–34. New York: Guilford, 2010.

Index of Authors

Note: Page numbers followed by n and a number indicate endnotes.

Index of Subjects

Note: Page numbers followed by n and a number indicate endnotes.

Index of Scripture Citations